A Complet ...ue to United States Military Medals 1939 to Present

By

Colonel Frank C. Foster (USA, Ret'd)
and
Lawrence H. Borts

5th Edition

Dedicated to America's finest citizens; her veterans and active military with the families who support them . . .
God Bless You All!

Hardcover Edition ISBN — 1-884452-18-3
Softcover Edition ISBN — 1-884452-19-1

Library of Congress
Catalog Card Number — 00-105970

Published by:
MOA Press (Medals of America Press)
114 South Chase Blvd., Fountain Inn, S.C. 29644
(864) 862-6051
www.moapress.com
www.usmedals.com

Printed in the United States of America

About the Authors

LONNY BORTS

FRANK FOSTER

Lawrence "Lonny" Borts developed a lifelong interest in military awards as a boy in New York City during World War II. After graduating from the New York University College of Engineering, he spent most of his professional life with the Grumman Corporation, retiring in 1992 as an Engineering Specialist in Airborne Surveillance Systems. He maintains one of the largest collections of military ribbons in the world and is consultant to several U. S. Armed Forces directorates and medals research societies. He is also the Awards Program Director of Vanguard, Inc., a major U.S. supplier of military uniform equipment, and realized every collector's dream when he co-designed the Coast Guard "E" Ribbon. Lonny is the author of *United Nations Medals and Missions*, the most comprehensive reference work on the subject and has contributed to a number of other well-known works on military awards. He and Beverly, his bride of over 44 years, now reside in Melbourne, Florida.

Col. Frank C. Foster (USA , Ret.), obtained his BS from The Citadel , MBA from the University of Georgia and is a graduate of the Army's Command and General Staff College and War College. He saw service as a Battery Commander in Germany and served in Vietnam with the 173rd Airborne Brigade and USARV General Staff. In the Adjutant General's Corps, he served as the Adjutant General of the Central Army Group, the 4th Infantry Division and was the Commandant and Chief of the Army's Adjutant General's Corps from 1986 to 1990. His military service provided him a unique understanding of the Armed Forces Awards System. He currently operates Medals of America Press and is the author of the *The Decorations, Medals, Badges and Insignia of the United States Army* and co author of *The Decorations and Medals of the Republic of Vietnam* . He and his wife Linda, who was decorated with the Army Commander's Medal in 1990, for service to the Army, live in Fountain Inn, South Carolina.

GRATEFUL ACKNOWLEDGMENTS

The authors wish to express their deepest appreciation to the following individuals for their invaluable contributions. Without their unselfish efforts, this book would have ended as an unfilled dream.

The entire Medals of America team with special thanks to: Mrs. Linda Foster, Mrs. Lois Owens for custom mounting, Mrs. Bonnie Crocker - Art Director and LTC (Ret.) Tony Aldebol for suggestions.

Mr.Thomas B. Proffitt, Retired Director of The Institute of Heraldry, U.S. Army, COL. (Ret.) Gerald T. Luchino and Mr. Robert L. Hopkins and Mr. Steve Hass.

COL. (Ret.) F. P. Anthony and Mrs. Charlene Rose formerly of the U.S. Marine Corps Military Awards Branch.

Ms. Phyllis Dula, U.S. Coast Guard Military Personnel Management Specialist and her predecessor, Ms. Diane E. Porter.

Mr. Lee Graves, Air Force veteran and President of GRACO Industries, one of the leading medal manufacturers in the United States.

Mrs. Arlette King and her fine team at the U. S. Army Awards Branch.

Mr. Bill Gershen, President and CEO, Mr. Michael Harrison, Vice-President, Mr. Gary Duncan, General Manager of Vanguard, Inc.

Ms. Patricia A. Thomas, Office of Maritime Labor & Training, Maritime Administration, Department of Transportation.

Donna J. Neary - Lieutenant Colonel, USMCR - Artist Marine Corps Art Collection

Mr. Dan Soares - Award Policy J1 (Personnel) DOD Joint Staff

Mr. John Royston - Present OMSA Ribbon Bank Manager

CDR Jerome Mahar USN - Head Awards & Special Projects Branch

CMSgt. Steve Haskin, former Ribbon Bank Manager of the Orders and Medals Society of America.

Table of Contents

TITLE **PAGE**

Introduction to the 5th Edition 4
History 5
Types of Military Medals & Devices 9
Different Forms of a Military Medal 9
How to Determine Veteran's Military Medals 10
Displaying Military Awards 11
Wear of Medals, Insignia and the Uniform by Veterans, Retirees and Former Service Members 13
Wearing Ribbons and Medals 14
U.S. Military Awards 16
Armed Forces Ribbon Displays 34
Right Breast Displays on the Full Dress Uniform 50
Issue of U.S. Medals to Veterans, Retirees and Their Families 52
Medal Descriptions 53
Attachments and Devices 124
Medal Clasps and Bars 128
Understanding U.S. Awards 129
Notes and Comments 139
Bibliography 139
Index 140

List of Illustrations

TITLE **PAGE**

Medals of Honor 17
U.S. Personal Decorations 18
U.S. Special Service, Good Conduct & Reserve Awards 24
U.S. Service Medals 26
U.S. Military Marksmanship Awards 30
Foreign Decorations and Non-U.S. Service Awards 32
U.S. Awards Having No Medals ("Ribbons-Only") 34
Correct Manner of Wear- Ribbons of the U.S. Merchant Marine 38
United Nations Awards Currently Authorized for U.S. Personnel 38
Correct Manner of Wear- Ribbons of the U.S. Army 40
Correct Manner of Wear- Ribbons of the U.S. Navy 42
Correct Manner of Wear- Ribbons of the U.S. Marine Corps 44
Correct Manner of Wear- Ribbons of the U.S. Air Force 46
Correct Manner of Wear- Ribbons of the U.S. Coast Guard 48
Right Breast Displays on Full Dress Uniforms 50
U.S. Merchant Marine Medals and Decorations 51
Attachments/Devices Used on American Ribbons 124
Placement of Silver Devices on the Ribbon 124
Placement of Silver Campaign Stars on the Ribbon 132
Placement of the Bronze Letter "V" on the Ribbon 132
Placement of the Letter "V" With Other Ribbon Devices 133
Former Device Usage on the Navy Air Medal 133
Placement of Devices on the Armed Forces Reserve Medal 137

Introduction to the 5th Edition

One evening in 1992, just as I was wrapping up my day's activities at Medals of America, I received a telephone call which started off: "Why haven't I heard of you before?" The caller introduced himself as a Mr. Lonny Borts and, when I said that I had never heard of **him** either, we both laughed. While the world of military medals is small, it is specialized. The obvious answer is that Medals of America focuses on veterans awards, rather than collectors and researchers, so there was little likelihood that we would cross paths in spite of our mutual membership in several organizations.

When Lonny described some of his work in the decorations and awards field, my level of excitement rose and I asked for a copy. Reading the material, I realized that Lonny is one of the foremost experts in the U.S. military awards field. I was so impressed by the level of detail and completeness of his efforts that I immediately proposed a book to cover the entire spectrum of U. S. Military awards since World War II.

The collaborative effort from that initial exchange of ideas culminated in four previous editions of this book. This book is designed to be a definitive reference covering United States decorations, medals and ribbons for veterans and active duty personnel. It is also designed to be a single source for the military decorations and medals of each service. Most of the material was derived from the latest military awards and uniform manuals and other authoritative sources, although the authors' personal opinions may have slipped in from time to time.

When the first edition was conceived, the perils of producing an absolutely up-to-date, definitive reference on any subject were fully recognized. This was especially true in the dynamic world of U.S. military awards which, up to that time, had produced 75 awards in 47 years, an average of 1.5 new awards per year since the unification of the Armed Forces in 1947.

Almost as predictable as the tides, since this book's original publication date, the U.S. military has issued a number of new awards thus increasing the number created since 1947 to 84. Just as important, the number of updated regulations that were issued by the U.S. military since the fourth printing virtually ordained that another edition, containing the very latest information, be made available to veterans, military personnel, collectors and enthusiasts everywhere.

Owing to the complimentary reviews enjoyed by the first four editions, the original format has been improved while the contents have been updated to reflect the current state of U.S. awards and decorations. In addition, most pages have been revamped to improve readability and a new text section on medals and ribbons has been added to enhance the reader's knowledge of this very complex subject. Finally, in what has become a trade mark, we are pleased to present the graphic debut of three new items never before seen in any reference, the Kosovo Campaign Medal, Navy Recruit Training Service Ribbon and the Air Force Military Training Instructor Ribbon.

And then there's that ugly word; **MISTEAKS**. Every book in print, probably dating back to the Gutenberg Bible, no matter how high-sounding, brilliantly conceived or well-intentioned, is bound to possess its share of factual errors and mispelled words. A few errors were discovered in the first four editions and appropriate corrections made in the text and graphical presentations. If any further errors are detected, please accept our apologies, drop us a line and be assured that they will be corrected in future editions. In this spirit, we will start the ball rolling by pointing out that the words "MISTEAKS" and "mispelled" in the second sentence of this paragraph are both misspelled.

It is hoped that this fifth edition will provide the reader with the same insights and informational value as its predecessors. We look forward to help from our readers to improve future editions.

Col. Frank C. Foster
(USA, Ret.)
Fountain Inn, SC

Lonny Borts
Melbourne, FL

Background of the United States Awards

John Paul Jones Medal

AMERICAN REVOLUTION — The chronicle of military decorations in the United States begins early in the American Revolution, when Congress voted to award gold medals to outstanding military leaders. The first such medal was struck to honor George Washington for his service in driving the British from Boston in 1776. Similar medals were bestowed upon General Horatio Gates for his victory at the Battle of Saratoga and Captain John Paul Jones after his famous naval engagement with the *Serapis* in 1779. Unlike present practice, however, these were large, presentation medals not designed to be worn on the military uniform. Interestingly, once the dies were cut, many copies were manufactured and distributed as commemorative medals to instill patriotic pride in the new country's victories. As a matter of interest, many of these early commemorative medallions are still being struck and offered for sale by the U. S. Mint.

The Andre Medal awarded to patriots Van Wert, Paulding and Williams by the Continental Congress in 1780.

The "Andre" medal broke the custom of restricting the award of medals to successful senior officers and is doubly unique in that it was designed for wear around the neck. The medal was presented by Congress in 1780 to the three enlisted men who captured British Major John Andre with the plans of the West Point fortifications in his boot.

In August, 1782, George Washington established the Badge of Military Merit, the first U. S. decoration which had general application to all enlisted men and one which he hoped would inaugurate a permanent awards system. At the same time, he expressed his fundamental awards philosophy when he issued an order from his headquarters at Newburgh, New York, which read:

"The General, ever desirous to cherish a virtuous ambition in his soldiers, as well as to foster and

encourage every species of military merit, directs that, whenever any singularly meritorious action is performed, the author of it shall be permitted to wear on his facings, over his left breast, the figure of a heart in purple cloth or silk, edged with narrow lace or binding. Not only instances of unusual gallantry, but also of extraordinary fidelity, and essential service in any way, shall meet with a due reward...the road to glory in a patriot army and a free country is thus opened to all. This order is also to have retrospect to the earliest days of the war, and to be considered a permanent one."*

Although special and commemorative medals had been awarded previously, until this point no decoration had been established which honored the private soldier with a reward for special merit. The wording of the order is worth careful study. The object was "to cherish a virtuous ambition" and "to foster and encourage every species of military merit." Note also, that Washington appreciated that every kind of service was important by proposing to reward, "not only instances of unusual gallantry, but also of extraordinary fidelity and essential service in any way." And finally, the wonderfully democratic sentence, "the road to glory in a patriotic army and free country is thus opened to all."

Coming as it did, almost a year after Cornwallis' surrender at Yorktown, the message was never given widespread distribution and, as a result, there were only three known recipients of this badge, Sergeants Elijah Churchill, William Brown and Daniel Bissell. Unfortunately, after the Revolution, the award fell into disuse and disappeared for 150 years.

However, it did not die, primarily due to the efforts of the Army's then Chief of Staff, General Douglas MacArthur, (and, by no accident, one of its first recipients). On the 200th anniversary of Washington's birth, February 22, 1932, the War Department announced that:

"By order of the President of the United States, the Purple Heart, established by Gen. George Washington at Newburgh, New York. . . is hereby revived out of respect to his memory and military achievements."

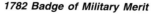

1782 Badge of Military Merit

1932 Purple Heart

Washington's "figure of a heart in purple" was retained as the medal's central theme and embellished with Washington's likeness and his coat of arms. The words "For Military Merit" appear on the reverse as a respectful reference to its worthy predecessor.

CIVIL WAR - In the eighty years after the Revolution, the United States engaged in at least two major conflicts with foreign nations (War of 1812, War with Mexico), but no attempt was made to revive or reestablish a comprehensive awards program. The Certificate of Merit was established by the Army in 1847 to reward soldiers who distinguished themselves in battle, but this was not translated into medallic form until 1905. In 1861, the Medal of Honor was established for enlisted personnel of the U. S. Navy, followed the next year by the creation of its Army counterpart for NCO's and private soldiers. Officers were made eligible for the award in later years.

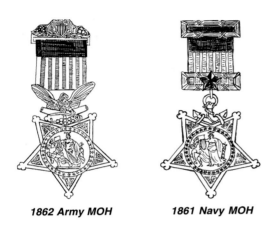

1862 Army MOH   *1861 Navy MOH*

SPANISH AMERICAN WAR — For nearly twenty years, the Medal of Honor remained the sole American military award of any kind. Although the Navy and Marine Corps had authorized the first Good Conduct Medals in the 1880's, it was not until the eve of the 20th Century that a host of medals were authorized to commemorate the events surrounding the Spanish-American War. This was future President Theodore Roosevelt's "Bully Little War" that produced seven distinct medals for only four months of military action.

The first of these was the medal to commemorate the victory of the naval forces under the command of Commodore Dewey over the Spanish fleet at Manila Bay. This award was notable as it was the first such medal in U. S. history to be awarded to all officers and enlisted personnel present during a specific military expedition.

When Roosevelt, an ardent supporter of the military, ultimately reached the White House, he took it upon himself to legislate for the creation of medals to honor all those who had served in America's previous conflicts. Thus, by 1908, the U.S. had authorized campaign medals, some retroactive, for the Civil War, Indian Wars, War with Spain, Philippine Insurrection and China Relief Expedition of 1900-01. While the services used the same ribbons, different medals were struck. Also, the custom of wearing service ribbons on the tunic was adopted during this same time frame (using different precedences). Thus, the Services managed to establish the principle of independence in the creation and wearing of awards that is virtually unchanged today.

WORLD WAR I — At the time of the U. S. entry into World War I, the Medal of Honor, Certificate of Merit and Navy/Marine Good Conduct Medals still represented America's entire inventory of personal decorations. This presented the twin dangers that the Medal of Honor might be cheapened by being awarded too often and that other deeds of valor might go unrecognized. By 1918, popular agitation forced the authorization of two new awards, the Army's Distinguished Service Cross and Distinguished Service Medal, created by Executive Order in 1918. In the same year, the traditional U. S. refusal to permit the armed forces to accept foreign decorations was rescinded, allowing military personnel to accept awards from the grateful Allied governments. In 1919, the Navy created the Navy Cross and its own Distinguished Service Medal for Navy and Marine Corps personnel.

Army Distinguished   *Navy Cross*
Service Cross

The issuance of the World War I Victory Medal established another precedent, that of wearing clasps with the names of individual battles on the suspension ribbon of a general campaign medal. This was an ongoing practice in many countries, most notably Britain and France, since the 19th Century. When the ribbon bar alone was worn, each clasp was represented by a small (3/16" diameter) bronze star. Fourteen such clasps were adopted along with five clasps to denote service in specific countries. However, the latter were issued only if no battle clasp was earned. Only one service clasp could be issued to any individual and they were not represented by a small bronze star on the ribbon bar.

World War I Victory Medal with Ribbon Bars

It is a final irony that the British, who were the greatest proponents of the practice, never issued a single bar with their own version of the Victory Medal.

During this same period, the Army used a 3/16" diameter silver star to indicate a citation for gallantry during any previous campaign, dating back to the Civil War. An officer or enlisted man so cited was also presented with a Silver Star citation, which evolved into the Silver Star Medal in 1932.

Between the two World Wars, American troops were dispatched to such areas as Haiti, Nicaragua and China to quell rebellions and deal with civil unrest and appropriate medals were authorized to commemorate these events.

WORLD WAR II — On September 8, 1939, in response to the growing threat of involvement in World War II, the President proclaimed a National Emergency in order to increase the size of the U. S. military forces. For the first time, a peacetime service award, the American Defense Service Medal, was authorized for wear by those personnel who served in the military prior to the attack on Pearl Harbor on December 7, 1941.

The onset of America's participation in World War II saw a significant increase in both personal decorations and campaign medals. Since U. S. forces were serving all over the world, a campaign medal was designed for each major (and carefully defined) area. The three medals for the American, Asiatic-Pacific and European-African-Middle Eastern Campaigns encompassed the globe. However, the World War I practice of using campaign bars was discarded in favor of 3/16" bronze stars that could denote each designated military campaign, from a major invasion to a submarine war patrol.

World War II introduced the first (and only!) service medal unique to female military personnel. Known as the Women's Army Corps Service Medal, it was authorized for service in both the W.A.C. and its predecessor, the Women's Army Auxiliary Corps. In addition, the war saw the large scale award of foreign medals and decorations to American servicemen. The Philippine Government, for one, authorized awards to commemorate the Defense and Liberation of their island country. The first foreign award designed strictly for units, the Philippine

Asiatic-Pacific and European-African-Middle East Campaign Medals.

Presidential Unit Citation, patterned after a similar American award, was also approved for wear by American forces at this time. In the European Theater, France and Belgium made many presentations of their War Crosses (Croix de Guerre) to U. S. military personnel.

The next mid-war period, from 1945 to 1950, saw the introduction of two counterparts of previous World War I awards, the Victory and Occupation Medals. This time, no bars or clasps were authorized for the Victory Medal, but bars were issued with the Occupation Medal to denote the recipient's area of service.

KOREA — The Korean Conflict, fought under the United Nations banner, added two new medals to the inventory. The first was the Korean Service Medal, which continued the practice of using 3/16" bronze stars on the ribbon to denote major engagements. The second, the National Defense Service Medal, set another record when it was later reinstated for the Vietnam and Gulf Wars to become the most awarded medal in U. S. history. Some units received the Korean Presidential Unit Citation and all participants were awarded the United Nations Service Medal, but more than 45 years elapsed before the U.S. accepted the War Service Medal issued by the South Korean Government.

U.S. Korean Service & United Nations Korean Service Medal

In the late 1950's and early 1960's, another substantial increase in awards took place as the Air Force, a separate service since 1947, created a flood of unique honors to replace their Army counterparts.

VIETNAM — The first American advisors in the Republic of South Vietnam were awarded the new Armed Forces Expeditionary Medal which was created in 1961 to cover campaigns for which no specific medal was instituted. However, as the U. S. involvement in the Vietnamese conflict grew, a unique award, the Vietnam Service Medal was authorized, thus giving previous recipients of the Expeditionary Medal the option of which medal to accept. The Government also authorized the acceptance of the Republic of Vietnam Campaign Medal by all who served for six months in-country, in the surrounding waters or the air after 1960.

After Vietnam, many new decorations, medals and ribbons came into being as the Department of Defense and the individual Services developed a complete structure to reward performance from the newest enlistee to the most senior Pentagon Staffer. Some of the awards, such as the Army Service Ribbon and the Air Force Training Ribbon have little meaning, except to give the recruit something to wear on his chest. Conversely, the Achievement and Commendation Medals provide a useful means for a field commander to recognize younger individuals for outstanding performance.

U.S. Vietnam Service and RVN Campaign Medals.

GULF WAR — The conflict in the Gulf, as previously noted, saw the reinstitution of the National Defense Service Medal (this time it also covered the Reserves) and the creation of the Southwest Asia Service Medal for the personnel in theater. The Department of Defense also approved the wear of the Saudi Arabian Medal for the Liberation of Kuwait, which probably wins the award as the "Most Colorful Medal" hanging on any military chest. Later the Department of Defense also authorized the Kuwait Medal for the Liberation of Kuwait.

U.S. Southwest Asia Service Medal, Saudi Arabian Medal and the Kuwait Medal for Liberation of Kuwait

TYPE OF AWARDS — The terms, "Decoration" and "Medal" are used almost interchangeably today, but there was once a recognizable distinction between them. Decorations, were awarded for acts of valor and meritorious service, while medals were awarded for participation in specific battles or campaigns. The fact that some very prestigious awards have the word "medal" in their titles (e.g. <u>Medal</u> of Honor, Marine Corps Brevet <u>Medal</u>, Distinguished Service <u>Medal</u>, etc.) can cause some confusion to the novice.

Another type of award is a badge, indicating special proficiency in specific areas such as marksmanship. The Services have also developed a system by which entire units, such as an Army battalion or a Navy ship can be recognized for outstanding performance in the field. Members of the cited unit are entitled to wear an appropriate insignia representing the award (e.g.: Presidential Unit Citation, Navy Unit Commendation) or the French Fourragere, worn in perpetuity by members of many Army and Marine units to honor it's award during one of the World Wars.

PURPOSE — It is the purpose of this book to provide the reader with a clear road map of U. S. military awards and decorations. Starting on Page 14, details involved in wearing and displaying military awards are presented. The narrative continues on Page 16, with the personal decorations starting with the Medal of Honor and proceeding through the various levels of the "Pyramid of Honor". After personal decorations are the Good Conduct, Special Service and Reserve Meritorious Awards, followed by the service medals in chronological order from 1939 to the present.

The Marksmanship medals and ribbons of the Navy, Coast Guard and Air Force are presented next (note that both the Army and Marine Corps award metal badges for shooting excellence, but these are beyond the scope of this book). This is followed by sections on the awards of various foreign governments to U.S. personnel, ribbons which have no associated medals ("ribbon only" awards) and, lastly, U. S. and foreign unit awards.

Finally, to complete the awards picture, sections depicting the proper wear of ribbons, describing devices, and further expanding information on medals and attachments are included. Details of the U. S. awards systems for the various services complete the book.

From the earliest orders of knighthood to the present day commendations, the purpose of awards has always been twofold; the first is to promote good service, pride and courageous conduct among military personnel. The second is to create a mystique that will surround these symbols of a nation's appreciation, and thus provide recognition for the recipients, their comrades, and their families.

All the service medals and ribbons, even the so-called "I Was There and Survived" awards have an important purpose. The display on a serviceman's chest can tell a commander at a glance the level of experience possessed by his subordinates. When a commander reviews his officers and NCO's, it only takes a minute or so to evaluate their backgrounds and predict performance from their ribbons.

It is, therefore, the authors' hope that this book will allow the reader, whether novice or veteran, to gain a new understanding of American Military awards, their evolution and history up to the present time.

Types of Military Medals, Ribbons and Devices

There are two general categories of medals awarded by the United States to its military personnel, namely, decorations and service medals. Since the establishment of our first awards, decorations for valorous or meritorious actions have traditionally been in the shape of a star, cross, hexagon or similar heraldic configuration. Although a small number of decorations are round, (e.g., Navy Distinguished Service Medal, Airman's Medal, Coast Guard Achievement Medal, etc.) the circular shape has been used almost exclusively for service medals. These can be awarded for good conduct, participation in a particular campaign or expedition or any noncombatant service on foreign soil.

Decoration   Service Medal

The three basic methods for wearing awards on the uniform are the full-size medal, the miniature medal and the ribbon bar. On civilian clothing, the miniature medal and the enameled lapel pin, in the colors of a specific ribbon, have been in vogue since the early part of the 20th Century. Additionally, since World War II, the enamel hat pin in the form of the appropriate medal has found favor with veterans' organizations.

Small metal devices are worn on the ribbon bar or the medal's suspension ribbon to denote additional awards, campaigns, additional honors or subsequent service. These attachments come in the form of ☆ stars, 🍂 oak leaf clusters, 3 numerals, ▲ arrowheads, etc. and are another means to indicate the level and extent of the medal holder's service to his country. The attachments and the manner of their placement are shown in detail in subsequent pages as well as the ribbon displays prescribed by the individual Armed Services.

Different Forms of a Military Medal

Enamel Lapel Pin

Basic Ribbon Bar

Hat Pin

Miniature Medal

Full Size Medal

Reverse of Medal

Ribbon Bar with Appropriate Devices

How to Determine a Veteran's Military Medals

Many veterans and their families are unsure of which military medals they were awarded and often for good reasons. Twenty five, thirty, even fifty years after military service it is often difficult to remember or clearly identify the awards a veteran may have earned the right to wear or display. Thousands of veterans have been heard to say "I don't want any awards I'm not authorized, but I want everything I am authorized". So the question is, "What are the medals authorized the veteran for his military service during each conflict?

There are a number of reasons besides the passage of time that veterans are not always sure of their military awards. At the end of World War II many campaign medals had not yet been struck and were available in ribbon only issue due to the restriction on brass and other metals for the war effort. Many unit awards had not yet been authorized, and, on the whole, most soldiers, sailors, marines and airmen were more interested in going home than they were in their military records. Other changes such as Congress' decision in the 1947s to authorize a Bronze Star Medal for meritorious service to all recipients of the combat infantryman and combat medical badge often meant many veterans never realized that they had earned a Bronze Star Medal. Another example is the recently-approved South Korean War Service Medal which the Republic of Korea offered to the United States at the end of the Korean War but was not accepted until 50 years later. In other cases, veterans came home and stuffed their medals and awards into a cigar box which usually found its way into the hands of children and these symbols of valor and service from a grateful nation simply disappeared over time.

Today there has been a wonderfully renewed interest in wearing and displaying United States military medals, both to honor veterans' patriotic service and to display their family pride in military service. World War II, Korean and

Vietnam veterans now wear their medals at formal social and patriotic events and a display of military medals and insignia is often in the place of honor of the family home.

As mentioned earlier, military medals are divided into two categories: Decorations, awarded for valor or meritorious service and Campaign and Service medals awarded for a particular service or event. Additionally there are Unit Awards which are for unit valor and meritorious service and ribbon-only awards presented for completing special training or recognizing certain service.

Decorations are individual awards and are of such singularly significance that most veterans will well remember and their family will remember when such awards have been presented. Decorations are noted on a veteran's official discharge papers (called a DD Form 214) as well as published in official unit orders. However there are exceptions, such as the Bronze Star Medal issued for meritorious service after World War II and in some cases Purple Heart medals that were never officially presented. If someone is unsure if they received a decoration, a request to the National Records Center in St. Louis or other veterans records holding areas are the only places to locate that information. Other than The Medal of Honor and the Distinguished Service Crosses there are no centralized lists recording awards of other U.S. military decorations. Decorations such as the Silver Star, Bronze Star, Air Medal, Purple Heart, Commendation and Achievement medals are announced in unit orders which are normally found in the individual's military service record.

Campaign and service medals, unit awards and ribbon only awards are more clearly identifiable. The Army, for example, has a campaign register which provides a clear indication of which campaign medals, unit awards, campaign stars and foreign unit awards are authorized a particular unit during certain periods of time. To aid in identifying the campaign medals authorized veterans of different conflicts and to show how they can be displayed, the United States and Allied campaign medals authorized since World War II are summarized below. Exact details of each medal and the campaigns associated with it are shown in detail later in the book.

World War II

World War II saw Good Conduct Medals for all four services. The Navy , Marine Corps and Coast Guard had already established Good Conduct Medals while the Army which included the Army Air Force established a Good Conduct Medal in 1941.

Army & AAF   WW II Navy   WW II Marine   USCG

WW II Good Conduct Medals

American Campaign Medal   Europe-Africa-Middle East   Victory Medal WWII   Occupation Medal, Army

Europe, Middle East, Africa

The American Defense Service Medal was authorized for the period of national emergency prior to 7 December 1941. After America declared war, the conflict was divided into three theaters (1) the American theater, (2) the European, African, Middle East theater, and the (3) Asiatic Pacific Theater. Examples of the medals awarded for each theater are shown below. Additionally allied medals such as those presented by the Philippines are shown.

American Campaign Medal   Asiatic Pacific Campaign   WW2 Victory   Occupation Medal Army   Occupation Medal Navy

Asiatic Pacific Theater

American Defense Service   American Campaign Medal   Victory Medal WWII

American Theater Medals

Philippine Defense Medal   Philippine Liberation Medal   Philippine Independence Medal   Philippine Presidential Unit Citation

US Veteran's Philippine Medals

National Defense Service   US Korean Service   UN Korean Service   ROK War Service   Korean Presidential Unit Citation

Korean War Basic Medals

Army Good Conduct   Navy Good Conduct   Marine Good Conduct   USAF Good Conduct   USCG Good Conduct

Good Conduct Medals Since 1963

National Defense Service Medal   U.S. Vietnam Service Medal   RVN Campaign Medal   RVN Gallantry Cross Unit Citation

Vietnam Basic Medals

National Defense Service Medal   South West Asia Service   Saudi Arabian Liberation of Kuwait   Kuwait Liberation of Kuwait

Gulf War Basic Medals

Displaying Military Awards

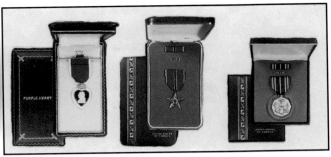

emblazoned on the front. At the present time, the more common decorations, (e.g., Achievement and Commendation Medals), come in small plastic cases, suitable only for initial presentation and storage of the medal.

The most appropriate use of military medals after active service is to mount the medals for permanent display in home or office. This reflects the individual's patriotism and the service rendered the United States.

Decorations are usually awarded in a presentation set which normally consists of a medal, ribbon bar and lapel pin, all contained in a special case. During World War II, the name of the decoration was stamped in gold on the front of the case. However, as budget considerations assumed greater importance, this practice was gradually phased out and replaced by a standard case with "United States of America"

The most effective method of protecting awards involves the use of a shadow box or glass front display case with at least 1/2 inch between the medals and the glass. This provides a three dimensional view and protects the medal display in a dust-free environment.

Any physical alteration destroys the integrity of the medal and the use of glues ruins the back of the ribbon and medal. The best way to mount medals is in a display case especially designed for that purpose.

The mounting board is absolutely critical. Acid-free Gator board at least 1/4 inch thick covered with a high quality velour-type material to which velcro will adhere will allow the medals to be mounted using velcro tape which locks the medal firmly into place without damage. The added advantage is the medals and insignia can be moved without damage.

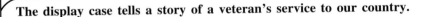

The display case tells a story of a veteran's service to our country.

★ What branch and unit, ship or squadron.

★ What awards and campaigns.

★ What skills and rank.

★ Where and when.

This display case of Army service in Korea is a good example.

★ Good Conduct Medal shows his exemplary service

★ National Defense Service Medal

★ Korean Service Medal with 2 campaign stars

★ Korean Service Ribbons with Unit citation

★ Early Korean Era Sergeant's rank

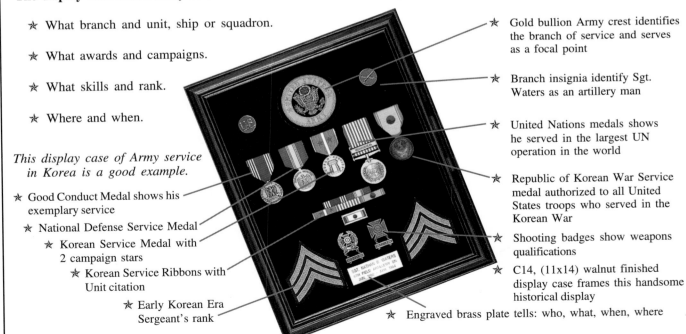

★ Gold bullion Army crest identifies the branch of service and serves as a focal point

★ Branch insignia identify Sgt. Waters as an artillery man

★ United Nations medals shows he served in the largest UN operation in the world

★ Republic of Korean War Service medal authorized to all United States troops who served in the Korean War

★ Shooting badges show weapons qualifications

★ C14, (11x14) walnut finished display case frames this handsome historical display

★ Engraved brass plate tells: who, what, when, where

Each display case will be different just as each veterans' service was different and each service will have different insignia. Each case will show the honors a grateful nation has bestowed on her veterans. Turn to page 39 for examples from each war and conflict.

Wear of Medals, Insignia and the Uniform by Veterans, Retirees and Former Service Members

Introduction

One of the first lessons taught to new recruits is proper wear of the uniform and its insignia. The same principle applies to wear of military awards on their old uniform by veterans and retirees. There are a number of occasions when tradition, patriotism, ceremonies and social occasions call for the wear of military awards.

Civilian Dress

The most common manner of wearing a decoration or medal is as a lapel pin, in the left lapel of a civilian suit  jacket. The small enameled lapel pin represents the ribbon bar of a single decoration or ribbon an individual has received (usually the highest award or one having special meaning to the wearer). Many well-known veterans such as former Senator Bob Dole, a World War II Purple Heart recipient, wear a lapel pin. Pins are available for all awards and some ribbons such as the Combat Action Ribbon or Presidential Unit Citation. Small miniature wings, parachute badges and Combat Infantry Badges are also worn in the lapel or as a tie tac. Additionally, retirees are encouraged to wear their retired pin and World War II veterans are encouraged to wear their Honorable Discharge Pin (affectionately referred to as the "ruptured duck").

WW2 Honorable Discharge Pin

U.S. Air Force Retired Pin

Honorably discharged and retired Armed Force members may wear full-size or miniature medals on civilian suits on appropriate occasions such as Memorial Day and Armed Forces Day. Female members may wear full-size or miniature medals on equivalent dress. It is not considered appropriate to wear skill or qualification badges on civilian attire.

Formal Civilian Wear

For more formal occasions, it is correct and encouraged to wear miniature decorations and medals. For a black or white tie occasion, the rule is quite simple: if the lapel is wide enough wear the miniatures on the left lapel or, in the case of a shawl lapel on a tuxedo, the miniature medals are worn over the left breast pocket. The center of the holding bar of the bottom row of medals should be parallel to the ground immediately above the pocket. Do not wear a pocket handkerchief. Miniature medals  really do make a handsome statement of patriotic service at weddings and other social events.

Miniature medals can also be worn on a civilian suit at veterans' functions, memorial events, formal occasions of ceremony and social functions of a military nature.

Wear of the Uniform

On certain occasions retired Armed Forces personnel may wear either the uniform prescribed at the date of retirement or any of the current active duty authorized uniforms. Retirees should adhere to the same grooming standards as Armed Forces active duty personnel when wearing the uniform (for example, a beard is inappropriate while in uniform). Whenever the uniform is worn, it must be done in such a manner as to reflect credit upon the individual and the service from which he/she is retired. (Do not mix uniform items.)

The occasions are for wear by retirees are:
- military ceremonies.
- military funerals, weddings, memorial services and inaugurals.
- patriotic parades on national holidays.
- military parades in which active or reserve units are participating.
- educational institutions when engaged in giving military instruction or responsible for military discipline.
- social or other functions when the invitation has obviously been influenced by the member's earlier active service.

Honorably separated wartime veterans may wear the uniform authorized at the time of their service.

The occasions are:
- military funerals, memorial services, and inaugurals.
- patriotic parades on national holidays.
- any occasion authorized by law.
- military parades in which active or reserve units are participating.

Non-wartime service personnel separated (other than retired, ANG and Reserve) are not authorized to wear the uniform but may wear the medals.

UNITED STATES ARMY

Wear Of Service Ribbons — Ribbons may be worn on the Army green, blue and white uniform coats. The ribbons are worn in one or more rows in order of precedence with either no space or 1/8 inch between rows, no more than four ribbons to a row. The top row is centered or aligned to left edge of the row underneath, whichever looks the best. Unit awards are centered above the right breast pocket with a maximum of three per row.

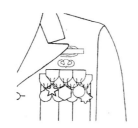

Wear Of Full Size Decorations & Service Medals — Decorations and service medals may be worn on the Army blue or white uniform after retreat and by enlisted personnel on the dress green uniform for social functions. The medals are mounted in order of precedence, in rows with not more than four medals in a row. The top row cannot have more medals than the one below. Rows are separated by 1/8 inch. Medals may not overlap (as Navy and Marines do), so normally there are only three to a row due to the size of the coat. Service and training ribbons are not worn with full size medals.

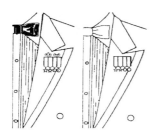

Wear Of Miniature Decorations & Service Medals — Miniature medals are scaled down replicas of full size medals. Only miniature medals are authorized for wear on the mess and evening uniform jackets (and with the blue and white uniform after retreat on formal occasions.)

Miniature medals are mounted on bars with the order of precedence from the wearer's right to left. The medals are mounted side by side if there are four or less. They may be overlapped up to 50% when five, six or seven are in a row. Overlapping is equal for all medals with the right one fully displayed. When two or more rows are worn, the bottom pendants must be fully visible.

UNITED STATES NAVY

(The Coast Guard generally follows U.S. Navy guidelines)

Wear Of Service Ribbons — Wear up to 3 in a row; if more than three ribbons wear in horizontal rows of three each. The top row contains the lesser number, centered above the row below, no spaces between ribbon rows. Rows of ribbons covered by coat lapel may contain two ribbons each and be aligned. Wear ribbons with lower edge of bottom row centered 1/4 inch above left breast and parallel to the deck.

Coast Guard members may either wear the senior three ribbons or all ribbons when they are covered by lapel by 1/3 or more. Rows can be decreased to 2 or 1 if all ribbons are worn in this situation.

Wear Of Full Size Decorations And Service Medals — Wear large medals on full dress uniforms. Align bottom row same as ribbon bars. All rows may contain maximum of 3 medals side by side or up to 5 overlapping. Overlapping is proportional with inboard medal showing in full. Mount medals so they cover suspension ribbon of the medal below.

Wear Of Miniature Medals — Wear miniature medals with all formal and dinner dress uniforms. Place holding bar of lowest row of miniatures 3 inches below the notch, centered on the lapel. Center the holding bar immediately above the left breast pocket on the blue and white service coat. You may wear up to five miniature medals in a row with no overlap on the dinner jacket, center up to 3 miniature medals on the lapel. Position 4 or more miniatures at the inner edge of the lapel extending beyond the lapel to the body of the jacket.

UNITED STATES MARINE CORPS

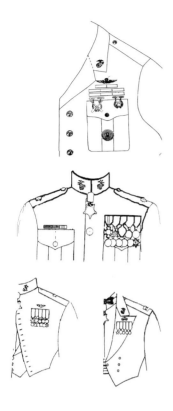

Wear Of Service Ribbons — Ribbons are authorized on Marine dress "B", dress "A" or shirts when prescribed as an outer garment. They are normally worn in rows of 3 or rows of 4 when displaying a large number of awards. If the lapel conceals any ribbons, they may be placed in successively decreasing rows (i.e.: 4, 3, 2, 1). All aligned vertically on center, except if the top row can be altered to present the neatest appearance. Ribbon rows may be spaced 1/8 inch apart or together. Ribbon bars are centered 1/8 inch above the upper left pocket. When marksmanship badges are worn, the ribbon bars are 1/8 inch above them.

Full Size Medals — Marines wear up to 4 medals side by side on a 3 1/4 inch bar. A maximum of 7 medals may be overlapped (not to exceed 50% with the right or inboard medal shown in full). Full size medals are worn on blue or white dress coat centered on the left breast pocket with the upper edge of the holding bar on line midway between the 1st and 2nd button of the coat. When large medals are worn, all unit citations and ribbons with no medal authorized are centered over the right breast pocket the bottom edge 1/8 inch above the top of the pocket.

Wear Of Miniature Medals — When miniature medals are worn, no ribbons will be worn. On evening dress jackets miniature medals will be centered on the left front jacket panel midway between the inner edge and the left armhole seam, with the top of the bar on line with the 2nd blind button hole. On mess dress and SNCO's evening and mess dress the miniature medals are centered on the left lapel with the top of the holding bar 1 inch below the lapel notch. Maximum of 10 overlapped.

UNITED STATES AIR FORCE

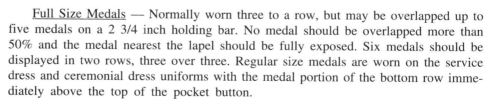

Wear Of Service Ribbons — Ribbons may be worn on service dress and blue shirt. Ribbons are normally worn in rows of three with the bottom bar centered and resting on the top edge of the pocket. Ribbons may be worn four-in-a-row with the left edge of the ribbons aligned with the left edge of pocket to keep lapel from covering ribbons. There is no space between rows of ribbons. Current regulations stipulate that members may choose which ribbons to wear, if any.

Full Size Medals — Normally worn three to a row, but may be overlapped up to five medals on a 2 3/4 inch holding bar. No medal should be overlapped more than 50% and the medal nearest the lapel should be fully exposed. Six medals should be displayed in two rows, three over three. Regular size medals are worn on the service dress and ceremonial dress uniforms with the medal portion of the bottom row immediately above the top of the pocket button.

Miniature Medals — Miniature Medals are worn on the blue mess dress or on formal dress. The miniatures are centered between lapel and arm seam and midway between top shoulder seam and top button of jacket. If more than four miniatures, the wearer has the option of mounting up to seven by overlapping or going to a 2nd bar. Seven is the maximum on one bar, however, many in the Air Force prefer only a maximum of four to a bar.

U. S. Military Awards

THE PYRAMID OF HONOR

The awards system of the United States, described in the introduction, has evolved into a structured program often called the "Pyramid of Honor." The system is designed to reward services ranging from heroism on the battlefield to superior performance of noncombat duties and even includes the completion of entry level training.

Far from being disturbed by the award proliferation, the Armed Services have embraced Napoleon's concept of liberally awarding medals and ribbons in great profusion to enhance morale and esprit de corps. This expanded and specifically-tailored awards program is generally very popular in the all-volunteer armed forces and has played a significant part in improving morale, job performance, recruitment and reenlistments amongst junior officers and enlisted personnel.

The decorations and awards which represent the rich United States military heritage from 1939 onward are presented on the following pages in an overall order of precedence (individual service orders of precedence start on Page 40). These awards paint a wonderful portrait of this country's dedication to the ideals of freedom and the honors and sacrifices required of the military to support those ideals.

In the award descriptions, the numbers in parentheses on the "Device" line refer to the tables contained in the "Attachments and Devices" section, starting on page 124. Additional, the page number after the name of the award refers to a detailed description of the decoration, medal or ribbon.

THE MEDAL OF HONOR

In a country whose Government is based on a totally democratic society, it is fitting that the first medal to reward meritorious acts on the field of battle should be for private soldiers and seamen (although extended in later years to officers).

The Congressional Medal of Honor (referred to universally as the Medal of Honor in all statutes, awards manuals, and uniform regulations) was born in conflict, steeped in controversy during its early years and finally emerged, along with Britain's Victoria Cross, as one of the world's premier awards for bravery.

The medal is actually a statistical oddity, proving the unlikely equation that "Three equals One". Although there are three separate medals representing America's highest reward for bravery (illustrated on the next page), there is now only a single set of directives governing the award of this, the most coveted of all U.S. decorations.

The medal was created during the Civil War as a reward for "gallantry in action and other soldier-like qualities" ("...seamanlike qualities..." in the case of the Navy). However, the reference to "other qualities" led to many awards for actions which would seem less than heroic, including the bestowal of 864 awards upon the entire membership of the 27th Maine Volunteer Infantry for merely reenlisting.

The inconsistencies in those and other dubious cases were apparently resolved in the early 20th Century when 910 names were removed from the lists (including the 864 to the 27th Maine). At the same time, the statutes which govern the award of the medal were revised to reflect the present-day criteria of "Gallantry and intrepidity at the risk of one's own life above and beyond the call of duty".

ARMY MEDAL OF HONOR

1862

The Army Medal of Honor was first awarded in 1862 but, owing to extensive copying by veterans groups, was redesigned in 1904 and patented by the War Department to ensure the design exclusivity.

The present medal, a five pointed golden star, lays over a green enamelled laurel wreath. The center of the star depicts Minerva, Goddess of righteous war and wisdom, encircled by the words: "United States of America". The back of the medal is inscribed, "The Congress to", with a place for the recipient's name. The medal hangs from a bar inscribed: "Valor", which is held by an American Eagle with laurel leaves (denoting peace) in its right talon and arrows (war) in its left. The eagle is fastened by a hook to a light blue silk pad on which are embroidered 13 stars.

NAVY MEDAL OF HONOR

1861

The 1861 Navy Medal of Honor, was redesigned by Tiffany in 1917, but returned to the basic 1861 design in 1942, and a neck ribbon added. The design is a five point bronze star, with a central circular plaque depicting Minerva repulsing Discord. The reverse is engraved, "Personal Valor", with room for the recipient's name, rank, ship or unit and date. The medal hangs from the flukes of an anchor, which is attached to the neck ribbon.

AIR FORCE MEDAL OF HONOR

Congress established the Air Force Medal of Honor in 1960, 13 years after the establishment of the Air Force as an independent Service (prior to 1960, airmen received the Army medal). The medal design is fashioned after the Army version and is a five pointed star with a green enamelled laurel wreath. The center depicts the head of the Statue of Liberty surrounded by 34 stars. The star hangs from a representation of the Air Force coat of arms and is suspended from a bar inscribed, VALOR.

Medals of Honor

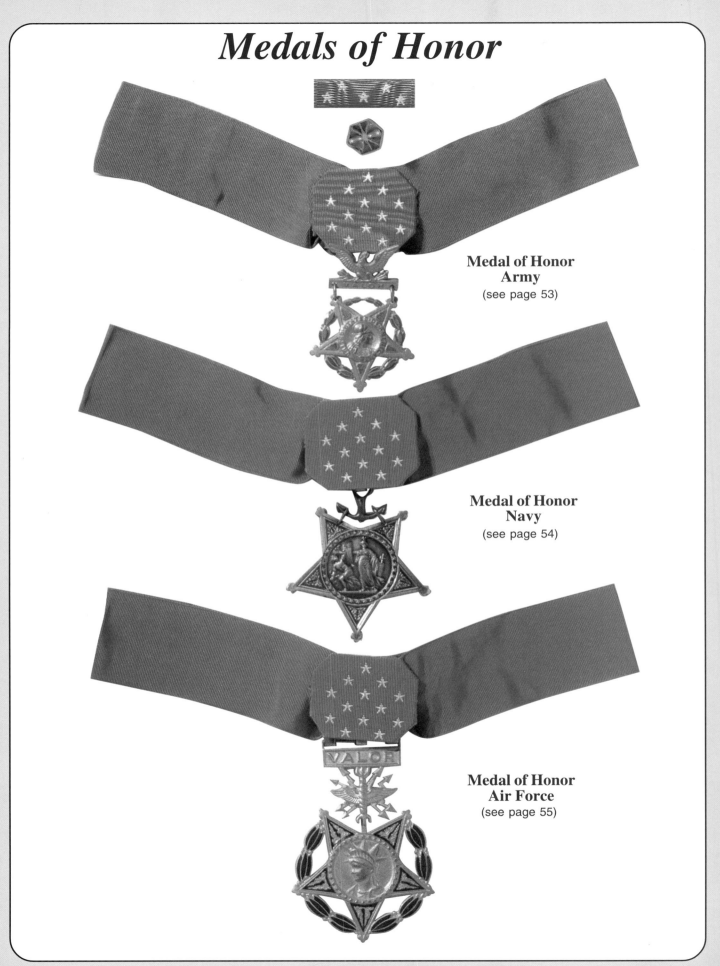

**Medal of Honor
Army**
(see page 53)

**Medal of Honor
Navy**
(see page 54)

**Medal of Honor
Air Force**
(see page 55)

Distinguished Service Cross
(see page 56)

Service: Army

Instituted: 1918

Criteria: Extraordinary heroism in action against an enemy of the U.S. while engaged in military operations involving conflict with an opposing foreign force or while serving with friendly foreign forces.

Devices: Bronze, silver oak leaf cluster (27, 29)

Notes: 100 copies of earlier design cross issued with a European-style (unedged) ribbon ("French Cut")

Navy Cross
(see page 56)

Service: Navy/Marine Corps/Coast Guard

Instituted: 1919

Criteria: Extraordinary heroism in action against an enemy of the U.S. while engaged in military operations involving conflict with an opposing foreign force or while serving with friendly foreign forces.

Devices: Gold, silver star (49, 50)

Notes: Originally issued with a 1 1/2" wide ribbon

Air Force Cross
(see page 57)

Service: Air Force

Instituted: 1960

Criteria: Extraordinary heroism in action against an enemy of the U.S. while engaged in military operations involving conflict with an opposing foreign force or while serving with friendly foreign forces.

Devices: Bronze, silver oak leaf cluster (27, 29)

Notes: Created under the same legislation which established the Distinguished Service Cross 42 years earlier

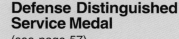

Defense Distinguished Service Medal
(see page 57)

Service: All Services (by Secretary of Defense)

Instituted: 1970

Criteria: Exceptionally meritorious service to the United States while assigned to a Joint Activity in a position of unique and great responsibility.

Devices: All Services: bronze & silver oak leaf cluster (27, 29)

Army Distinguished Service Medal
(see page 58)

Service: Army

Instituted: 1918

Criteria: Exceptionally meritorious service to the United States Government in a duty of great responsibility

Devices: Bronze, silver oak leaf cluster (27, 29)

Notes: Originally issued with European (unedged) ribbon ("French Cut")

Navy Distinguished Service Medal
(see page 58)

Service: Navy/Marine Corps

Instituted: 1919

Criteria: Exceptionally meritorious service to the United States Government in a duty of great responsibility

Devices: Gold, silver star (49, 50)

Notes: 107 copies of earlier medal design issued but later withdrawn. First ribbon design was 1 1/2" wide

Air Force Distinguished Service Medal

(see page 59)

<u>Service:</u> Air Force

<u>Instituted:</u> 1960

<u>Criteria:</u> Exceptionally meritorious service to the United States Government in a duty of great responsibility

<u>Devices:</u> Bronze, silver oak leaf cluster (27, 29)

<u>Notes:</u> Original design was modified and used as the Airman's Medal

Transportation Distinguished Service Medal

(see page 59)

<u>Service:</u> Coast Guard

<u>Instituted:</u> 1992

<u>Criteria:</u> Exceptionally meritorious service in a duty of great responsibility while assigned to the Department of Transportation or other activities under the responsibility of the Secretary of Transportation

<u>Devices:</u> Gold star (49)

Coast Guard Distinguished Service Medal

(see page 60)

<u>Service:</u> Coast Guard

<u>Instituted:</u> 1961

<u>Criteria:</u> Exceptionally meritorious service to the United States Government in a duty of great responsibility

<u>Devices:</u> Gold, silver star (49, 50)

<u>Notes:</u> Originally authorized in 1949 but the design was not approved until 1961

Silver Star

(see page 60)

<u>Service:</u> All Services (originally Army only)

<u>Instituted:</u> 1932

<u>Criteria:</u> Gallantry in action against an armed enemy of the United States or while serving with friendly foreign forces

<u>Devices:</u> Army/Air Force: bronze, silver oak leaf cluster (27, 29); Navy/Marine Corps/Coast Guard: gold, silver star (49, 50)

<u>Notes:</u> Derived from the 3/16" silver "Citation Star" previously worn on Army campaign medals

Defense Superior Service Medal

(see page 61)

<u>Service:</u> All Services (by Secretary of Defense)

<u>Instituted:</u> 1976

<u>Criteria:</u> Superior meritorious service to the United States while assigned to a Joint Activity in a position of significant responsibility

<u>Devices:</u> All Services: bronze, silver oak leaf cluster (27, 29)

Legion of Merit

(see page 61)

<u>Service:</u> All Services

<u>Instituted:</u> 1942

<u>Criteria:</u> Exceptionally meritorious conduct in the performance of outstanding services to the United States

<u>Devices:</u> Army/Air Force: bronze, silver oak leaf cluster (27, 29); Navy/Marine Corps/Coast Guard: bronze letter "V" (for valor) (18), gold, silver star (49, 50)

<u>Notes:</u> Issued in four degrees (Legionnaire, Officer, Commander & Chief Commander) to foreign nationals

Distinguished Flying Cross

(see page 62)

Service: All Services

Instituted: 1926

Criteria: Heroism or extraordinary achievement while participating in aerial flight

Devices: Army/Air Force: bronze, silver oak leaf cluster (27, 29); Navy/Marine Corps: bronze letter "V" (for valor) (18), Navy/Marine Corps/Coast Guard: gold, silver star (49, 50)

Soldier's Medal

(see page 62)

Service: Army

Instituted: 1926

Criteria: Heroism not involving actual conflict with an armed enemy of the United States.

Devices: Bronze, silver oak leaf cluster (27, 29)

Notes: Award requires personal hazard or danger and voluntary risk of life.

Navy and Marine Corps Medal

(see page 63)

Service: Navy/Marine Corps

Instituted: 1942

Criteria: Heroism not involving actual conflict with an armed enemy of the United States.

Devices: Gold, silver star (49, 50)

Notes: For acts of lifesaving, action must be at great risk to one's own life.

Airman's Medal

(see page 63)

Service: Air Force

Instituted: 1960

Criteria: Heroism involving voluntary risk of life under conditions other than those of actual conflict with an armed enemy.

Devices: Bronze, silver oak leaf cluster (27, 29)

Notes: Derived from original design of Air Force Distinguished Service Medal.

Coast Guard Medal

(see page 64)

Service: Coast Guard

Instituted: 1958

Criteria: Heroism not involving actual conflict with an armed enemy of the United States.

Devices: Gold, silver star (49, 50)

Notes: Authorized in 1949 but not designed and issued until 1958.

Ribbon design used for a few months in 1999.

Gold Lifesaving Medal

(see page 64)

Service: All Services and Civilians

Instituted: 1874 (modified 1882 and 1946)

Criteria: Heroic conduct at the risk of life during the rescue or attempted rescue of a victim of drowning or shipwreck.

Devices: Coast Guard: gold star (49)

Notes: Normally a "Non-Military Decoration" but considered a personal decoration by the Coast Guard. Originally a "table" (non-wearable) medal, then worn with a 2" wide ribbon.

Bronze Star Medal

(see page 65)

<u>Service:</u> All Services

<u>Instituted:</u> 1944

<u>Criteria:</u> Heroic or meritorious achievement or service not involving participation in aerial flight.

<u>Devices:</u> Army/Air Force: bronze letter "V" (for valor) (17), bronze, silver oak leaf cluster (27, 29); Navy/Marine Corps/Coast Guard: bronze letter "V" (for valor) (17), gold, silver star (49, 50)

<u>Notes:</u> Awarded to World War II holders of Army Combat Infantryman Badge or Combat Medical Badge.

Purple Heart

(see page 66)

<u>Service:</u> All Services (originally Army only)

<u>Instituted:</u> 1932

<u>Criteria:</u> Awarded to any member of the U.S. Armed Forces killed or wounded in an armed conflict.

<u>Devices:</u> Army/Air Force: bronze, silver oak leaf cluster (27, 29); Navy/ Marine Corps/ Coast Guard: gold, silver star (49, 50)

<u>Notes:</u> Wound Ribbon appeared circa 1917-18 but was never officially authorized. (Army used wound chevrons during World War I).

Defense Meritorious Service Medal

(see page 67)

<u>Service:</u> All Services (by Secretary of Defense)

<u>Instituted:</u> 1977

<u>Criteria:</u> Noncombat meritorious achievement or service while assigned to Joint Activity.

<u>Devices:</u> All Services: bronze, silver oak leaf cluster (27, 29)

Meritorious Service Medal

(see page 67)

<u>Service:</u> All Services

<u>Instituted:</u> 1969

<u>Criteria:</u> Outstanding non-combat meritorious achievement or service to the United States.

<u>Devices:</u> Army/Air Force: bronze, silver oak leaf cluster (27, 29); Navy/ Marine Corps/ Coast Guard: gold, silver star (49, 50); Coast Guard: silver letter "O" (15).

Air Medal

(see page 68)

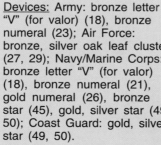

<u>Service:</u> All Services

<u>Instituted:</u> 1942

<u>Criteria:</u> Heroic actions or meritorious service while participating in aerial flight.

<u>Devices:</u> Army: bronze letter "V" (for valor) (18), bronze numeral (23); Air Force: bronze, silver oak leaf cluster (27, 29); Navy/Marine Corps: bronze letter "V" (for valor) (18), bronze numeral (21), gold numeral (26), bronze star (45), gold, silver star (49, 50); Coast Guard: gold, silver star (49, 50).

Silver Lifesaving Medal

(see page 69)

<u>Service:</u> All Services and Civilians

<u>Instituted:</u> 1874 (modified 1882 and 1946)

<u>Criteria:</u> Heroic conduct during rescue or attempted rescue of a victim of drowning or shipwreck.

<u>Devices:</u> Coast Guard: gold star (49)

<u>Notes:</u> Normally a "Non-Military Decoration" but considered a personal decoration by the Coast Guard. Originally a "table" (non-wearable) medal, then worn with a 2" wide ribbon.

Aerial Achievement Medal

(see page 69)

Service: Air Force

Instituted: 1988

Criteria: Sustained meritorious achievement while participating in aerial flight.

Devices: Bronze, silver oak leaf cluster (27, 29)

Notes: Considered on a par with the Air Medal but more likely to be awarded for peacetime actions.

Joint Service Commendation Medal

(see page 70)

Service: All Services (by Secretary of Defense)

Instituted: 1963

Criteria: Meritorious service or achievement while assigned to a Joint Activity.

Devices: All Services: bronze letter "V" (for valor) (18), bronze, silver oak leaf cluster (27, 29)

Army Commendation Medal

(see page 70)

Service: Army

Instituted: 1945 (retroactive to 1941)

Criteria: Heroism, meritorious achievement or meritorious service.

Devices: Bronze letter "V" (for valor) (18), bronze, silver oak leaf cluster (27, 29)

Notes: Originally a ribbon-only award then designated "Army Commendation Ribbon with Metal Pendant". Redesignated: "Army Commendation Medal" in 1960.

Navy & Marine Corps Commendation Medal

(see page 71)

Service: Navy/Marine Corps

Instituted: 1944 (retroactive to 1941)

Criteria: Heroic or meritorious achievement or service.

Devices: Bronze letter "V" (for valor) (18), gold, silver star (49, 50)

Notes: Originally a ribbon-only award then designated "Navy Commendation Ribbon with Metal Pendant". Redesignated: "Navy Commendation Medal" in 1960. Change to present name was made in 1994.

Air Force Commendation Medal

(see page 71)

Service: Air Force

Instituted: 1958

Criteria: Outstanding achievement or meritorious service rendered on behalf of the United States Air Force.

Devices: Bronze, silver oak leaf cluster (27, 29), bronze letter "V" (for valor) (18)

Coast Guard Commendation Medal

(see page 72)

Service: Coast Guard

Instituted: 1947

Criteria: 1. Heroic or meritorious achievement or service. 2. Meritorious service resulting in unusual or outstanding achievement.

Devices: Silver letter "O" (15), bronze letter "V" (for valor) (18), gold, silver star (49, 50)

Notes: Originally "Commendation Ribbon with Metal Pendant". Redesignated: "Coast Guard Commendation Medal" in 1959.

Joint Service Achievement Medal

(see page 72)

Service: All Services (by Secretary of Defense)

Instituted: 1983

Criteria: Meritorious service or achievement while serving with a Joint Activity.

Devices: All Services: bronze, silver oak leaf cluster (27, 29)

Army Achievement Medal

(see page 73)

Service: Army

Instituted: 1981

Criteria: Meritorious service or achievement while serving in a non-combat area.

Devices: Bronze, silver oak leaf cluster (27, 29)

Navy & Marine Corps Achievement Medal

(see page 73)

Service: Navy/Marine Corps

Instituted: 1961

Criteria: Meritorious service or achievement in a combat or noncombat situation based on sustained performance of a superlative nature.

Devices: Bronze letter "V" (for valor) (18), gold, silver star (49, 50)

Notes: Originally a ribbon-only award: "Secretary of the Navy Commendation for Achievement Award with Ribbon". Changed to present form in 1967. Changed to present name in 1994.

Air Force Achievement Medal

(see page 74)

Service: Air Force

Instituted: 1980

Criteria: Outstanding achievement or meritorious service not warranting award of the Air Force Commendation Medal.

Devices: Bronze, silver oak leaf cluster (27, 29), bronze letter "V" (for valor) (18)

Coast Guard Achievement Medal

(see page 74)

Service: Coast Guard

Instituted: 1968

Criteria: Professional and/or leadership achievement in a combat or noncombat situation.

Devices: Silver letter "O" (15), bronze letter "V" (for valor) (18), gold, silver star (49, 50)

Notes: Originally a ribbon-only award. Present configuration adopted in 1968.

Commandant's Letter of Commendation Ribbon

(see page 74)

Service: Coast Guard   Instituted: 1979

Criteria: Receipt of a letter of commendation for an act or service resulting in unusual and/or outstanding achievement.

Devices: Silver letter "O" (15), gold, silver star (49, 50)

Combat Action Ribbon

(see page 75)

Service: Navy/Marine Corps   Instituted: 1969 (Retroactive to 6th Dec 1941)

Criteria: Active participation in ground or air combat during specifically listed military operations.

Devices: Gold, silver star (49, 50)

Notes: This is the only Navy personal decoration which has no associated medal (a "ribbon-only" award).

Prisoner of War Medal

(see page 75)

Service: All Services

Instituted: 1985

Criteria: Awarded to any member of the U.S. Armed Forces taken prisoner during any armed conflict dating from World War I.

Devices: Bronze, silver star (42, 47)

Combat Readiness Medal

(see page 75)

Service: Air Force

Instituted: 1964

Criteria: Awarded for specific periods of qualifying service in a combat or mission-ready status.

Devices: Bronze, silver oak leaf cluster (27, 29)

Army Good Conduct Medal

(see page 76)

Service: Army (also Air Force until 1963)

Instituted: 1941

Criteria: Exemplary conduct, efficiency and fidelity during three years of active enlisted service with the U.S. Army (1 year during wartime).

Devices: Bronze, silver, gold knotted bar (4)

Reserve Special Commendation Ribbon (obsolete)

(see page 77)

Service: Navy/Marine Corps   Instituted: 1946

Criteria: Awarded to Reserve Officers with 4 years of successful command and a total Reserve service of 10 years.

Devices: None

WW II Navy Good Conduct Medal

WW II Marine Good Conduct Medal

WW II Coast Guard Good Conduct Medal

Navy Good Conduct Medal

(see page 77)

Service: Navy

Instituted: 1888

Criteria: Outstanding performance and conduct during 4 years of continuous active enlisted service in the U.S. Navy.

Devices: Bronze, silver star (42, 47)

Notes: Earlier ribbon was a brighter shade of red.

Marine Corps Good Conduct Medal

(see page 78)

Service: Marine Corps

Instituted: 1896

Criteria: Outstanding performance and conduct during 3 years of continuous active enlisted service in the U.S. Marine Corps.

Devices: Bronze, silver star (42, 47)

Notes: Earlier ribbon was 1 1/4" wide.

Air Force Good Conduct Medal

(see page 78)

Service: Air Force

Instituted: 1963

Criteria: Exemplary conduct, efficiency and fidelity during three years of active enlisted service with the U.S. Air Force.

Devices: Bronze, silver oak leaf cluster (27, 29)

Notes: Air Force used Army Good Conduct Medal until 1963.

Coast Guard Good Conduct Medal

(see page 79)

Service: Coast Guard

Instituted: 1921

Criteria: Outstanding proficiency, leadership and conduct during 3 continuous years of active enlisted Coast Guard service.

Devices: Bronze, silver star (42, 47)

Notes: Earlier ribbon was 1 1/2" wide.

Army Reserve Components Achievement Medal

(see page 79)

Service: Army

Instituted: 1971

Criteria: Exemplary conduct, efficiency and fidelity during 3 years of service with the U.S. Army Reserve or National Guard.

Devices: Bronze, silver oak leaf cluster (27, 29)

Naval Reserve Meritorious Service Medal

(see page 80)

Service: Navy

Instituted: 1964

Criteria: Outstanding performance and conduct during 4 years of enlisted service in the Naval Reserve.

Devices: Bronze, silver star (42, 47)

Notes: Originally a ribbon-only award.

Selected Marine Corps Reserve Medal

(see page 80)

Service: Marine Corps

Instituted: 1939

Criteria: Outstanding performance and conduct during 4 years of enlisted service in the Marine Corps Selected Reserve.

Devices: Bronze, silver star (42, 47)

Notes: Formerly: "Organized Marine Corps Reserve Medal".

Air Reserve Forces Meritorious Service Medal

(see page 80)

Service: Air Force

Instituted: 1964

Criteria: Exemplary behavior, efficiency and fidelity during three years of active enlisted service with the Air Force Reserve.

Devices: Bronze, silver oak leaf cluster (27, 29)

Coast Guard Reserve Good Conduct Medal

(see page 81)

Service: Coast Guard

Instituted: 1963

Criteria: Outstanding proficiency, leadership and conduct during 3 years of enlisted service in the Coast Guard Reserve.

Devices: Bronze, silver star (42, 47))

Notes: Originally a ribbon-only award- "Coast Guard Reserve Meritorious Service Ribbon".

Fleet Marine Force Ribbon

(see page 81)

Service: Navy   Instituted: 1984

Criteria: Active participation by professionally skilled Navy personnel with the Fleet Marine Force.

Devices: None

Outstanding Airman of the Year Ribbon

(see page 81)

Service: Air Force   Instituted: 1968

Criteria: Awarded to airmen for selection to the "12 Outstanding Airmen of the Year" Competition Program.

Devices: Bronze, silver oak leaf cluster (27, 29), bronze star (43)

Air Force Recognition Ribbon

(see page 81)

Service: Air Force   Instituted: 1980

Criteria: Awarded to individual recipients of Air Force-level special trophies and awards.

Devices: Bronze, silver oak leaf cluster (27, 29)

Navy Expeditionary Medal

(see page 82)

Service: Navy

Instituted: 1936

Dates: 1936 to Present

Criteria: Landings on foreign territory and operations against armed opposition for which no specific campaign medal has been authorized.

Devices: Silver letter "W" (19) (denotes bar below), bronze, silver star (42, 47)

Bars: "Wake Island" (see page128)

Marine Corps Expeditionary Medal

(see page 82)

Service: Marine Corps

Instituted: 1919

Dates: 1919 to Present

Criteria: Landings on foreign territory and operations against armed opposition for which no specific campaign medal has been authorized.

Devices: Silver letter "W" (19) (denotes bar below), bronze, silver star (42, 47)

Notes: Originally a "ribbon-only" award.

Bars: "Wake Island" (see page 128)

China Service Medal

(see page 83)

Service: Navy/Marine Corps/ Coast Guard

Instituted: 1940

Dates: 1937-39, 1945-57

Criteria: Service ashore in China or on-board naval vessels during either of the above periods.

Devices: Bronze star (39)

Notes: Medal was reinstituted in 1947 for extended service during dates shown above.

American Defense Service Medal

(see page 83)

Service: All Services

Instituted: 1941

Dates: 1939-41

Criteria: Army: 12 months of active duty service during the above period; Naval Services: Any active duty service.

Devices: All Services: bronze star (41) (denotes bars below); All Naval Services: bronze letter "A" (8) (not worn with bronze star [device no. 41] above)

Bars: "Foreign Service", "Base", "Fleet", "Sea" (see page 128)

Women's Army Corps Service Medal

(see page 84)

<u>Service:</u> Army

<u>Instituted:</u> 1943

<u>Dates:</u> 1941-46

<u>Criteria:</u> Service with both the Women's Army Auxiliary Corps and Women's Army Corps during the above period.

<u>Devices:</u> None

<u>Note:</u> Only U.S. award authorized for women only.

American Campaign Medal

(see page 84)

<u>Service:</u> All Services

<u>Instituted:</u> 1942

<u>Dates:</u> 1941-46

<u>Criteria:</u> Service outside the U.S. in the American theater for 30 days, or within the continental U.S. for one year.

<u>Devices:</u> All Services: bronze star (40,)

Asiatic-Pacific Campaign Medal

(see page 85)

<u>Service:</u> All Services

<u>Instituted:</u> 1942

<u>Dates:</u> 1941-46

<u>Criteria:</u> Service in the Asiatic-Pacific theater for 30 days or receipt of any combat decoration.

<u>Devices:</u> All Services: bronze, silver star (40, 46); Army/Air Force: bronze arrowhead (2); Navy: bronze Marine Corps device (20)

European-African-Middle Eastern Campaign Medal

(see page 86)

<u>Service:</u> All Services

<u>Instituted:</u> 1942

<u>Dates:</u> 1941-45

<u>Criteria:</u> Service in the European-African-Middle Eastern theater for 30 days or receipt of any combat decoration.

<u>Devices:</u> All Services: bronze, silver star (40, 46); Army/Air Force: bronze arrowhead (2); Navy: bronze Marine Corps device (20)

World War II Victory Medal

(see page 87)

<u>Service:</u> All Services

<u>Instituted:</u> 1945

<u>Dates:</u> 1941-46

<u>Criteria:</u> Awarded for service in the U.S. Armed Forces during the above period.

<u>Devices:</u> None

U.S. Antarctic Expedition Medal

(see page 87)

<u>Service:</u> Navy/Coast Guard

<u>Instituted:</u> 1945

<u>Dates:</u> 1939-41

<u>Criteria:</u> Awarded in gold, silver and bronze to members of the U.S. Antarctic Expedition of 1939-41.

<u>Devices:</u> None

Army of Occupation Medal

(see page 88)

Service: Army/Air Force
Instituted: 1946
Dates: 1945-55 (Berlin: 1945-90)
Criteria: 30 consecutive days of service in occupied territories of former enemies during above period.

Devices: Gold airplane (1)
Bars: "Germany", "Japan" (see page128)

Navy Occupation Service Medal

(see page 88)

Service: Navy/Marine Corps/Coast Guard
Instituted: 1947
Dates: 1945-55 (Berlin: 1945-90)
Criteria: 30 consecutive days of service in occupied territories of former enemies during above period.

Devices: Gold airplane (1)
Bars: "Europe", "Asia" (see page 128)

Medal for Humane Action

(see page 89)

Service: All Services
Instituted: 1949
Dates: 1948-49
Criteria: 120 consecutive days of service participating in the Berlin Airlift or in support thereof. Was also awarded posthumously
Devices: None
Notes: This medal was only awarded for Berlin Airlift service and is not to be confused with the Humanitarian Service Medal (established in 1977)

National Defense Service Medal

(see page 89)

Service: All Services
Instituted: 1953
Dates: 1950-54, 1961-74, 1990-95
Criteria: Any honorable active duty service during any of the above periods

Devices: All Services: bronze star (39); Army: bronze oak leaf cluster (28) (obsolete)
Notes: Reinstituted in 1966 and 1991 for Vietnam and Southwest Asia (Gulf War) actions respectively

Korean Service Medal

(see page 90)

Service: All Services
Instituted: 1950
Dates: 1950-54
Criteria: Participation in military operations within the Korean area during the above period

Devices: All Services: bronze, silver star (40, 46); Army/Air Force: bronze arrowhead (2); Navy: bronze Marine Corps device (20)

Antarctica Service Medal

(see page 91)

Service: All Services
Instituted: 1960
Dates: 1946 to Present
Criteria: 30 calendar days of service on the Antarctic Continent

Devices: Bronze, gold, silver disks (5) (denote bars below)

WINTERED OVER

Bars: "Wintered Over" in bronze, gold, silver (see page 128)

Arctic Service Medal

(see page 91)

Service: Coast Guard
Instituted: 1976
Dates: 1946 to Present
Criteria: Awarded for 21 days of service on vessels operating in polar waters north of the Arctic Circle.

Devices: For all deployments after 1 January 1989: bronze, silver star (42, 47)

Armed Forces Expeditionary Medal

(see page 92)

Service: All Services
Instituted: 1961
Dates: 1958 to Present
Criteria: Participation in military operations not covered by specific war medal.

Devices: All Services: bronze, silver star (42, 47); Army: bronze arrowhead (2); Navy: bronze Marine Corps device (20)
Notes: Authorized for service in Vietnam until establishment of Vietnam Service Medal.

Vietnam Service Medal

(see page 93)

Service: All Services
Instituted: 1965
Dates: 1965-73
Criteria: Service in Vietnam, Laos, Cambodia or Thailand during the above period.

Devices: All Services: bronze, silver star (40, 46); Army: bronze arrowhead (2); Navy: bronze Marine Corps device (20)

Southwest Asia Service Medal

(see page 94)

Service: All Services
Instituted: 1991
Dates: 1991 to 1995
Criteria: Active participation in, or support of, Operations Desert Shield and/or Desert Storm.

Devices: All Services: bronze star (40); Navy: bronze Marine Corps device (20)
Notes: Terminal date of service was 30 Nov 95.

Kosovo Campaign Medal

(see page 94)

Service: All Services
Instituted: 2000
Dates: 1999-TBD
Criteria: Service in Kosovo, Former Yugoslavia during the above period.

Devices: All Services: bronze star (42)

Armed Forces Service Medal

(see page 95)

Service: All Services
Instituted: 1996
Dates: 1995 to Present
Criteria: Participation in military operations not covered by specific war medal or the Armed Forces Expeditionary Medal.

Devices: All Services: bronze, silver star (42, 47)

Humanitarian Service Medal
(see page 95)

Service: All Services
Instituted: 1977
Dates: 1975 to Present
Criteria: Direct participation in specific operations of a humanitarian nature.

  3

Devices: All Services: bronze, silver star (42, 47); Army/Air Force/Navy/Marine Corps: bronze numeral (22) (obsolete)

Outstanding Volunteer Service Medal
(see page 96)

Service: All Services
Instituted: 1993
Dates: 1993 to Present
Criteria: Awarded for outstanding and sustained voluntary service to the civilian community.

Devices: All Services: bronze, silver star (42, 47)

Armed Forces Reserve Medal
(see page 96)

Service: All Services
Instituted: 1950
Dates: 1949 to Present
Criteria: 10 years of honorable service in any reserve component of the United States Armed Forces Reserve or award of "M" device.

Devices: Bronze, silver, gold hourglass (7), bronze letter "M" (13); bronze numeral (24)

Naval Reserve Medal (obsolete)
(see page 97)

Service: Navy
Instituted: 1938
Dates: 1938-58
Criteria: 10 years of honorable service in the U.S. Naval Reserve.

Devices: Bronze star (42)
Notes: Replaced by the Armed Forces Reserve Medal (at left). Some earlier versions had deep red ("plum") ribbon.

Navy Expert Rifleman Medal
(see page 97)

Service: Navy
Criteria: Attainment of the minimum qualifying score for the expert level during prescribed shooting exercises.
Devices: None on medal (but see Navy Rifle Marksmanship Ribbon on next page)

Navy Expert Pistol Shot Medal
(see page 97)

Service: Navy
Criteria: Attainment of the minimum qualifying score for the expert level during prescribed shooting exercises.
Devices: None on medal (but see Navy Pistol Marksmanship Ribbon on next page)

 **Navy Distinguished Marksman and Pistol Shot Ribbon (obsolete)**

Service: Navy
Criteria: Attainment of the minimum qualifying score during prescribed shooting exercises.
Devices: None

 Navy Rifle Marksmanship Ribbon

(see page 98)

 **Navy Pistol Marksmanship Ribbon**

(see page 98)

Service: Navy
Criteria: Attainment of the minimum qualifying score during prescribed shooting exercises.

Devices: Bronze, silver letter "E" (9, 10), bronze letter "S" (16)

 **Coast Guard Rifle Marksmanship Ribbon**

(see page 99)

Service: Coast Guard
Criteria: Attainment of the minimum qualifying score during prescribed shooting exercises.

Devices: Bronze, silver letter "E" (9, 10), silver letter "S" (17), bronze, silver rifle (35, 36), gold rifle target (53)

 **Coast Guard Expert Rifleman Medal**

(see page 98)

Service: Coast Guard
Criteria: Attainment of the minimum qualifying score for the expert level during prescribed shooting exercises.

Devices: None on medal (but see Coast Guard Rifle Marksmanship Ribbon directly above)

 **Navy Distinguished Marksman Ribbon (obsolete)**

 **Navy Distinguished Pistol Shot Ribbon (obsolete)**

Service: Navy
Criteria: Attainment of the minimum qualifying score during prescribed shooting exercises.
Devices: None

 **Small Arms Expert Marksmanship Ribbon**

(see page 98)

Service: Air Force
Instituted: 1962
Criteria: Qualification as expert with either the M-16 rifle or standard Air Force issue handgun.

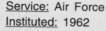

Devices: Bronze star (44)

 **Coast Guard Pistol Marksmanship Ribbon**

(see page 99)

Service: Coast Guard
Criteria: Attainment of the minimum qualifying score during prescribed shooting exercises.

Devices: Bronze, silver letter "E" (9, 10), silver letter "S" (17), bronze, silver pistol (33, 34), gold pistol target (52)

 **Coast Guard Expert Pistol Shot Medal**

(see page 99)

Service: Coast Guard
Criteria: Attainment of the minimum qualifying score for the expert level during prescribed shooting exercises.

Devices: None on medal (but see Coast Guard Pistol Marksmanship Ribbon directly above)

Commonly Awarded Allied Awards

Croix de Guerre

(see page 100)

Country: France

Instituted: 1941

Criteria: Individual feats of arms as recognized by mention in dispatches.

Devices: Bronze palm similar to (31), bronze, silver, gold stars similar to (51) denote level of award and additional awards

Notes: Belgium awarded their own Croix de Guerre to selected U.S. personnel.

Philippine Defense Medal

(see page 102)

Country: Republic of the Philippines

Instituted: 1945 (Army: 1948)

Criteria: Service in defense of the Philippines between 8 December 1941 and 15 June 1942.

Devices: Bronze star (40)

Notes: Only the ribbon may be worn on the U.S. military uniform.

Philippine Liberation Medal

(see page 102)

Country: Republic of the Philippines

Instituted: 1945 (Army: 1948)

Criteria: Service in the liberation of the Philippines between 17 October 1944 and 3 September 1945.

Devices: Bronze star (40)

Notes: Only the ribbon may be worn on the U.S. military uniform.

Philippine Independence Medal

(see page 103)

Country: Republic of the Philippines

Instituted: 1946 (Army: 1948)

Criteria: Receipt of both the Philippine Defense and Liberation Medals/Ribbons. Originally presented to those present for duty in the Philippines on 4 July 1946.

Devices: None

Notes: Only the ribbon may be worn on U.S. military uniform.

United Nations Service Medal (Korea)

(see page 103)

Service: All Services

Instituted: 1951

Criteria: Service on behalf of the United Nations in Korea between 27 June 1950 and 27 July 1954.

Devices: None

Notes: Above date denotes when award was authorized for wear by U.S. military personnel.

Republic of Korea War Service Medal

(see page 106)

Service: All Services

Instituted: 1953

Criteria: Service on the Korean Peninsula between 1950 and 1953

Devices: None

Notes: Not accepted by the United States Government for wear on the military uniform until 1999

 * Some original 1953 medals had a taeguk in the center of the drape like the ribbon bar

Inter-American Defense Board Medal

(see page 103)

Service: All Services

Instituted: 1981

Criteria: Service with the Inter-American Defense Board for at least 1 year.

Devices: Gold star (67)

Notes: Above date denotes when award was authorized for wear by U.S. military personnel.

United Nations Medal

(see page 104)

Service: All Services

Instituted: 1964

Criteria: 6 months service with any authorized UN Peacekeeping mission

Devices: Bronze star (49)

Notes: Medal worn with appropriate mission ribbon. (See pages 38 & 107 for complete list)

NATO Medal

(see page 104)

<u>Service:</u> All Services

<u>Instituted:</u> 1992

<u>Criteria:</u> 30 days service in or 90 days outside the former Republic of Yugoslavia and the Adriatic Sea under NATO command in direct support of NATO operations.

<u>Devices:</u> Bronze Star (42)

<u>Notes:</u> Above date denotes when award was authorized for wear by U.S. military personnel. "Former Yugoslavia" and "Kosovo" Bars not authorized for wear by U.S. Military personnel.

Gallantry Cross

(see page 100)

<u>Country:</u> Republic of Vietnam

<u>Instituted:</u> 1950

<u>Criteria:</u> Deeds of valor and acts of courage/heroism while fighting the enemy.

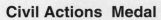

<u>Devices:</u> Bronze palm similar to (31), bronze, silver, gold stars similar to (51)denote level of award and additional awards (see page 127 for further data on Gallantry Cross devices)

Civil Actions Medal

(see page 101)

<u>Country:</u> Republic of Vietnam

<u>Instituted:</u> 1964

<u>Criteria:</u> For outstanding achievements in the field of civic actions.

<u>Devices:</u> None

<u>Notes:</u> 1st Class for officers is shown; the 2nd Class ribbon has no center red stripes.

Saudi Arabian Medal for the Liberation of Kuwait

(see page 106)

<u>Service:</u> All Services

<u>Instituted:</u> 1991

<u>Criteria:</u> Participation in, or support of, Operation Desert Storm (1991 Jan.-Feb.).

<u>Devices:</u> Gold palm tree device (37)

Multinational Force and Observers Medal

(see page 105)

<u>Service:</u> All Services

<u>Instituted:</u> 1982

<u>Criteria:</u> 6 months service with the Multinational Force & Observers peacekeeping force in the Sinai Desert.

<u>Devices:</u> Bronze numeral (23)

<u>Notes:</u> Above date denotes when award was authorized for wear by U.S. military personnel.

Armed Forces Honor Medal

(see page 101)

<u>Country:</u> Republic of Vietnam

<u>Instituted:</u> 1953

<u>Criteria:</u> For outstanding contributions to the training and development of RVN Armed Forces.

<u>Devices:</u> None

<u>Notes:</u> 1st Class for officers is shown; the 2nd Class ribbon does not have the yellow edge stripes.

Republic of Vietnam Campaign Medal

(see page 105)

<u>Service:</u> All Services

<u>Instituted:</u> 1966

<u>Criteria:</u> 6 months service in the Republic of Vietnam between 1965 and 1973 or if wounded, captured or killed in action during the above period.

<u>Devices:</u> Silver date bar (3)

<u>Notes:</u> Bar inscribed "1960-" is the only authorized version.

Kuwaiti Medal for the Liberation of Kuwait

(see page 107)

<u>Service:</u> All Services

<u>Instituted:</u> 1995

<u>Criteria:</u> Participation in, or support of, Operations Desert Shield and/or Desert Storm (1990-93).

<u>Devices:</u> None

<u>Notes:</u> Above date denotes when award was authorized for wear by U.S. military personnel.

The "Ribbon Only" Award Syndrome

The next chapter in this review of the totally unique American awards system will deal with the ribbons depicted on the following pages. These items fall into a special class of honors known as "ribbon-only" awards since there is no associated medal. Although the U.S. is not the only country which has employed this variety of award, it has certainly become the world's greatest proponent of the format.

The practice seems to stem from the late 19th century when various German States, among them Baden, Bavaria, Mecklenburg and Prussia, issued "schnalle" or buckles to members of their Landwehr (militia) as a reward for long and faithful service. The award usually consisted of a unicolored ribbon on which the sovereign's initials were embroidered along with other forms of ornamentation (e.g.: Maltese crosses, the class of the award (II), etc). The ribbon was surrounded by a metal frame and affixed to the uniform by a simple pin back, thus giving the impression of a belt buckle (hence the name).

The first such items in the U.S. inventory were the Presidential Unit Citations established by the Army and Navy during World War II, both as a reward to units/ships cited for collective battle honors and as visual recognition of the individuals who served in such units. As an interesting sidelight, it will be noted that all U.S. Army unit awards, whether by design or pure accident, reintroduce the buckle format by surrounding each ribbon with a gold frame containing a design of laurel leaves. The influence of the Senior Service on others may also be seen in the unit awards issued by the Department of Defense, by our wartime allies (The Republics of the Philippines, Korea and Vietnam) and most recently, the Coast Guard, all of which emulate the Army's gold frame arrangement.

The Marine Corps Reserve Ribbon (now obsolete) was the first non-unit award to appear in this form and, as can be seen, was the forerunner of a large number of ribbons having no medallic counterparts. Whether the form was selected because of simplicity, to provide decorations and service medals a higher degree of stature or forced by budgetary considerations, it has certainly become a major element in the U.S. award structure. It may be expected to continue as a major factor in future awards policies.

Joint Meritorious Unit Award
(see page 116)

Service: All Services (Inst: 1981)
Criteria: Awarded to Joint Service units for meritorious achievement or service in combat or extreme circumstances.

Devices: Army/Air Force/ Navy/Marine Corps: bronze, silver oakleaf cluster (27, 29); Coast Guard: bronze, silver star (42, 47)

Army Valorous Unit Award
(see page 117)

Service: Army (Inst: 1963)
Criteria: Awarded to U.S. Army units for outstanding heroism in armed combat against an opposing armed force.

Devices: Bronze, silver oak leaf cluster (27, 29)

Army Superior Unit Award
(see page 119)

Service: Army (Inst: 1985)
Criteria: Awarded to U.S. Army units for meritorious performance in difficult and challenging peacetime missions.

Devices: Bronze, silver oak leaf cluster (27, 29)

Army Service Ribbon
(see page109)

Service: Army (Inst: 1981)
Criteria: Successful completion of initial entry training.
Devices: None

Army Reserve Components Overseas Training Ribbon
(see page 110)

Service: Army (Inst: 1984)
Criteria: Successful completion of annual training or active duty training for 10 consecutive duty days on foreign soil.

Devices: Bronze numeral (23)

Army Presidential Unit Citation
(see page 116)

Service: Army (Inst: 1942)
Criteria: Awarded to U.S. Army units for extraordinary heroism in action against an armed enemy.
Devices: Bronze, silver oak leaf cluster (27, 29)
Notes: Original designation: Distinguished Unit Citation. Renamed in 1966.

Army Meritorious Unit Commendation
(see page 118)

Service: Army (Inst: 1944)
Criteria: Awarded to U.S. Army units for exceptionally meritorious conduct in the performance of outstanding service.

Devices: Bronze, silver oak leaf cluster (27, 29)
Notes: Originally a golden wreath worn on the lower sleeve. Authorized in its present form in 1961.

N.C.O. Professional Development Ribbon
(see page 109)

Service: Army (Inst: 1981)
Criteria: Successful completion of designated NCO professional development courses.
Devices: Bronze numeral (25)

Army Overseas Service Ribbon
(see page 110)

Service: Army (Inst: 1981)
Criteria: Successful completion of normal overseas tours not recognized by any other service award.

Devices: Bronze numeral (23)

Navy Presidential Unit Citation (see page 116)

Service: Navy/Marine Corps/ Coast Guard (Inst: 1942)
Criteria: Awarded to Navy/ Marine Corps units for extraordinary heroism in action against an armed enemy.

Devices: Gold globe (6), gold letter "N" (14), blue star (38), bronze, silver star (42, 47)

Navy Unit Commendation
(see page117)

Service: Navy/Marine Corps (Inst: 1944)
Criteria: Awarded to Navy & Marine Corps units for outstanding heroism in action or extremely meritorious service.

Devices: Bronze, silver star (42, 47)

Navy "E" Ribbon
(see page 119)

Service: Navy/Marine Corps   (Inst: 1976)
Criteria: Awarded to ships or squadrons which have won battle efficiency competitions.

Devices: Silver letter "E" (11), wreathed silver letter "E" (12)

Navy Arctic Service Ribbon (see page 110)

Service: Navy/Marine Corps (Inst: 1987)
Criteria: 28 days of service on naval vessels operating above the Arctic Circle.

Devices: None

Navy and Marine Corps Overseas Service Ribbon
(see page 111)

Service: Navy/Marine Corps (Inst: 1987)
Criteria: 12 months consecutive or accumulated duty at an overseas shore base duty station.

Devices: Bronze, silver star (42, 47)

Navy Recruit Training Service Ribbon
(see page 111)

Service: Navy (Inst. 1998 - retroactive to 1995)
Criteria: Successful service as Recruit Division Commander (RDC) and training at least nine Divisions over a minimum tour of three years.

Devices: Bronze, silver star (42, 47)

Marine Corps Drill Instructor Ribbon
(see page 112)

Service: Marine Corps (inst: 1997-retroactive to 1952)
Criteria: Successful completion of a tour of duty as a drill instructor (staff billets require completion of 18 months to be eligible).

Devices: Bronze, silver star (42, 47)

Marine Corps Reserve Ribbon (obsolete)
(see page 112)

Service: Marine Corps (Inst: 1945)
Criteria: Successful completion of 10 years of honorable service in any class of the Marine Corps Reserve.

Devices: Bronze star (42)

Navy Meritorious Unit Commendation
(see page 118)

Service: Navy/Marine Corps (Inst: 1967)
Criteria: Awarded to Navy/ Marine Corps units for valorous actions or meritorious achievement (combat or noncombat).

Devices: Bronze, silver star (42, 47)

Navy Sea Service Deployment Ribbon
(see page 110)

Service: Navy/Marine Corps (Inst: 1981)
Criteria: 12 months active duty on deployed vessels operating away from their home port for extended periods.

Devices: Bronze, silver star (42, 47)

Naval Reserve Sea Service Ribbon
(see page 111)

Service: Navy (Inst: 1987)
Criteria: 24 months of cumulative service embarked on Naval Reserve vessels or an embarked Reserve unit.

Devices: Bronze, silver star (42, 47)

Navy Recruiting Service Ribbon
(see page 111)

Service: Navy (Inst: 1989)
Criteria: Successful completion of 3 consecutive years of recruiting duty.

Devices: Bronze, silver star (42, 47)

Marine Corps Recruiting Ribbon
(see page 112)

Service: Marine Corps (inst:1995-retroactive to 1973)
Criteria: Successful completion of 3 consecutive years of recruiting duty.

Devices: Bronze, silver star (42, 47)

Marine Security Guard Ribbon
(see page 112)

Service: Marine Corps (inst: 1997-retroactive to 1949)
Criteria: Successful completion of 24 months of cumulative security guard duty service at a foreign service establishment.

Devices: Bronze, silver star (42, 47)

Air Force Presidential Unit Citation
(see page 116)

Service: Air Force (Inst: 1957)
Criteria: Awarded to Air Force units for extraordinary heroism in action against an armed enemy.
Devices: Bronze, silver oak leaf cluster (27, 29)
Notes: Original designation: Distinguished Unit Citation. Renamed in 1966.

Air Force Outstanding Unit Award
(see page 117)

Service: Air Force (Inst: 1954)

Criteria: Awarded to U.S. Air Force units for exceptionally meritorious achievement or meritorious service.

Devices: Bronze letter "V" (18), bronze, silver oak leaf cluster (27, 29)

Overseas Ribbon (Short Tour)
(see page 113)

Service: Air Force (Inst: 1980)

Criteria: Successful completion of an overseas tour designated as "short term" by appropriate authority.

Devices: Bronze, silver oak leaf cluster (27, 29)

Air Force Longevity Service Award
(see page 113)

Service: Air Force (Inst: 1957)

Criteria: Successful completion of an aggregate total of four years of honorable active service.

Devices: Bronze, silver oak leaf cluster (27, 29)

N.C.O. Professional Military Education Graduate Ribbon
(see page114)

Service: Air Force (Inst: 1962)

Criteria: Successful completion of a certified NCO professional military education school.

Devices: Bronze, silver oak leaf cluster (27, 29)

Air Force Training Ribbon
(see page 114)

Service: Air Force (Inst: 1980)

Criteria: Successful completion of an Air Force accession training program.

Devices: Bronze, silver oak leaf cluster (27, 29)

Coast Guard Unit Commendation
(see page 118)

Service: Coast Guard (Inst: 1963)

Criteria: Awarded to U.S. Coast Guard units for valorous or extremely meritorious service not involving combat.

Devices: Silver letter "O" (15), gold, silver star (49, 50)

Coast Guard Meritorious Team Commendation
(see page 119)

Service: Coast Guard (Inst: 1993)

Criteria: Awarded to smaller U.S. Coast Guard units for valorous or meritorious achievement (combat or noncombat).

Devices: Silver letter "O" (15), gold, silver star (49, 50)

Air Force Organizational Excellence Award
(see page 118)

Service: Air Force (Inst: 1969)

Criteria: Same as Outstanding Unit Award but awarded to unique unnumbered organizations performing staff functions.

Devices: Bronze letter "V" (18), bronze, silver oak leaf cluster (27, 29)

Overseas Ribbon (Long Tour)
(see page 113)

Service: Air Force (Inst: 1980)

Criteria: Successful completion of an overseas tour designated as "long term" by appropriate authority.

Devices: Bronze, silver oak leaf cluster (27, 29)

Air Force Military Training Instructor Ribbon
(see page 113)

Service: Air Force (Inst. 1998)

Criteria: Graduation from Military Training Instructor (MTI) School. Permanently worn after completion of a 12 month tour of duty as an MTI.

Devices: Bronze, silver oak leaf cluster (27, 29)

Basic Military Training Honor Graduate Ribbon
(see page 114)

Service: Air Force (Inst: 1976)

Criteria: Demonstration of excellence in all academic and military training phases of basic Air Force entry training.

Devices: None

Dept. of Transportation Outstanding Unit Award
(see page 117)

Service: Coast Guard (Inst: 1995)

Criteria: Awarded to U.S. Coast Guard units for valorous or extremely meritorious service on behalf of the Transportation Dept.

Devices: Silver letter "O" (15), gold, silver star (49, 50)

Coast Guard Meritorious Unit Commendation
(see page 119)

Service: Coast Guard (Inst: 1973)

Criteria: Awarded to U.S. Coast Guard units for valorous or meritorious achievement (combat or noncombat).

Devices: Silver letter "O" (15), gold, silver star (49, 50)

Coast Guard "E" Ribbon
(see page 120)

Service: Coast Guard (Inst: 1990)

Criteria: Awarded to U.S. Coast Guard ships and cutters which earn the overall operational readiness efficiency award.

Devices: Gold, silver star (49, 50)

Coast Guard Bicentennial Unit Commendation
(see page 120)

Service: Coast Guard (Inst: 1990)

Criteria: Awarded to all Coast Guard personnel serving satisfactorily at any time between 4 June 1989 and 4 June 1990.

Devices: None

Coast Guard Sea Service Ribbon
(see page 115)

Service: Coast Guard (Inst: 1984)

Criteria: Satisfactory completion of a minimum of 12 months of cumulative sea duty.

Devices: Bronze, silver star (42, 47)

Coast Guard Basic Training Honor Graduate Ribbon
(see page 115)

Service: Coast Guard (Inst: 1984)

Criteria: Successful attainment of the top 3 percent of the class during Coast Guard recruit training.

Devices: None

Philippine Republic Presidential Unit Citation (see page 120)

Service: All Services (Inst: 1948)

Criteria: Awarded to units of the U.S. Armed Forces for service in the war against Japan and/or for 1970 and 1972 disaster relief.

Devices: All Services (except Army) bronze star (39)

Republic of Vietnam Presidential Unit Citation (see page 120)

Service: Army/Navy/Marine Corps/Coast Guard (Inst: 1954)

Criteria: Awarded to certain units of the U.S. Armed Forces for humanitarian service in the evacuation of civilians from North and Central Vietnam.

Devices: None

Republic of Vietnam Civil Actions Unit Citation (see page 121)

Service: All Services (Inst: 1966)

Criteria: Awarded to certain units of the U.S. Armed Forces for meritorious service during the Vietnam War, 1 March 1961 to 28 March 1974.

Devices: Bronze palm (30)

Special Operations Service Ribbon
(see page 114)

Service: Coast Guard (Inst: 1987)

Criteria: Participation in a Coast Guard special noncombat operation not recognized by another service award.

Devices: Bronze, silver star (42, 47)

Restricted Duty Ribbon (see page 115)

Service: Coast Guard (Inst: 1984)

Criteria: Successful completion of a tour of duty at remote shore stations (LORAN stations, light ships, etc.) without family.

Devices: Bronze, silver star (42, 47)

Coast Guard Recruiting Service Ribbon
(see page 115)

Service: Coast Guard (Inst. -1995)

Criteria: Successful completion of 3 consecutive years of recruiting duty.

Devices: Bronze, silver star (42, 47)

Korean Republic Presidential Unit Citation
(see page 120)

Service: All Services (Inst: 1951)

Criteria: Awarded to certain units of the U.S. Armed Forces for services rendered during the Korean War.

Devices: None

Republic of Vietnam Gallantry Cross Unit Citation (see page 121)

Service: All Services (Inst: 1966)

Criteria: Awarded to certain units of the U.S. Armed Forces for valorous combat achievement during the Vietnam War, 1 March 1961 to 28 March 1974.

Devices: All Services: Bronze palm, (30, 31),
Army: gold, silver, bronze star (51)

Correct Manner of Wear — Ribbons of the Merchant Marine

 = Silver Service Star Indicates crew member forced to abandon ship

 = Bronze Service Star Denotes second and subsequent awards of a service award or participation in a campaign or operation

 = Silver Seahorse Worn in Gallant Ship Citation Bar upon initial issue but has no significance

	Distinguished Service Medal None		
Meritorious Service Medal None	Mariner's Medal None	Gallant Ship Citation Bar Silver	Merchant Marine Combat Bar Silver
Prisoner of War Medal Bronze	Merchant Marine Defense Medal None	Atlantic War Zone None	Pacific War Zone None
Mediterranean-Middle East War Zone	World War II Victory Medal None	Korean Service Medal None	Vietnam Service Medal None
Merchant Marine Expeditionary Medal Bronze	Philippine Defense Ribbon Bronze	Philippine Liberation Ribbon Bronze	40th Anniversary of World War II (USSR) None

United Nations Medals Currently Authorized for U.S. Personnel

Korean War
1950-1953

UN Palestine Truce Supervision Organization
1948-Present

UN Military Observer Group, in India and Pakistan
1949-Present

UN Security Force in West New Guinea
1962-1963

UN Iraq-Kuwait Observation Mission
1991-Present

UN Mission for the Referendum in Western Sahara
1991-Present

UN Advance Mission in Cambodia
1991-1992

UN Protective Force in Former Yugoslavia
1992-1995

UN Transitional Authority in Cambodia
1992-1993

UN Operation in Somalia
1993-1995

UN Mission in Haiti
1993-1996

UN Special Service Medal

Examples of Medal Displays

World War II

Korean War

Vietnam War

Liberation of Kuwait

U.S. Army
Correct Order Of Ribbon Wear (Left Breast)

Medal of Honor   Distinguished Service Cross

| Defense Distinguished Service Medal | Army Distinguished Service Medal | Silver Star | Defense Superior Svc. Medal | Legion of Merit |

| Distinguished Flying Cross | Soldier's Medal | Bronze Star Medal | Purple Heart | Defense Meritorious Service Medal |

| Meritorious Service Medal | Air Medal | Joint Service Commendation Medal | Army Commendation Medal | Joint Service Achievement Medal |

| Army Achievement Medal | Prisoner of War Medal | Army Good Conduct Medal | Rsv. Components Achievement Medal | American Defense Service |

| Women's Army Corps Service | American Campaign Medal | Asiatic-Pacific Campaign Medal | Eur.-African-Middle Eastern Campaign Medal | World War II Victory Medal |

| Army of Occupation Medal | Medal For Humane Action | National Defense Service Medal | Korean Service Medal | Antarctica Service Medal |

| Armed Forces Expeditionary Medal | Vietnam Service Medal | Southwest Asia Service Medal | Kosovo Campaign Medal | Armed Forces Service Medal |

| Humanitarian Service Medal | Outstanding Volunteer Service Medal | Armed Forces Reserve Medal | NCO Professional Development Ribbon | Army Service Ribbon |

| Overseas Service Ribbon | Rsv. Components Overseas Training Ribbon | Foreign Decoration | Philippine Defense Ribbon | Philippine Liberation Ribbon |

| Philippine Independence Ribbon | United Nations Service Medal | Inter-American Defense Board Medal | United Nations Medal | NATO Medal |

| Multinational Force & Observers Medal | Republic of Vietnam Campaign Medal | Kuwait Liberation Medal (Saudi Arabia) | Kuwait Liberation Medal (Emirate of Kuwait) | Republic of Korea War Service Medal |

U.S. Army
Unit Awards (Right Breast)

Army Presidential Unit Citation

| Joint Meritorious Unit Award | Army Valorous Unit Award | Army Meritorious Unit Commendation |

| Army Superior Unit Award | Philippine Presidential Unit Citation | Korean Presidential Unit Citation |

| Vietnam Presidential Unit Citation | Vietnam Gallantry Cross Unit Citation | Vietnam Civil Actions Unit Citation |

Note: Per Army regulations, no row may contain more than four (4) ribbons. The above display is arranged solely to conserve space on the page.

40

U.S. Army Ribbon Devices

Left Breast

	Medal of Honor Bronze	**Distinguished Service Cross** Silver Bronze		
Defense Distinguished Service Medal Bronze	**Army Distinguished Service Medal** Silver Bronze	**Silver Star** Silver Bronze	**Defense Superior Service Medal** Silver Bronze	**Legion of Merit** Silver Bronze
Distinguished Flying Cross Silver Bronze	**Soldier's Medal** Bronze	**Bronze Star Medal** V Bronze Silver Bronze	**Purple Heart** Silver Bronze	**Defense Meritorious Service Medal** Silver Bronze
Meritorious Service Medal Silver Bronze	**Air Medal** V Bronze 3 Bronze	**Joint Svc. Commendation Medal** V Bronze Silver Bronze	**Army Commendation Medal** V Bronze Silver Bronze	**Joint Service Achievement Medal** Silver Bronze
Army Achievement Medal Silver Bronze	**Prisoner of War Medal** Silver Bronze	**Army Good Conduct Medal** Gold, Silver or Bronze Clasp	**Reserve Components Achievement Medal** Silver Bronze	**American Defense Service Medal** Bronze
Women's Army Corps Service Medal None	**American Campaign Medal** Bronze	**Asiatic-Pacific Campaign Medal** Bronze Silver Bronze	**European-African-Mid. Est. Campaign** Bronze Silver Bronze	**World War II Victory Medal** None
Army of Occupation Medal Gold Airplane	**Medal For Humane Action** None	**National Defense Service Medal** Bronze	**Korean Service Medal** Bronze Silver Bronze	**Antarctica Service Medal** Bronze, Gold, or Silver
Armed Forces Expeditionary Medal Bronze Silver Bronze	**Vietnam Service Medal** Bronze Silver Bronze	**Southwest Asia Service Medal** Bronze	**Kosovo Campaign Medal** Bronze	**Armed Forces Service Medal** Silver Bronze
Humanitarian Service Medal Silver Bronze	**Outstanding Volunteer Service Medal** Silver Bronze	**Armed Forces Reserve Medal** Bronze, Silver, Gold Hourglass 3 M Bronze	**NCO Professional Development Ribbon** Bronze 3	**Army Service Ribbon** None
Overseas Service Ribbon 3 Bronze	**Reserve Components Overseas Training Ribbon** 3 Bronze	**Foreign Decoration** As specified by the Awarding Government	**Philippine Defense Ribbon** Bronze	**Philippine Liberation Ribbon** Bronze
Philippine Independence Ribbon None	**United Nations Service Medal** None	**Inter-American Defense Board Medal** Gold	**United Nations Medal** Bronze	**NATO Medal** Bronze
Multinational Force & Observers Medal 3 Bronze Numeral	**Republic of Vietnam Campaign Medal** Silver Date Bar	**Kuwait Liberation Medal (Saudi Arabia)** Gold Palm Tree	**Kuwait Liberation Medal (Emirate of Kuwait)** None	**ROK War Service Medal** None

Army Unit Awards

Right Breast

	Army Presidential Unit Citation Silver Bronze	
Joint Meritorious Unit Award Silver Bronze	**Army Valorous Unit Award** Silver Bronze	**Army Meritorious Unit Commendation** Silver Bronze
Army Superior Unit Award Silver Bronze	**Philippine Presidential Unit Citation** None	**Republic of Korea Presidential Unit Citation** None
Republic of Vietnam Presidential Unit Citation None	**Vietnam Gallantry Cross Unit Citation** Bronze Palm Gold, Silver, Bronze	**Vietnam Civil Actions Unit Citation** Bronze Palm

- **= Bronze Oak Leaf Cluster** Denotes second and subsequent awards of a decoration or unit citation
- **= Silver Oak Leaf Cluster** Worn in lieu of five bronze oak leaf clusters
- ★ **= Bronze Service Star** Denotes second and subsequent awards of a service award or participation in a campaign or major operation
- ★ **= Silver Service Star** Worn in lieu of five gold or bronze service stars
- V **= Bronze Letter "V"** Awarded for distinguished actions in combat (valor)
- M **= Letter "M"** Denotes Reservists mobilized and called to active duty
- ▲ **= Bronze Arrowhead** Denotes participation in parachute, glider or amphibious landing or assault
- **= Antarctica Disk** Denotes personnel who "winter-over" on the Antarctic continent
- 3 **= Bronze Numeral** Denotes total number of awards of the Air Medals and other awards
- **= Hourglass** Issued after each 10 years of reserve service
- **= Good Conduct Medal Clasp** Number of loops and color denote number of awards of Good Conduct Medal. Bronze, second-fifth; silver, sixth-10th; gold, 11th - 15th
- **= Palm**
- **= Date Bar, Silver**

U.S. Navy
Correct Order Of Ribbon
Wear (Left Breast)

Medal of Honor   Navy Cross

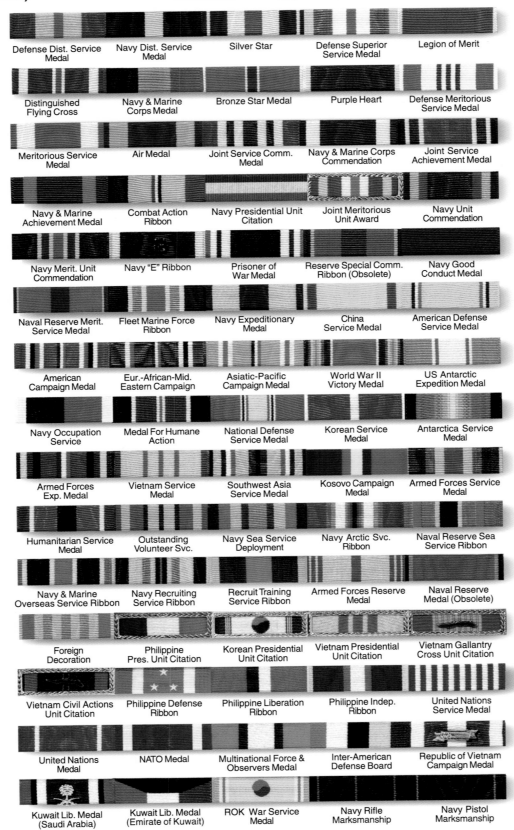

Defense Dist. Service Medal	Navy Dist. Service Medal	Silver Star	Defense Superior Service Medal	Legion of Merit
Distinguished Flying Cross	Navy & Marine Corps Medal	Bronze Star Medal	Purple Heart	Defense Meritorious Service Medal
Meritorious Service Medal	Air Medal	Joint Service Comm. Medal	Navy & Marine Corps Commendation	Joint Service Achievement Medal
Navy & Marine Achievement Medal	Combat Action Ribbon	Navy Presidential Unit Citation	Joint Meritorious Unit Award	Navy Unit Commendation
Navy Merit. Unit Commendation	Navy "E" Ribbon	Prisoner of War Medal	Reserve Special Comm. Ribbon (Obsolete)	Navy Good Conduct Medal
Naval Reserve Merit. Service Medal	Fleet Marine Force Ribbon	Navy Expeditionary Medal	China Service Medal	American Defense Service Medal
American Campaign Medal	Eur.-African-Mid. Eastern Campaign	Asiatic-Pacific Campaign Medal	World War II Victory Medal	US Antarctic Expedition Medal
Navy Occupation Service	Medal For Humane Action	National Defense Service Medal	Korean Service Medal	Antarctica Service Medal
Armed Forces Exp. Medal	Vietnam Service Medal	Southwest Asia Service Medal	Kosovo Campaign Medal	Armed Forces Service Medal
Humanitarian Service Medal	Outstanding Volunteer Svc.	Navy Sea Service Deployment	Navy Arctic Svc. Ribbon	Naval Reserve Sea Service Ribbon
Navy & Marine Overseas Service Ribbon	Navy Recruiting Service Ribbon	Recruit Training Service Ribbon	Armed Forces Reserve Medal	Naval Reserve Medal (Obsolete)
Foreign Decoration	Philippine Pres. Unit Citation	Korean Presidential Unit Citation	Vietnam Presidential Unit Citation	Vietnam Gallantry Cross Unit Citation
Vietnam Civil Actions Unit Citation	Philippine Defense Ribbon	Philippine Liberation Ribbon	Philippine Indep. Ribbon	United Nations Service Medal
United Nations Medal	NATO Medal	Multinational Force & Observers Medal	Inter-American Defense Board	Republic of Vietnam Campaign Medal
Kuwait Lib. Medal (Saudi Arabia)	Kuwait Lib. Medal (Emirate of Kuwait)	ROK War Service Medal	Navy Rifle Marksmanship	Navy Pistol Marksmanship

Note: Per Navy regulations, no row may contain more than three (3) ribbons. The above display is arranged solely to conserve space on the page.

U.S. Navy Ribbon Devices

Medal of Honor	Navy Cross	
Gold	Silver	Gold

Defense Distinguished Service Medal	Navy Distinguished Service Medal	Silver Star	Defense Superior Service Medal	Legion of Merit
Bronze	Silver · Gold	Silver · Gold	Silver · Bronze	Bronze · Silver · Gold
Distinguished Flying Cross	Navy & Marine Corps Medal	Bronze Star Medal	Purple Heart	Defense Meritorious Service Medal
Bronze · Silver · Gold	Gold	Bronze · Silver · Gold	Silver · Gold	Silver · Bronze
Meritorious Service Medal	Air Medal	Joint Service Commendation Medal	Navy & Marine Corps Commendation Medal	Joint Service Achievement Medal
Silver · Gold	Bronze · Silver · Gold	Bronze · Silver · Bronze	Bronze · Silver · Gold	Silver · Bronze
Navy & Marine Corps Achievement Medal	Combat Action Ribbon	Navy Presidential Unit Citation	Joint Meritorious Unit Award	Navy Unit Commendation
Bronze · Silver · Gold	Silver · Gold	Gold · Gold · Silver · Bronze	Silver · Bronze	Silver · Bronze
Navy Meritorious Unit Commendation	Navy "E" Ribbon	Prisoner of War Medal	Reserve Special Commendation Ribbon (Obsolete)	Navy Good Conduct Medal
Silver · Bronze	Silver · Silver	Silver · Bronze	None	Silver · Bronze
Naval Reserve Meritorious Service Medal	Fleet Marine Force Ribbon	Navy Expeditionary Medal	China Service Medal	American Defense Service Medal
Silver · Bronze	None	Silver · Silver · Bronze	Bronze	Bronze · Bronze
American Campaign Medal	European-African-Middle Eastern Campaign	Asiatic-Pacific Campaign Medal	World War II Victory Medal	US Antarctic Expedition Medal
Bronze	Bronze · Silver · Bronze	Bronze · Silver · Bronze	None	None
Navy Occupation Service Medal	Medal For Humane Action	National Defense Service Medal	Korean Service Medal	Antarctica Service Medal
Gold Airplane	None	Bronze	Bronze · Silver · Bronze	Bronze, Gold, or Silver
Armed Forces Expeditionary Medal	Vietnam Service Medal	Southwest Asia Service Medal	Kosovo Campaign Medal	Armed Forces Service Medal
Bronze · Silver · Bronze	Bronze · Silver · Bronze	Bronze · Bronze	Bronze · Bronze	Silver · Bronze
Humanitarian Service Medal	Outstanding Volunteer Service Medal	Navy Sea Service Deployment Ribbon	Navy Arctic Service Ribbon	Naval Reserve Sea Service Ribbon
Silver · Bronze	Silver · Bronze	Silver · Bronze	None	Silver · Bronze
Navy & Marine Corps Overseas Service Ribbon	Navy Recruiting Service Ribbon	Recruit Training Service Ribbon	Armed Forces Reserve Medal	Naval Reserve Medal (Obsolete)
Silver · Bronze	Silver · Bronze	Silver · Bronze	Bronze, Silver, Gold Hourglass · Bronze	Bronze
Foreign Decoration — As Specified by the Awarding Government	Philippine Presidential Unit Citation	Republic of Korea Presidential Unit Citation	Republic of Vietnam Presidential Unit Citation	Vietnam Gallantry Cross Unit Citation
	Bronze	None	None	Bronze Palm
Vietnam Civil Actions Unit Citation	Philippine Defense Ribbon	Philippine Liberation Ribbon	Philippine Independence Ribbon	United Nations Service Medal
Bronze Palm	Bronze	Bronze	None	None
United Nations Medal	NATO Medal	Multinational Force & Observers Medal	Inter-American Defense Board Medal	Republic of Vietnam Campaign Medal
Bronze	Bronze	Bronze Numeral	Gold	Silver Date Bar
Kuwait Liberation Medal (Saudi Arabia)	Kuwait Liberation Medal (Emirate of Kuwait)	ROK War Service Medal	Navy Rifle Marksmanship Ribbon	Navy Pistol Marksmanship Ribbon
Gold Palm Tree	None	None	Silver · Bronze	Silver · Bronze

Legend

 =Gold Star
Denotes second and subsequent awards of a decoration

 = Silver Star
Worn in the same manner as the gold star, in lieu of five gold stars

 = Bronze Service Star
Denotes second and subsequent awards of a service award or participation in a campaign or major operation

 = Silver Service Star
Worn in lieu of five gold or bronze service stars

 = Bronze Oak Leaf Cluster
Denotes second and subsequent awards of a Joint Service decoration or unit citation

 = Silver Oak Leaf Cluster
Worn in lieu of five bronze oak leaf clusters

 = Bronze Letter "V"
Awarded for distinguished actions in combat (valor)

 = Letter "A"
Denotes service with Atlantic Fleet prior to World War II

 = Bronze Letter "M"
Denotes reservists mobilized and called to active duty

 = Antarctica Disk
Denotes personnel who "winter-over" on the Antarctic continent

 = Marine Corps Device
Denotes combat service with Marine Corps Units

 = Bronze Numeral
Denotes total number of strike/flight awards of the Air Medals and other awards

Marksmanship Devices

 = Letter "S"

 = Letter "E"

 = Hourglass
Issued after each 10 years of reserve service

U.S. Marine Corps
Correct Order Of Ribbon Wear (Left Breast)

Medal of Honor   Navy Cross

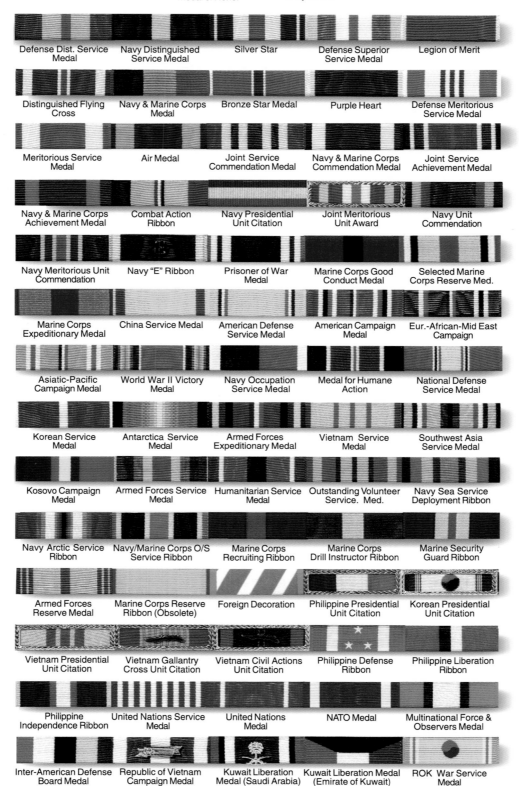

Defense Dist. Service Medal	Navy Distinguished Service Medal	Silver Star	Defense Superior Service Medal	Legion of Merit
Distinguished Flying Cross	Navy & Marine Corps Medal	Bronze Star Medal	Purple Heart	Defense Meritorious Service Medal
Meritorious Service Medal	Air Medal	Joint Service Commendation Medal	Navy & Marine Corps Commendation Medal	Joint Service Achievement Medal
Navy & Marine Corps Achievement Medal	Combat Action Ribbon	Navy Presidential Unit Citation	Joint Meritorious Unit Award	Navy Unit Commendation
Navy Meritorious Unit Commendation	Navy "E" Ribbon	Prisoner of War Medal	Marine Corps Good Conduct Medal	Selected Marine Corps Reserve Med.
Marine Corps Expeditionary Medal	China Service Medal	American Defense Service Medal	American Campaign Medal	Eur.-African-Mid East Campaign
Asiatic-Pacific Campaign Medal	World War II Victory Medal	Navy Occupation Service Medal	Medal for Humane Action	National Defense Service Medal
Korean Service Medal	Antarctica Service Medal	Armed Forces Expeditionary Medal	Vietnam Service Medal	Southwest Asia Service Medal
Kosovo Campaign Medal	Armed Forces Service Medal	Humanitarian Service Medal	Outstanding Volunteer Service. Med.	Navy Sea Service Deployment Ribbon
Navy Arctic Service Ribbon	Navy/Marine Corps O/S Service Ribbon	Marine Corps Recruiting Ribbon	Marine Corps Drill Instructor Ribbon	Marine Security Guard Ribbon
Armed Forces Reserve Medal	Marine Corps Reserve Ribbon (Obsolete)	Foreign Decoration	Philippine Presidential Unit Citation	Korean Presidential Unit Citation
Vietnam Presidential Unit Citation	Vietnam Gallantry Cross Unit Citation	Vietnam Civil Actions Unit Citation	Philippine Defense Ribbon	Philippine Liberation Ribbon
Philippine Independence Ribbon	United Nations Service Medal	United Nations Medal	NATO Medal	Multinational Force & Observers Medal
Inter-American Defense Board Medal	Republic of Vietnam Campaign Medal	Kuwait Liberation Medal (Saudi Arabia)	Kuwait Liberation Medal (Emirate of Kuwait)	ROK War Service Medal

Note: Per Marine Corps regulations, no row may contain more than four (4) ribbons. The above display is arranged solely to conserve space on the page.

U.S. Marine Corps Ribbon Devices

	Medal of Honor	Navy Cross	
	Gold	Silver	Gold

Defense Distinguished Service Medal Bronze	**Navy Distinguished Service Medal** Silver / Gold	**Silver Star** Silver / Gold	**Defense Superior Service Medal** Silver / Bronze	**Legion of Merit** V Gold / Silver / Gold
Distinguished Flying Cross V Gold / Silver / Gold	**Navy & Marine Corps Medal** Gold	**Bronze Star Medal** V Gold / Silver / Gold	**Purple Heart** Silver / Gold	**Defense Meritorious Service Medal** Silver / Bronze
Meritorious Service Medal Silver / Gold	**Air Medal** V Gold / 3 Bronze / Silver Gold	**Joint Service Commendation Medal** V Gold / Silver / Bronze	**Navy & Marine Corps Commendation Medal** V Gold / Silver / Gold	**Joint Service Achievement Medal** Silver / Bronze
Navy & Marine Corps Achievement Medal V Gold / Silver / Gold	**Combat Action Ribbon** Silver / Gold	**Navy Presidential Unit Citation** Silver / Bronze	**Joint Meritorious Unit Award** Silver / Bronze	**Navy Unit Commendation** Silver / Bronze
Navy Meritorious Unit Commendation Silver / Bronze	**Navy "E" Ribbon** Silver / Silver	**Prisoner of War Medal** Silver / Bronze	**Marine Corps Good Conduct Medal** Silver / Bronze	**Selected Marine Corps Reserve Medal** Silver / Bronze
Marine Corps Expeditionary Medal W Silver / Silver / Bronze	**China Service Medal** Bronze	**American Defense Service Medal** Bronze / A Bronze	**American Campaign Medal** Bronze	**European-African-Middle Eastern Campaign** Silver / Bronze
Asiatic-Pacific Campaign Medal Silver / Bronze	**World War II Victory Medal** None	**Navy Occupation Service Medal** Gold Airplane	**Medal For Humane Action** None	**National Defense Service Medal** Bronze
Korean Service Medal Silver	**Antarctica Service Medal** Bronze, Gold, or Silver	**Armed Forces Expeditionary Medal** Silver / Bronze	**Vietnam Service Medal** Silver / Bronze	**Southwest Asia Service Medal** Bronze
Kosovo Campaign Medal Bronze	**Armed Forces Service Medal** Silver / Bronze	**Humanitarian Service Medal** Silver / Bronze	**Outstanding Volunteer Service Medal** Silver / Bronze	**Navy Sea Service Deployment Ribbon** Silver / Bronze
Navy Arctic Service Ribbon None	**Navy & Marine Corps Overseas Service Ribbon** Silver / Bronze	**Marine Corps Recruiting Ribbon** Silver / Bronze	**Marine Corps Drill Instructor Ribbon** Silver / Bronze	**Marine Security Guard Ribbon** Silver / Bronze
Armed Forces Reserve Medal Bronze, Silver, Gold Hourglass / Bronze	**Marine Corps Reserve Ribbon (Obsolete)** Bronze	**Foreign Decoration** As Specified by the Awarding Government	**Philippine Presidential Unit Citation** Bronze	**Republic of Korea Presidential Unit Citation** None
Republic of Vietnam Presidential Unit Citation None	**Vietnam Gallantry Cross Unit Citation** Bronze Palm	**Vietnam Civil Actions Unit Citation** Bronze Palm	**Philippine Defense Ribbon** Bronze	**Philippine Liberation Ribbon** Bronze
Philippine Independence Ribbon None	**United Nations Service Medal** None	**United Nations Medal** Bronze	**NATO Medal** Bronze	**Multinational Force & Observers Medal** 3 Bronze Numeral
Inter-American Defense Board Medal Gold	**Republic of Vietnam Campaign Medal** Silver Date Bar	**Kuwait Liberation Medal (Saudi Arabia)** Gold Palm Tree	**Kuwait Liberation Medal (Emirate of Kuwait)** None	**ROK War Service Medal** None

Legend

 =Gold Star
Denotes second and subsequent awards of a decoration

 = Silver Star
Worn in the same manner as the gold star, in lieu of five gold stars

 = Bronze Service Star
Denotes second and subsequent awards of a service award or participation in a campaign or major operation

= Silver Service Star
Worn in lieu of five gold or bronze service stars

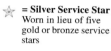 **= Bronze Oak Leaf Cluster**
Denotes second and subsequent awards of a Joint Service decoration or unit citation

= Silver Oak Leaf Cluster
Worn in lieu of five bronze oak leaf clusters

 = Gold Letter "V"
Awarded for distinguished actions in combat (valor)

 = Letter "W"
Denotes participation in Defense of Wake Island

 = Bronze Letter "M"
Denotes reservists mobilized and called to active duty

 = Antarctica Disk
Denotes personnel who "winter-over" on the Antarctic continent

 = Bronze Numeral
Denotes total number of strike/flight awards of the Air Medals and other awards

 = Hourglass
Issued after each 10 years of reserve service

 = Palm

U.S. Air Force
Correct Order Of
Ribbon Wear
(Left Breast)

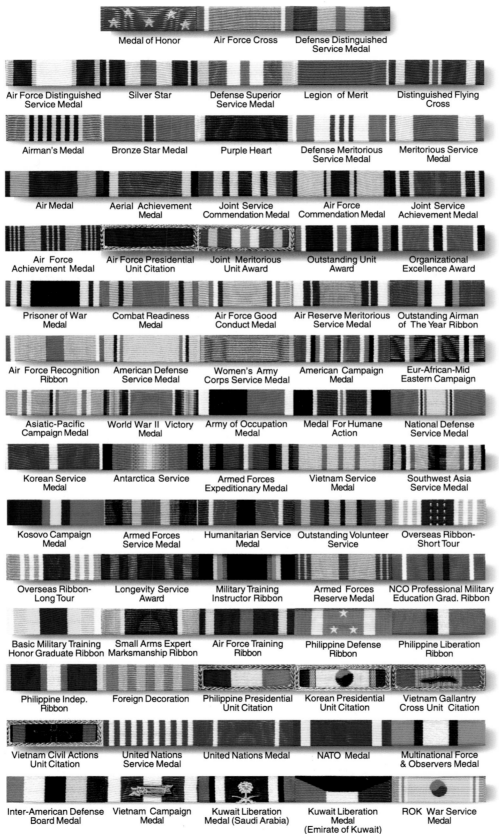

Medal of Honor   Air Force Cross   Defense Distinguished Service Medal

Air Force Distinguished Service Medal   Silver Star   Defense Superior Service Medal   Legion of Merit   Distinguished Flying Cross

Airman's Medal   Bronze Star Medal   Purple Heart   Defense Meritorious Service Medal   Meritorious Service Medal

Air Medal   Aerial Achievement Medal   Joint Service Commendation Medal   Air Force Commendation Medal   Joint Service Achievement Medal

Air Force Achievement Medal   Air Force Presidential Unit Citation   Joint Meritorious Unit Award   Outstanding Unit Award   Organizational Excellence Award

Prisoner of War Medal   Combat Readiness Medal   Air Force Good Conduct Medal   Air Reserve Meritorious Service Medal   Outstanding Airman of The Year Ribbon

Air Force Recognition Ribbon   American Defense Service Medal   Women's Army Corps Service Medal   American Campaign Medal   Eur-African-Mid Eastern Campaign

Asiatic-Pacific Campaign Medal   World War II Victory Medal   Army of Occupation Medal   Medal For Humane Action   National Defense Service Medal

Korean Service Medal   Antarctica Service   Armed Forces Expeditionary Medal   Vietnam Service Medal   Southwest Asia Service Medal

Kosovo Campaign Medal   Armed Forces Service Medal   Humanitarian Service Medal   Outstanding Volunteer Service   Overseas Ribbon- Short Tour

Overseas Ribbon- Long Tour   Longevity Service Award   Military Training Instructor Ribbon   Armed Forces Reserve Medal   NCO Professional Military Education Grad. Ribbon

Basic Military Training Honor Graduate Ribbon   Small Arms Expert Marksmanship Ribbon   Air Force Training Ribbon   Philippine Defense Ribbon   Philippine Liberation Ribbon

Philippine Indep. Ribbon   Foreign Decoration   Philippine Presidential Unit Citation   Korean Presidential Unit Citation   Vietnam Gallantry Cross Unit Citation

Vietnam Civil Actions Unit Citation   United Nations Service Medal   United Nations Medal   NATO Medal   Multinational Force & Observers Medal

Inter-American Defense Board Medal   Vietnam Campaign Medal   Kuwait Liberation Medal (Saudi Arabia)   Kuwait Liberation Medal (Emirate of Kuwait)   ROK War Service Medal

Note: Per Air Force regulations, no row may contain more than four (4) ribbons. The above display is arranged solely to conserve space on the page.

46

U.S. Air Force Ribbon Devices

	Medal of Honor — Bronze	Air Force Cross — Silver, Bronze	Defense Distinguished Service Medal — Bronze	
Air Force Distinguished Service Medal — Silver, Bronze	Silver Star — Silver, Bronze	Defense Superior Service Medal — Silver, Bronze	Legion of Merit — Silver, Bronze	Distinguished Flying Cross — Silver, Bronze
Airman's Medal — Bronze	Bronze Star Medal — Bronze (V), Silver, Bronze	Purple Heart — Silver, Bronze	Defense Meritorious Service Medal — Silver, Bronze	Meritorious Service Medal — Silver, Bronze
Air Medal — Silver, Bronze	Aerial Achievement Medal — Silver, Bronze	Joint Svc. Commendation Medal — Bronze (V), Silver, Bronze	Air Force Commendation Medal — Bronze (V), Silver, Bronze	Joint Svc. Achievement Medal — Silver, Bronze
Air Force Achievement Medal — Bronze (V), Silver, Bronze	Air Force Presidential Unit Citation — Silver, Bronze	Joint Meritorious Unit Award — Silver, Bronze	Outstanding Unit Award — Bronze (V), Silver, Bronze	Organizational Excellence Award — Bronze (V), Silver, Bronze
Prisoner of War Medal — Silver, Bronze	Combat Readiness Medal — Silver, Bronze	Air Force Good Conduct Medal — Silver, Bronze	Air Reserve Forces Meritorious Service Medal — Silver, Bronze	Outstanding Airman of the Year Ribbon — Bronze, Silver, Bronze
Air Force Recognition Ribbon — Silver, Bronze	American Defense Service Medal — Bronze	Women's Army Corps Service Medal — None	American Campaign Medal — Bronze	European-African-Middle Eastern Campaign — Bronze (arrowhead), Silver, Bronze
Asiatic-Pacific Campaign Medal — Bronze (arrowhead), Silver, Bronze	World War II Victory Medal — None	Army of Occupation Medal — Gold Airplane	Medal For Humane Action — None	National Defense Service Medal — Bronze
Korean Service Medal — Bronze (arrowhead), Silver, Bronze	Antarctica Service Medal — Bronze, Gold, or Silver	Armed Forces Expeditionary Medal — Silver, Bronze	Vietnam Service Medal — Silver, Bronze	Southwest Asia Service Medal — Bronze
Kosovo Campaign Medal — Bronze	Armed Forces Service Medal — Silver, Bronze	Humanitarian Service Medal — Silver, Bronze	Outstanding Volunteer Service — Silver, Bronze	Overseas Ribbon - Short Tour — Silver, Bronze
Overseas Ribbon - Long Tour — Silver, Bronze	Longevity Service Award Ribbon — Silver, Bronze	Military Training Instructor Ribbon — Silver, Bronze	Armed Forces Reserve Medal — Bronze, Silver, Gold Hourglass; Bronze, M	NCO Prof. Mil. Education Grad. Ribbon — Silver, Bronze
Basic Military Training Honor Graduate Ribbon — None	Small Arms Expert Marksmanship Ribbon — Bronze	Air Force Training Ribbon — Silver, Bronze	Philippine Defense Ribbon — Bronze	Philippine Liberation Ribbon — Bronze
Philippine Independence Ribbon — None	Foreign Decoration — As specified by the Awarding Government	Philippine Presidential Unit Citation — Bronze	Republic of Korea Presidential Unit Citation — None	Vietnam Gallantry Cross Unit Citation — Bronze Palm
Vietnam Civil Actions Unit Citation — Bronze Palm	United Nations Service Medal — None	United Nations Medal — Bronze	NATO Medal — Bronze	Multinational Force & Observers Medal — Bronze Numeral
Inter-American Defense Board Medal — Gold	Republic of Vietnam Campaign Medal — Silver Date Bar	Kuwait Liberation Medal (Saudi Arabia) — Gold Palm Tree	Kuwait Liberation Medal (Emirate of Kuwait) — None	ROK War Service Medal — None

Legend

 = **Bronze Oak Leaf Cluster**
Denotes second and subsequent awards of a decoration or unit citation

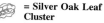 = **Silver Oak Leaf Cluster**
Worn in lieu of five bronze oak leaf clusters

= **Bronze Service Star**
Denotes second and subsequent awards of a service award or participation in a campaign or major operation

= **Silver Service Star**
Worn in lieu of five gold or bronze service stars

 = **Bronze Letter "V"**
Awarded for distinguished actions in combat (valor)

 = **Bronze Letter "M"**
Denotes reservists mobilized and called to active duty

 = **Bronze Arrowhead**
Denotes participation in parachute, glider or amphibious landing or assault

 = **Antarctica Disk**
Denotes personnel who "winter-over" on the Antarctic continent

 = **Bronze Numeral**
Denotes total number of mobilizations

 = **Berlin Airlift Device**

 = **Palm**

 = **Date Bar, Silver**

 = **Hourglass**
Issued after each 10 years of reserve service

U.S. Coast Guard
Correct Order of Ribbon Wear (Left Breast)

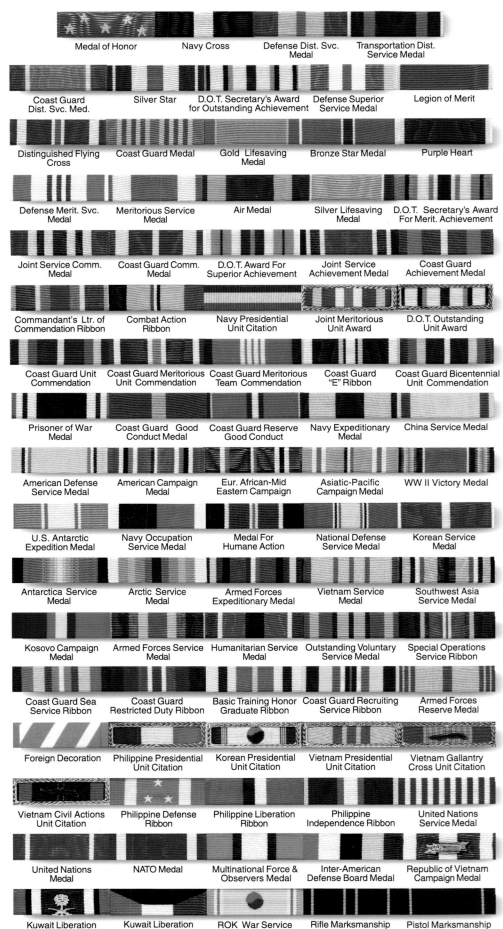

Medal of Honor	Navy Cross	Defense Dist. Svc. Medal	Transportation Dist. Service Medal	
Coast Guard Dist. Svc. Med.	Silver Star	D.O.T. Secretary's Award for Outstanding Achievement	Defense Superior Service Medal	Legion of Merit
Distinguished Flying Cross	Coast Guard Medal	Gold Lifesaving Medal	Bronze Star Medal	Purple Heart
Defense Merit. Svc. Medal	Meritorious Service Medal	Air Medal	Silver Lifesaving Medal	D.O.T. Secretary's Award For Merit. Achievement
Joint Service Comm. Medal	Coast Guard Comm. Medal	D.O.T. Award For Superior Achievement	Joint Service Achievement Medal	Coast Guard Achievement Medal
Commandant's Ltr. of Commendation Ribbon	Combat Action Ribbon	Navy Presidential Unit Citation	Joint Meritorious Unit Award	D.O.T. Outstanding Unit Award
Coast Guard Unit Commendation	Coast Guard Meritorious Unit Commendation	Coast Guard Meritorious Team Commendation	Coast Guard "E" Ribbon	Coast Guard Bicentennial Unit Commendation
Prisoner of War Medal	Coast Guard Good Conduct Medal	Coast Guard Reserve Good Conduct	Navy Expeditionary Medal	China Service Medal
American Defense Service Medal	American Campaign Medal	Eur. African-Mid Eastern Campaign	Asiatic-Pacific Campaign Medal	WW II Victory Medal
U.S. Antarctic Expedition Medal	Navy Occupation Service Medal	Medal For Humane Action	National Defense Service Medal	Korean Service Medal
Antarctica Service Medal	Arctic Service Medal	Armed Forces Expeditionary Medal	Vietnam Service Medal	Southwest Asia Service Medal
Kosovo Campaign Medal	Armed Forces Service Medal	Humanitarian Service Medal	Outstanding Voluntary Service Medal	Special Operations Service Ribbon
Coast Guard Sea Service Ribbon	Coast Guard Restricted Duty Ribbon	Basic Training Honor Graduate Ribbon	Coast Guard Recruiting Service Ribbon	Armed Forces Reserve Medal
Foreign Decoration	Philippine Presidential Unit Citation	Korean Presidential Unit Citation	Vietnam Presidential Unit Citation	Vietnam Gallantry Cross Unit Citation
Vietnam Civil Actions Unit Citation	Philippine Defense Ribbon	Philippine Liberation Ribbon	Philippine Independence Ribbon	United Nations Service Medal
United Nations Medal	NATO Medal	Multinational Force & Observers Medal	Inter-American Defense Board Medal	Republic of Vietnam Campaign Medal
Kuwait Liberation Medal (Saudi Arabia)	Kuwait Liberation Medal (Emirate of Kuwait)	ROK War Service Medal	Rifle Marksmanship Ribbon	Pistol Marksmanship Ribbon

Note:
Per Coast Guard regulations, no row may contain more than three (3) ribbons. The above display is arranged solely to conserve space on the page.

U.S. Coast Guard Ribbon Devices

Medal of Honor	Navy Cross	Defense Distinguished Service Medal	Transportation Distinguished Service Medal
Gold	Silver · Gold	Bronze	Gold

Coast Guard Distinguished Service Medal	Silver Star	D.O.T. Secretary's Award For Outstanding Achievement	Defense Superior Service Medal	Legion of Merit
Gold	Silver · Gold	Gold	Silver · Bronze	Bronze · Silver · Gold
Distinguished Flying Cross	**Coast Guard Medal**	**Gold Lifesaving Medal**	**Bronze Star Medal**	**Purple Heart**
Silver · Gold	Gold	Gold	Bronze · Silver · Gold	Silver · Gold
Defense Meritorious Service Medal	**Meritorious Service Medal**	**Air Medal**	**Silver Lifesaving Medal**	**D.O.T. Secretary's Award For Merit. Achievement**
Silver · Bronze	Silver · Silver · Gold	Bronze · Silver · Gold	Gold	Gold
Joint Service Commendation Medal	**Coast Guard Commendation Medal**	**D.O.T. Award For Superior Achievement**	**Joint Service Achievement Medal**	**Coast Guard Achievement Medal**
Bronze · Silver · Bronze	Bronze · Silver · Silver · Gold	Gold	Silver · Bronze	Bronze · Silver · Silver · Gold
Commandant's Ltr. of Com. Ribbon	**Combat Action Ribbon**	**Navy Presidential Unit Citation**	**Joint Meritorious Unit Award**	**D.O.T. Outstanding Unit Award**
Silver · Silver · Gold	Silver · Gold	Silver · Bronze	Silver · Bronze	Gold
Coast Guard Unit Commendation	**Coast Guard Meritorious Unit Commendation**	**Coast Guard Meritorious Team Commendation**	**Coast Guard "E" Ribbon**	**Coast Guard Bicentennial Unit Commendation**
Silver · Silver · Gold	Silver · Silver · Gold	Silver · Silver · Gold	Silver · Gold	None
Prisoner of War Medal	**Coast Guard Good Conduct Medal**	**Coast Guard Reserve Good Conduct Medal**	**Navy Expeditionary Medal**	**China Service Medal**
Silver · Bronze	Silver · Bronze	Silver · Bronze	Silver · Bronze	Bronze
American Defense Service Medal	**American Campaign Medal**	**European-African-Middle East. Campaign**	**Asiatic-Pacific Campaign Medal**	**World War II Victory Medal**
Bronze · Bronze (A)	Bronze	Silver · Bronze	Silver · Bronze	None
U.S. Antarctic Expedition Medal	**Navy Occupation Service Medal**	**Medal For Humane Action**	**National Defense Service Medal**	**Korean Service Medal**
None	Gold Airplane	None	Bronze	Silver · Bronze
Antarctica Service Medal	**Arctic Service Medal**	**Armed Forces Expeditionary Medal**	**Vietnam Service Medal**	**Southwest Asia Service Medal**
Bronze, Gold, or Silver	Silver	Silver · Bronze	Silver · Bronze	Bronze
Kosovo Campaign Medal	**Armed Forces Service Medal**	**Humanitarian Service Medal**	**Outstanding Volunteer Service Medal**	**Special Operations Service Ribbon**
Bronze	Silver · Bronze	Silver · Bronze	Silver · Bronze	Silver · Bronze
Coast Guard Sea Service Ribbon	**Coast Guard Restricted Duty Ribbon**	**Basic Training Honor Graduate Ribbon**	**Coast Guard Recruiting Service Ribbon**	**Armed Forces Reserve Medal**
Silver · Bronze	Silver · Bronze	Silver · Bronze	Silver · Bronze	Bronze, Silver, Gold Hourglass · 3 M Bronze
Foreign Decoration	**Philippine Presidential Unit Citation**	**Republic of Korea Presidential Unit Citation**	**Republic of Vietnam Presidential Unit Citation**	**Vietnam Gallantry Cross Unit Citation**
As Specified by the Awarding Government	Bronze	None	None	Bronze Palm
Vietnam Civil Actions Unit Citation	**Philippine Defense Ribbon**	**Philippine Liberation Ribbon**	**Philippine Independence Ribbon**	**United Nations Service Medal**
Bronze Palm	Bronze	Bronze	None	None
United Nations Medal	**NATO Medal**	**Multinational Force & Observers Medal**	**Inter-American Defense Board Medal**	**Republic of Vietnam Campaign Medal**
Bronze	Bronze	Bronze Numeral	Gold	Silver Date Bar
Kuwait Liberation Medal (Saudi Arabia)	**Kuwait Liberation Medal (Emirate of Kuwait)**	**ROK War Service Medal**	**Rifle Marksmanship Ribbon**	**Pistol Marksmanship Ribbon**
Gold Palm Tree	None	None	Silver · Bronze · Gold	Silver · Bronze · Gold

Note: Per Coast Guard regulations, no row may contain more than three (3) ribbons. The above display is arranged solely to conserve space on the page.

Legend

 =**Gold Star** Denotes second and subsequent awards of a decoration

 = **Silver Star** Worn in the same manner as the gold star, in lieu of five gold stars

= **Bronze Service Star** Denotes second and subsequent awards of a service award or participation in a campaign or major operation

 = **Silver Service Star** Worn in lieu of five gold or bronze service stars

 = **Bronze Oak Leaf Cluster** Denotes second and subsequent awards of a decoration or unit citation

= **Silver Oak Leaf Cluster** Worn in lieu of five bronze oak leaf clusters

 = **Bronze Letter "V"** Awarded for distinguished actions in combat (valor)

 = **Operational Distinguishing Service** Denotes superior operational performance

 = **Letter "A"** Denotes service with Atlantic Fleet prior to World War II

= **Bronze Letter "M"** Denotes reservists mobilized and called to active duty

 = **Antarctica Disk** Denotes personnel who "winter-over" on the Antarctic continent

 = **Hourglass** Issued after each 10 years of reserve service

Marksmanship Devices

 = Letter "S"

 = Letter "E"

 = M-14 Rifle

 = M1911A1 Pistol

 = Rifle Target

 = Pistol Target

Right Breast Displays on Full Dress Uniforms

The three Naval Services prescribe the wear of "ribbon-only" awards on the <u>right</u> breast of the full dress uniform when large medals are worn. The required displays are as follows:

NAVY

Joint Meritorious Unit Award	Navy Presidential Unit Citation	Combat Action Ribbon
Navy "E" Ribbon	Navy Meritorious Unit Commendation	Navy Unit Commendation
Sea Service Deployment Ribbon	Fleet Marine Force Ribbon	Reserve Special Commendation Ribbon
Navy & Marine Corps Overseas Service Ribbon	Naval Reserve Sea Service Ribbon	Arctic Service Ribbon
Philippine Presidential Unit Citation	Navy Recruit Training Service Ribbon	Navy Recruiting Service Ribbon
Vietnam Gallantry Cross Unit Citation	Vietnam Presidential Unit Citation	Korean Presidential Unit Ribbon
Philippine Liberation Ribbon	Philippine Defense Ribbon	Vietnam Civil Actions Unit Citation
Pistol Marksmanship Ribbon	Rifle Marksmanship Ribbon	Philippine Independence Ribbon

MARINE CORPS

Combat Action Ribbon	Navy Presidential Unit Citation	Joint Meritorious Unit Award
Navy Unit Commendation	Navy Meritorious Unit Commendation	Navy "E" Ribbon
Sea Service Deployment Ribbon	Arctic Service Ribbon	Navy & Marine Corps Overseas Service Ribbon
Marine Corps Recruiting Ribbon	Marine Corps Drill Instructor Ribbon	Marine Security Guard Ribbon
Marine Corps Reserve Ribbon	Philippine Presidential Unit Citation	Korean Presidential Unit Ribbon
Vietnam Presidential Unit Citation	Vietnam Gallantry Cross Unit Citation	Vietnam Civil Actions Unit Citation
Philippine Defense Ribbon	Philippine Liberation Ribbon	Philippine Independence Ribbon

COAST GUARD

	Commandant's Letter of Commendation Ribbon	
Joint Meritorious Unit Award	Navy Presidential Unit Citation	Combat Action Ribbon
Coast Guard Meritorious Unit Commendation	Coast Guard Unit Commendation	D.O.T. Outstanding Unit Award
Coast Guard Bicentennial Unit Commendation	Coast Guard "E" Ribbon	Coast Guard Meritorious Team Commendation
Restricted Duty Ribbon	Coast Guard Sea Service Ribbon	Special Operations Service Ribbon
Philippine Presidential Unit Citation	Coast Guard Recruiting Service Ribbon	Basic Training Honor Graduate Ribbon
Vietnam Gallantry Cross Unit Citation	Vietnam Presidential Unit Citation	Korean Presidential Unit Citation
Philippine Liberation Ribbon	Philippine Defense Ribbon	Vietnam Civil Actions Unit Citation
Pistol Marksmanship Ribbon	Rifle Marksmanship Ribbon	Philippine Independence Ribbon

U.S. MERCHANT MARINE
MEDALS AND DECORATIONS

To you who answered the call of your country and served in its Merchant Marine ... President Harry S. Truman

Distinguished Service Medal
The Merchant Marine's Highest Award
Under authority of Public Law 100-324, the Maritime Administration shall award this medal to seamen who distinguished themselves by outstanding conduct or service beyond the line of duty.

Meritorious Service Medal
Under authority of Public Law 100-324, the Maritime Administration shall award this medal to seamen for conduct or service of a meritorious nature.

Gallant Ship Plaque

Gallant Ship Citation Ribbon
Awarded to officers and seamen who served on a ship which, at the time of service, was cited for gallantry by the Maritime Administration. The bronze plaque is awarded to the ship.

Mariner's Medal
(World War II)
Awarded to a seaman who, while serving on a ship from December 7, 1941, and July 25, 1947, was wounded or suffered physical injury as a result of an act of an enemy of the United States.

Merchant Marine Defense Medal
(World War II)
Awarded for service in the U.S. Merchant Marine prior to Pearl Harbor. It may be worn by all merchant seamen who served as members of the crews of U.S. merchant ships from September 8, 1939, and December 7, 1941.

Atlantic War Zone Medal
(World War II)
Awarded for service in the Atlantic War Zone, including the North Atlantic, South Atlantic, Gulf of Mexico, Carribean, Barents Sea, and the Greenland Sea, during the period December 7, 1941, to November 8, 1945.

Mediterranean-Middle East War Zone Medal
(World War II)
Awarded for service in the zone including the Mediterranean Sea, Red Sea, Arabian Sea, and Indian Ocean west of 80 degrees east longitude, during the period December 7, 1941, to November 8, 1945.

Pacific War Zone Medal
(World War II)
Awarded for service in the Pacific War Zone, including the North Pacific, South Pacific, and the Indian Ocean east of 80 degrees east longitude, during the period December 7, 1941, to March 2, 1946.

Victory Medal
(World War II)
Awarded to members of the crews of ships who served for 30 days or more during the period December 7, 1941, to September 3, 1945.

Merchant Marine Combat Bar
(World War II)
Awarded to merchant seamen who served on a ship which at the same time of such service was attacked or damaged by an instrumentality of war from December 7, 1941, and July 25, 1947. A star is attached if the seaman was forced to abandon ship. For each additional abandonment a star is added.

Honorable Service Button
Awarded to members of the crews of ships who served for 30 days during the period December 7, 1941, to September 3, 1945.

Merchant Marine Emblem
(World War II)
The emblem is an identifying insigne that was issued to active merchant seamen for service from December 7, 1941, to July 25, 1947.

Korean Service Medal
Awarded to service in the merchant marine from June 30, 1950, and September 30, 1953 in waters adjacent to Korea.

Vietnam Service Medal
Awarded for service in the merchant marine from July 4, 1965, and August 15, 1973 in waters adjacent to Vietnam.

Merchant Marine Expeditionary Award
Awarded to American merchant seamen who serve on U.S.-flag ships in support of operations involving American and allied military forces as authorized by the Maritime Administration.

DEPARTMENT OF DEFENSE AND FOREIGN GOVERNMENTS RECOGNITION

Prisoner of War Medal
(U.S. Department of Defense)
Awarded to World War II merchant marine veterans held prisoners of war during the period December 7, 1941, to August 15, 1945. The medal recognizes the special service prisoners of war gave to their country and the suffering and anguish they endured while incarcerated.

Soviet Commemorative Medal
Awarded to merchant marine veterans who participated in convoys to Murmansk during World War II.

Philippine Defense Ribbon
Awarded to members of crews of ships who served in Phillippine waters for not less than 30 days from December 8, 1941, to June 15, 1942.

Phillippine Liberation Ribbon
Awarded to members of crews of ships who served in Phillippine waters for not less than 30 days from October 17, 1944, to September 3, 1945.

U.S. Department of Transportation
Maritime Administration

Applications for or inquiries relating to merchant marine medals and decorations should be directed to U.S. Department of Transportation, Maritime Administration, Office of Maritime Labor and Training, Washington, DC 20590.

Issue of U.S. Medals to Veterans, Retirees, and Their Families

The Armed Forces normally issue decorations and service medals as they are awarded or earned. The Services do not issue or replace any foreign awards, only United States awards.

Veterans of any U. S. military service may request replacement of medals which have been lost, stolen, destroyed or rendered unfit through no fault of the recipient. Requests may also be filed for awards that were earned but, for any reason, were never issued to the service member. The next-of-kin of deceased veterans may also make the same request.

AIR FORCE — The Air Force processes requests for medals through the National Personnel Records Center, which determines eligibility through the information in the veteran's records. Once verified, a notification of entitlement is forwarded to Randolph Air Force Base, Texas, from which the medals are mailed to the requestor. To request medals earned while in the Air Force or its predecessors, the Army Air Corps or Army Air Force veterans or their next-of-kin should write to:

> National Personnel Records Center
> Air Force Reference Branch
> 9700 Page Avenue
> St. Louis, MO 63132-5100

Where to write in case of a problem or an appeal and where medals are mailed from:

> Headquarters
> Air Force Personnel Center
> AFPC/DPPPR
> 550 C Street West, Suite 12
> Randolph AFB, TX 78150-4714

ARMY — The National Personnel Records Center does not determine eligibility for awards issued by the other services. If the person served in the Army, the request should be sent to:

> U. S. Army Reserve Personnel Center
> Attn.: ARPC-VSE-A (Medals)
> 9700 Page Avenue
> St. Louis, MO 63132-5200

ALL NAVAL SERVICES — Requests pertaining to persons who served in the Navy, Marine Corps or Coast Guard should be sent to:

> Navy Liaison Office (Navy medals)
> Room 5409
> 9700 Page Avenue
> St. Louis, MO 63132-5100

It is recommended that requesters use Standard Form 180, *Request Pertaining to Military Records*, when applying. Forms are available from offices of the Department of Veterans Affairs (VA). If the Standard Form 180 is not used, a letter may be sent, but it must include: the veteran's full name used while in service, the branch of service, approximate dates of service, and service number. The letter should indicate if the request is for a specific medal(s), or for all medals earned. The letter must be signed by the veteran or his next-of-kin, indicating the relationship to the deceased.

It is also helpful to include copies of any military service documents that indicate eligibility for medals, such as military orders or the veteran's report of separation (DD Form 214 or its earlier equivalent).

The DD Form 214, Report of Separation, is filed in the Official Military Personnel Record File. Copies of the DD214 can be made available upon request.

Veterans and next-of-kin of deceased veterans have the same rights to full access to the record. Next-of-kin are the unremarried widow or widower, son or daughter, father or mother, brother or sister of the deceased veteran.

Authorized third party requesters, e.g., lawyers, doctors, historians, etc., may submit requests for information from individual records with the veteran's (or next-of-kin's) signed and dated authorization. All authorizations should specify exactly what the veteran (or next-of-kin) is allowing to be released to a third party. Authorizations are valid one year from date of signature.

Information or copies of documents may be released from Official Military Personnel Files within the provisions of the law. The Freedom of Information Act (FOIA) and the Privacy Act provide balance between the right of the public to obtain information from military service records, and the right of the former military service member to protect his/her privacy. Please review these items for additional information. In all cases, you must sufficiently identify the person whose record is requested, so that the records can be located with reasonable effort.

Federal law [5 USC 552a(b)] requires that all requests for information from official military personnel files be submitted in writing. Each request must be signed (in cursive) and dated (within the last year). For this reason, no requests are accepted over the internet.

The Center may have a difficult time locating records since millions of records were lost in a fire at the National Personnel Records Center in 1973. The fire destroyed 80 per cent of the Army's discharge records between November 1912 and December 1959. World War II Army Air Force records were in this group. Seventy-five per cent of Air Force discharge records before 1964 and whose last names that fall alphabetically between Hubbard (James E.) and Z were also burned. Only four million records from this period were saved. Although the requested medals can often be issued on the basis of alternate records, the documents sent in with the request are sometimes the only means of determining proper eligibility.

Finally, requesters should exercise extreme patience. It may take several months or, in some cases, a year to determine eligibility and dispatch the appropriate medals. The Center asks that you not send a follow-up request for 90 days. Due to these delays, many veterans simply purchase their medals from a supplier.

MEDIAL OF HONOR ARMY

First MOH   Second MOH   Third MOH

ESTABLISHING AUTHORITY

The Army Medal of Honor was established by Joint Resolution of Congress, July 12, 1862 (as amended)

EFFECTIVE DATES: April 15, 1861

CRITERIA Awarded for conspicuous gallantry and intrepidity at the risk of one's life, above and beyond the call of duty. This gallantry must be performed either while engaged in action against an enemy of the United States, while engaged in military operations involving conflict with an opposing foreign force, or, while serving with friendly foreign forces engaged in an armed conflict against an opposing armed force in which the United States is not a belligerent party. Recommendation must be submitted within three years of the act, and the medal must be awarded within five years of the act.

The current Army Medal of Honor was designed by the firm of Arthus Bertrand, Beranger & Magdelaine of Paris, France and is based on the original design of the Medal of Honor created in 1862 by William Wilson & Son Company of Philadelphia, Pennsylvania.

The Medal of Honor is a five-pointed gold-finished star (point down) with each point ending in a trefoil. Every point of the star has a green enamel oak leaf in its center, and a green enamel laurel wreath surrounds the center of the star, passing just below the trefoils. In the center of the star is a profile of the Goddess Minerva encircled by the inscription UNITED STATES OF AMERICA with a small shield at the bottom. The star is suspended by links from a bar inscribed VALOR topped by a spread winged eagle grasping laurel leaves in its right talon and arrows in the left. The star represents each State in the United States. The oak leaf represents strength and the laurel leaf represents achievement. The head of Minerva represents wisdom, with the shield from the Great Seal of the United States representing lawful authority. The laurel leaves clasped in the right claw of the Federal eagle offer peace while the arrows represent military might if the country's offer of peace is rejected. The back of the bar holding the star is engraved THE CONGRESS TO. The rest of the medal is smooth to permit engraving the recipient's name. The ribbon is a light blue moired silk neck band one and three sixteenths inches wide and twenty four inches long, with a square pad in the center of the same ribbon. Thirteen white stars are woven into the pad.

The First Army Medal Of Honor (July 12, 1862 To May 1, 1896)

The first Army Medal of Honor had the same five-pointed star and flag ribbon as the Navy. The only differences were in the means of suspension. While the Navy medal was suspended by a fouled anchor, the Army's was suspended from an American eagle with outstretched wings with a stack of eight balls and a sabre in front of crossed cannon. The cannon, shot, and sabre represent the artillery and cavalry with the eagle as the national symbol. The top of the ribbon was held by a shield derived from the Great Seal of the United States flanked by two cornucopia, symbolizing America as the land of plenty. The reverse of the medal was engraved with the words, THE CONGRESS TO but was otherwise blank to permit engraving the recipient's name.

The Second Army Medal Of Honor (May 2, 1896 To April 23, 1904)

In the years following the Civil War, many veteran's organizations and other patriotic societies adopted membership badges and insignia which were thinly-disguised replicas of the Medal of Honor. To protect the sanctity of the Medal of Honor, Congress authorized a new ribbon for the Army Medal of Honor in 1896 to clearly distinguish it from veterans association's badges. The basic colors of the original ribbon were not changed, but simply altered.

The Third Army Medal Of Honor (April 23, 1904 To The Present)

Unfortunately, the Army Medal of Honor continued to be widely copied and its design criticized. On April 23, 1904 a new design was approved and was granted Patent Serial Number 197,369. In addition to the new planchet, the redesigned award was suspended from the now-familiar light blue moire ribbon symbolic of loyalty and vigilance, containing 13 embroidered white stars representing the 13 original states. This new, third version of the Medal of Honor is the design that is still used to the present day. The only change that has taken place since its adoption in 1904 is the suspension which was modified in 1942 from a pin-on breast ribbon to a neck ribbon.

MEDAL OF HONOR
NAVY

First

Second

Third

ESTABLISHING AUTHORITY

The Navy Medal of Honor arose from a Public Resolution signed into law by President Lincoln on 21 December 1861 authorizing the preparation of "200 medals of honor" to promote the efficiency of the Navy. It was followed by a Joint Resolution of Congress on July 12, 1862 (as amended) which actually approved the design and further defined the eligibility and required deeds of potential recipients

CRITERIA

For conspicuous gallantry and intrepidity at the risk of life, above and beyond the call of duty, in action, involving actual conflict with an opposing armed force. The Medal of Honor is worn before all other decorations and medals and is the highest honor that can be conferred on a member of the Armed Forces. Since its inception, 3,427 Medals of Honor have been awarded to 3,408 individuals. The Public Resolution cited above contained a provision for a Navy medal of valor which was originally intended to recognize gallantry in action by enlisted personnel. This was later amended to include officers. Congress also passed an act on 9 July 1918 which established criteria for the award that the act of heroism had to be above and beyond the call of duty and so unique as to clearly distinguish the recipient from his comrades. A recommendation for the Navy Medal of Honor must be made within three years from the date of the deed upon which it depends and award of the medal must be made within five years after the date of the deed. A stipulation for the medal is that there must be a minimum of two witnesses to the deed, who swear separately that the event transpired as stated in the final citation.

The Navy Medal of Honor is a five pointed star with a standing figure of the Goddess Minerva surrounded by a circle of stars representing the number of States in the Union at the outbreak of the Civil War. Minerva, the Roman Goddess of Strength and Wisdom, holds a shield taken from the Great Seal of the United States, and in her left hand she holds a fasces, representing the lawful authority of the state with which she is warding off a crouching figure representing Discord. The medal is suspended from an anchor and the reverse is plain for engraving the recipient's name. The ribbon is light blue ribbon containing thirteen white stars and has a light blue, eight-sided central pad with thirteen white stars.

The First Navy Medal Of Honor (December 21, 1861 to August 11, 1913)

Since its inception, the Navy Medal of Honor has been revised three times. The original version was quite similar to its Army counterpart with a planchet virtually identical to that used on the present Navy Medal of Honor. The same suspension ribbon ("Flag design") as the Army, a solid, dark blue field on its top half and thirteen alternating vertical stripes of red and white on the bottom was also fitted. The major differences lay in the hangers used for ribbon suspension. Where the Army used an eagle as its hanger (the transition between the ribbon and the medal), the Navy employed a gold rectangular frame on which was superimposed a gold star, both pieces supporting a gold anchor.

The Second Navy Medal Of Honor (August 12, 1913 to April 5, 1917)

The first modification to the Medal of Honor by the Navy was authorized on August 12, 1913 as part of a general update to their uniform regulations. In a change which was mostly cosmetic, the original ribbon was discarded in favor of the same light blue ribbon with white stars that was used on the Army medal since 1904. Along with a few minor changes to the planchet, the regulations now stated that the medal was to be worn from a cravat-style neck ribbon.

The Third Navy Medal Of Honor (April 6, 1917 to August 6, 1942)

In 1919, a new Medal of honor version, retroactive to the start of World War I, came into use and remained until 1942, when the current Navy Medal of Honor was reinstituted. This version was often referred to as the "Tiffany Cross," since the firm of Tiffany & Co. were the designers of the new award. The medal was a gold cross patee on a wreath of oak and laurel leaves. In the center of the cross was an octagon with the inscription UNITED STATES NAVY 1917-1918. Inside the octagon was an eagle design of the United States Seal and an anchor appeared on each arm of the cross. The reverse of the medal had the raised

Continued on Next Page

inscription AWARDED TO and space for the recipient's name. The medal was suspended from a light blue ribbon with thirteen white stars. The ribbon was suspended from a rectangular gold pin bar inscribed with the word VALOUR.

The Fourth Navy Medal Of Honor (August 7, 1942 to Present)

In 1942, Congress readopted the original, Civil War-style five-pointed star, adding a neckband of light blue and eight-sided pad charged with 13 white stars. Although some minor modifications have been made to the neck ribbon/pad in the interim, the award as adopted in 1942 is basically identical to the Medal of Honor design used by the Navy and Marine Corps today.

Many Americans today are confused with the term "Congressional Medal of Honor," when, in fact, the proper term is "Medal of Honor." A law passed in July 1918 authorized the President to present the medal in the name of Congress. Part of this confusion stems from the fact that all MOH recipients belong to the Congressional Medal of Honor Society chartered by Congress. An act of Congress in July 1963 clarified and amended the criteria for awarding the Medal of Honor to prevent award of the medal for deeds done "in line of profession," but not necessarily in actual conflict with an enemy. This act of Congress made the clarification by stating that the award was "for service in military operations involving conflict with an opposing force or for such service with friendly forces engaged in armed conflict."

MEDAL OF HONOR AIR FORCE

ESTABLISHING AUTHORITY

The Air Force design of the Medal of Honor was established by Congress on July 6, 1960 and presented to all Air Force recipients of the MOH on or after November 1, 1965. Air Force decorations are generally considered as deriving from their earlier comparable Army awards; that is, they are not legally "new" decorations but rather the Air Force design versions of previously established Army decorations. The Air Force is authorized to issue its own version of the Army Medal of Honor by Section 8741 of Title 10 of the U.S. Code.

CRITERIA

Criteria for awarding the Air Force Medal of Honor is the same as for the Army and Navy, to wit: "conspicuous gallantry and intrepidity at the risk of life above and beyond the call of duty." Each recommendation for the Medal of Honor must incontestably prove that the self sacrifice or personal bravery involved conspicuous risk of life. The Air Force Medal of Honor became effective on November 1, 1965, and was designed by Lewis J. King, Jr., of the Army's Institute of Heraldry. The first recipient of the Air Force Medal of Honor was Major Bernard E. Fisher on January 19, 1967 for his heroic actions in rescuing a fellow pilot who had crash landed on a landing strip in the A Shau Valley on March 10, 1966. Airman First Class John L. Levitow was the first USAF enlisted person to receive the Medal. He was awarded the MOH for saving his AC-47 gunship and crew in Vietnam. Five airmen received the Medal of Honor during the Vietnam War.

The medal is officially described as follows: within a wreath of laurel in green enamel, a gold-finished five-pointed star, one point down, tipped with trefoils and each point containing a crown of laurel and oak on a green enamel background. Centered upon the star is an annulet of thirty-four stars which surround the profile of the head from the Statue of Liberty. The star is suspended by a connecting bar and pinned hinge from a trophy consisting of a bar inscribed with the word VALOR above an adaptation of a thunderbolt. The bar is suspended from a pale blue moire silk neck band behind an elongated square pad in the center, with the corners turned back and charged with thirteen white stars in the form of a triple chevron. The star is a replica of the design originally adopted by the Navy and the Army. The profile taken from the Statue of Liberty represents those ideals for which the United States is known throughout the world. The thunderbolt is taken from the Air Force coat of arms and distinguishes the medal as an Air Force decoration. The medal is two inches in overall height and two and one-sixteenth inches in overall width, making it larger than either the Army or Navy Medals of Honor. The reverse is plain, providing space for the name of the recipient.

Although referred to here and in most texts as the "Air Force Medal of Honor", the nation's highest award for valor for Air Force personnel should more properly be referred to as the "Medal of Honor - Air Force design."

DISTINGUISHED SERVICE CROSS

Silver

Bronze

Service: Army
Instituted: 1918
Criteria: Extraordinary heroism in action against an enemy of the U.S. or while serving with friendly foreign forces
Devices: Bronze, silver oak leaf cluster
Notes: 100 copies of earlier design cross were issued with a European-style (unedged) ribbon

    Authorized by Congress on July 9, 1918. Awarded for extraordinary heroism against an armed enemy but of a level not justifying the award of the Medal of Honor. It may be awarded to both civilians and military serving in any capacity with the Army who distinguish themselves by heroic actions in combat. The act or acts of heroism must be so notable and have involved risk of life so extraordinary as to set the individual apart from his comrades. The medal had been initially proposed for award to qualifying members of the American Expeditionary Forces in Europe during World War I but was authorized permanently by Congress in the Appropriations Act of 1918. The Cross was designed by 1st Lt. Andre Smith and Captain Aymar Embury, with the final design sculpted by John R. Sinnock at the Philadelphia Mint.

    While DSCs were originally numbered, the practice was discontinued during World War II. In 1934 the DSC was authorized to be presented to holders of the Certificate of Merit which had been discontinued in 1918 when the Distinguished Service Medal was established. The medal is a cross with an eagle with spread wings centered on the cross behind which is a circular wreath of laurel leaves. The cross has decorative, fluted edges with a small ornamental scroll topped by a ball at the end of each arm. The laurel wreath is tied at its base by a scroll which upon which are written the words, FOR VALOR. The eagle represents the United States and the laurel leaves surrounding the eagle representing victory and achievement. The reverse of the cross features the same decorations at the edges that appear on the front. The eagle's wings, back and tips also show. Centered on the reverse of the cross is a laurel wreath . In the center of the wreath is a decorative rectangular plaque for engraving the soldier's name. The ribbon has a one inch wide center of national blue edged in white and red on the outer edge of the ribbon. The national colors taken from the flag stand for sacrifice (red), purity (white), and high purpose (blue).

NAVY CROSS

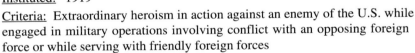
Silver   Gold

Instituted: 1919
Criteria: Extraordinary heroism in action against an enemy of the U.S. while engaged in military operations involving conflict with an opposing foreign force or while serving with friendly foreign forces
Devices: Gold, silver star
Notes: Originally issued with a 1-1/2" wide ribbon

    For extraordinary heroism in connection with military operations against an opposing armed force. The Navy Cross is worn after the Medal of Honor and before all other decorations.

    The Navy Cross was established by an Act of Congress and approved on 4 February 1919. Initially the Navy Cross was awarded for extraordinary heroism or distinguished service in either combat or peacetime. The criteria was upgraded in August 1942 to limit the award to those individuals demonstrating extraordinary heroism in connection with military operations against an armed enemy.

    The Navy Cross medal is a cross patee with the ends of the cross rounded. It has four laurel leaves with berries in each re-entrant angle, which symbolizes victory. In the center of the cross is a sailing ship on waves. The ship is a caravel, symbolic of ships of the fourteenth century. On the reverse are crossed anchors with cables attached with the letters USN amid the anchors. The ribbon is navy blue with a white center stripe. Additional awards of the Navy Cross are denoted by gold stars five-sixteenths of an inch in diameter.

AIR FORCE CROSS

Service: Air Force
Instituted: 1960
Criteria: Extraordinary heroism in action against an enemy of the U.S. or while serving with friendly foreign forces
Devices: Bronze, silver oak leaf cluster

Silver

Bronze

Authorized on November 1, 1965 for extraordinary heroism while engaged in a military action against an enemy of the United States; previous to the effective date of July 6, 1960, deserving Air Force personnel received the Army Distinguished Service Cross (DSC). It is awarded for heroic actions not justifying the Medal of Honor and is presented in the name of the President.

The first award of the Air Force Cross was made posthumously to Major Rudolf Anderson, Jr. who was shot down and killed over Cuba during the Cuban missile crisis while flying a U-2 aircraft. The first living enlisted man to receive the award was Sgt. Duane D. Hackney who received it for rescuing a downed Air Force pilot in Vietnam. T/Sgt Tim Wilkinson, an Air Force pararescueman, as of this writing, is the most recent USAF person to receive the Air Force Cross. He received his award for his heroic actions during the October 1993 firefight in Mogadishu, Somalia when, despite injuries and intense enemy fire, he treated injured Army helicopter crews and injured Army Rangers. The design of the Air Force Cross medal and ribbon are based on the design of the Army Distinguished Service Cross. The medal is a bronze cross containing a gold-plated American bald eagle with wings against a cloud formation encircled by a green laurel wreath. The Awardee's name may be engraved on the reverse. The blue in the center of the ribbon is a lighter shade than that of the DSC. Additional awards are denoted bronze and silver oak leaf clusters.

DEFENSE DISTINGUISHED SERVICE MEDAL

Service: All Services (by Secretary of Defense)
Instituted: July 9, 1970.
Criteria: Exceptionally meritorious service to the United States while assigned to a Joint Activity in a position of unique and great responsibility
Devices: All Services: bronze & silver oak leaf cluster

Silver

Bronze

Authorized on July 9, 1970 and awarded to military officers for exceptionally meritorious service while assigned to a Department of Defense joint activity. The Secretary of Defense is the awarding authority for the medal, usually awarded to the most senior officers. Examples of assignments that may allow qualification for this medal are: Chairman, Joint Chiefs of Staff; Chiefs and Vice Chiefs of the Military Services, including the Commandant and Assistant Commandant of the Marine Corps; and Commanders and Vice Commanders of Unified and Specified Commands. It may also be awarded to other senior officers who serve in positions of great responsibility, or to an officer whose direct and individual contributions to national security or defense are also recognized as being so exceptional in scope and value as to be equivalent to contributions normally associated with positions encompassing broader responsibilities. Subsequent awards are denoted by bronze and silver oak leaf clusters.

The medal depicts an American bald eagle with wings spread and the United States shield on its breast; the eagle is superimposed on a medium blue pentagon (which represents the five services) and is surrounded by a gold circle that has thirteen stars in the upper half and a laurel and olive wreath in the lower half. On the reverse of the medal is the inscription FROM THE SECRETARY OF DEFENSE TO...FOR DISTINGUISHED SERVICE. Space is provided between the TO and FOR for engraving of the recipient's name. The ribbon has a central stripe of red flanked by stripes of gold and blue. The red represents zeal and courageous action, the gold denotes excellence, and the medium blue represents the Department of Defense.

The Defense Distinguished Service Medal was designed by Mildred Orloff and sculpted by Lewis J. King, Jr., both of the Army's Institute of Heraldry.

DISTINGUISHED SERVICE MEDAL (ARMY)

Silver   Bronze

Service: Army
Instituted: 1918
Criteria: Exceptionally meritorious service to the United States Government in a duty of great responsibility
Devices: Bronze, silver oak leaf cluster
Notes: Originally issued with European (unedged) ribbon ("French Cut")

Authorized by Congress on July 9, 1918 for exceptionally meritorious service to the United States while serving in a duty of great responsibility with the U.S. Army. It was originally intended for award for qualifying actions during wartime only but was later authorized for qualifying actions during both wartime or peacetime. As this country's highest award for meritorious service or achievement, it has been awarded to both military and civilians, foreign and domestic. The first American to receive this medal was General John J. Pershing, commanding general of the American Expeditionary Forces during World War I, on October 12, 1918. Individuals who had received the Certificate of Merit before its disestablishment in 1918 were authorized to receive the DSM. The Army DSM is seldom awarded to civilians and personnel below the rank of Brigadier General.

The medal is a circular design containing the U.S. Coat of Arms encircled by a blue ring with the inscription: FOR DISTINGUISHED SERVICE MCMXVII. Subsequent awards are denoted by the attachment of a bronze oak leaf cluster to the medal and ribbon. In the center of the reverse of the medal, amidst several flags and weapons, is a blank scroll for engraving the awardee's name.

The ribbon has a central wide white stripe edged with blue and an outer red band representing the colors of the U.S. flag. The Army Distinguished Service Medal was designed by Captain Aymar E. Embury III and sculpted by Private Gaetano Cecere.

DISTINGUISHED SERVICE MEDAL (NAVY)

Silver   Gold

Instituted: 1919
Criteria: Exceptionally meritorious service to the U.S. Government in a duty of great responsibility
Devices: Gold, silver star
Notes: 107 copies of earlier medal design issued but later withdrawn. First ribbon design was 1 1/2" wide

For exceptionally meritorious service to the U.S. Government in a duty of great responsibility. The Navy Distinguished Service Medal is worn after the Defense Distinguished Service Medal and before the Silver Star.

The Navy Distinguished Service Medal was established by an Act of Congress and approved on 4 February 1919 and, like the Navy Cross, was made retroactive to 6 April 1917. During this period there was confusion about what criteria constituted the award of the Navy Distinguished Service Medal and what criteria constituted the award of the Navy Cross. At the outbreak of World War II, laws governing the award of naval decorations were changed with Public Law 702, which placed the Navy Cross above the Navy Distinguished Service Medal and clearly limited the Navy Distinguished Service Medal for exceptionally meritorious service and not for acts of heroism. The first Navy Distinguished Service Medal was awarded, posthumously, to Brigadier General Charles M. Doyen, USMC.

The Navy Distinguished Service Medal is a gold medallion with an American bald eagle with displayed wings in the center. The eagle is surrounded by a blue enameled ring which contains the words, UNITED STATES OF AMERICA with NAVY at the bottom. Outside the blue ring is a gold border of waves. The medal is suspended from its ribbon by a five pointed white enameled star with an anchor in the center. Behind the star are gold rays emanating from the re-entrant angles of the star. The reverse of the medal contains a trident surrounded by a wreath of laurel. The wreath is surrounded by a blue enamel ring with the inscription: FOR DISTINGUISHED SERVICE. The blue enamel ring is surrounded by a gold border of waves the same as on the front of the medal. The ribbon is navy blue with a gold stripe in the center. Additional awards of the Navy Distinguished Service Medal are denoted by gold stars five sixteenths of an inch in diameter.

DISTINGUISHED SERVICE MEDAL (AIR FORCE)

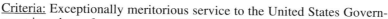

Silver   Bronze

Service: Air Force

Instituted: 1960

Criteria: Exceptionally meritorious service to the United States Government in a duty of great responsibility

Devices: Bronze, silver oak leaf cluster

Notes: Original design was modified and used as the Airman's Medal

The Air Force Distinguished Service Medal was authorized by Congress on July 6, 1960; it evolved from the Army Distinguished Service Medal authorized in 1918. The medal is awarded for exceptionally meritorious service to the U.S. in a duty of great responsibility; the term "great responsibility" denotes the success of a major operation or program attributed to the proper exercise of authority and judgement. This is the highest peacetime Air Force decoration awarded. It is presented to all recipients who are awarded this decoration on or after November 1, 1965; AAF and USAF personnel who were awarded this decoration prior to this date received the Army version. The Air Force Distinguished Service Medal is rarely awarded to officers below the rank of Brigadier General. The medal should be referred to as "Distinguished Service Medal - Air Force design." Major General Osmond J. Ritland, Air Force Systems Command, was the first recipient of the Air Force Distinguished Service Medal on November 30, 1965 for his efforts as Deputy Commander for Manned Space Flight. Subsequent awards are denoted by bronze and silver oak leaf clusters. The medal is a blue stone centered within 13 gold rays, each separated by 13 white stars. The recipient's name may be engraved on the reverse of the medal.

DISTINGUISHED SERVICE MEDAL (DEPT. OF TRANSPORTATION)

⭐ Gold

Service: Department of Transportation, Coast Guard

Instituted: 1992

Criteria: Exceptionally meritorious service to the Department of Transportation in a duty of great responsibility

Devices: Gold star

The Transportation Distinguished Service Medal was established by Executive Order 12824 signed by President George Bush on December 7, 1992. It may be awarded to any member of the Coast Guard who has provided exceptionally meritorious service in a duty of great responsibility while assigned to the Department of Transportation, or in other activities under the responsibility of the Secretary of Transportation, either national or international as may be assigned by the Secretary. The Transportation Distinguished Service Medal is worn only by Coast Guard officers. It is worn after the Defense Distinguished Service Medal and before the Coast Guard DSM.

The Transportation Distinguished Service Medal was designed by Nadine Russell of the Army Institute of Heraldry. In the center of the obverse is a silver medallion containing a narrow-bordered blue triskelion adapted from the Department of Transportation Seal . It is contained within a raised border of continuous cable in gold, superimposed over crossed anchors on a circular field. This field is in turn surrounded by a raised laurel wreath in green enamel, finished in gold.

The suspender which connects the medal to its ribbon is integral to the medal and consists of a miniature Coast Guard officer's cap device in gold. In the upper-central portion of the reverse there is a raised plaque for engraving the recipient's name. Above the plaque in two lines are the raised words, AWARDED TO; and below the plaque in four lines, the words FOR EXTRAORDINARY MERITORIOUS SERVICE. The plaque and inscription are contained within an incomplete circle (open at the bottom) consisting of the raised words, UNITED STATES DEPARTMENT OF TRANSPORTATION.

The ribbon to the Transportation Distinguished Service Medal is predominantly Old Glory Blue edged in white with two stripes of paprika near each edge, the colors traditionally associated with other Department of Transportation awards. Additional awards are denoted by gold stars.

DISTINGUISHED SERVICE MEDAL (COAST GUARD)

Service: Coast Guard

Instituted: 1961

Gold

Criteria: Exceptionally meritorious service to the United States Government in a duty of great responsibility

Devices: Gold star

Notes: Originally authorized in 1949 but the design was not approved until 1961

The Coast Guard Distinguished Service Medal was officially established by Act of Congress on August 4, 1949 . Although the medal was authorized in 1949, its design was not approved until February 1, 1961. It is awarded to any person who, while serving in any capacity with the Coast Guard, distinguishes himself or herself by exceptionally meritorious service to the United States in a duty of great responsibility. To justify an award of the Distinguished Service Medal, exceptional performance of duty, clearly above that normally expected, which has contributed materially to the success of a major command or project, is required. In general, the Coast Guard Distinguished Service Medal is normally awarded only to those officers in principal commands whose service is such as to justify the award. The Secretary of Transportation has retained the authority to approve, in the name of the President, all awards of the Coast Guard Distinguished Service Medal.

The Coast Guard Distinguished Service Medal was designed and sculpted by Thomas Hudson Jones of the Army's Institute of Heraldry. It is a gold disc which, on its obverse, shows a representation of the U.S. Revenue Cutter *Massachusetts* under full sail on a moderate sea. In a circle surrounding the ship are the words, U.S. COAST GUARD in the upper portion, and DISTIN-GUISHED SERVICE in the lower. On the reverse is the Coast Guard Seal above a blank streamer (used for engraving the recipient's name) which follows the contour of the lower half of the medal. In terms of its symbolism, the *Massachusetts,* was the first U.S. Revenue Cutter. Built in 1791, it was the forerunner of a long line of similar vessels which rendered distinguished service to U.S. Maritime history and was considered a fitting symbol to use on the Coast Guard Distinguished Service Medal. The ribbon consists of a central stripe of light blue, bordered on each side by a pinstripe of white. The ribbon is edged in purple. Additional awards are denoted by gold stars.

SILVER STAR

Silver   Gold   Silver   Bronze

Service: All Services (originally Army only)

Instituted: 1932

Criteria: Gallantry in action against an armed enemy of the United States or while serving with friendly foreign forces

Devices: Army/Air Force: bronze, silver oak leaf cluster; Navy/Marine Corps/Coast Guard: gold, silver star

Notes: Derived from the 3/16" silver "Citation Star" previously worn on Army campaign medals

Awarded for gallantry in action against an enemy of the United States or while engaged in military operations involving conflict against an opposing armed force in which the United States is not a belligerent party. The level of gallantry required, while of a high degree, is less than that required for the Medal of Honor, Distinguished Service Cross or Navy Cross. The Silver Star is derived from the Army's "Citation Star", a 3/16" dia. silver star device. It was worn on the ribbon bar and suspension ribbon of the "appropriate Army campaign medal " by any soldier cited in orders for gallantry in action. Although most applicable to the World War I Victory Medal, it was retroactive to all Army campaign medals dating back to the Civil War.

The actual Silver Star *Medal* was instituted in 1932 with the first award presented to General Douglas MacArthur, the Army's then-Chief-of-Staff. The Silver Star was designed by Rudolf Freund of the firm of Bailey, Banks and Biddle. On August 7, 1942, the award was extended to Navy personnel and, later that year, authorized for civilians serving with the armed forces who met the stated criteria specified in the initial regulation.

The medal is a five-pointed star finished in gilt-bronze. In the center of the star is a three-sixteenths inch silver five-pointed star within a wreath of laurel, representing the silver [citation] star prescribed by the original legislation . The rays of both stars align. The top of the medal has a rectangular-shaped loop for the suspension ribbon. The laurel wreath signifies achievement, and the larger gilt-bronze star represents military service. The reverse contains the inscription FOR GALLANTRY IN ACTION with a space to engrave the name of the recipient.

The ribbon, based on the colors of the National flag, has a center stripe of red flanked by a stripes of white which are flanked by blue bands with borders of white edged in blue. Additional awards are denoted by a bronze or silver oak leaf clusters or gold and silver stars depending on the recipient's Branch of Service.

DEFENSE SUPERIOR SERVICE MEDAL

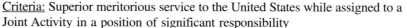

Silver   Bronze

Service: All Services (by Secretary of Defense)
Instituted: February 6, 1976.
Criteria: Superior meritorious service to the United States while assigned to a Joint Activity in a position of significant responsibility
Devices: All Services: bronze, silver oak leaf cluster

Authorized on February 6, 1976 by an executive order signed by President Gerald R. Ford. Awarded by the Secretary of Defense to any member of the armed forces for superior meritorious service after February 6, 1976 in a position of significant responsibility while assigned to a DOD joint activity, including the Office of the Secretary of Defense, the Joint Chiefs of Staff, and specified and unified commands. The medal was created to provide recognition to those assigned to joint duty on a level equivalent to that recognition provided by the Legion of Merit. Prior to establishment of the Defense Superior Service Medal, the Office of the Secretary of Defense had to provide recognition through equivalent awards that were approved through individual service channels. Although it was established as equivalent to the Legion of Merit, its precedence is before the Legion of Merit when both are worn. Oak leaf clusters denote additional awards.

The medal depicts a silver American bald eagle with wings spread and the United States shield on its breast; the eagle is superimposed on a medium blue pentagon (which represents the five services) and is surrounded by a silver circle that has thirteen stars in the upper half and a laurel and olive wreath in the lower half. On the reverse of the medal is the inscription FROM THE SECRETARY OF DEFENSE TO...FOR SUPERIOR SERVICE. Space is provided between the TO and FOR for engraving of the recipient's name. The ribbon consists of a central stripe of red, flanked on either side by stripes of white, blue and gold.

LEGION OF MERIT

Bronze   Silver   Gold   Silver   Bronze

Service: All Services
Instituted: 1942 retroactive to September 8, 1939
Criteria: Exceptionally meritorious conduct in the performance of outstanding services to the United States
Devices: Army/Air Force: bronze, silver oak leaf cluster; Navy/Marine Corps/ Coast Guard: bronze letter "V" (for valor), gold, silver star
Notes: Issued in four degrees (Legionnaire, Officer, Commander & Chief Commander) to foreign nationals

Authorized by Congress on July 20, 1942 for award to members of the Armed Forces of the United States for exceptionally meritorious conduct in the performance of outstanding service. Superior performance of normal duties will not alone justify award of this decoration. It is not awarded for heroism but rather service and achievement while performing duties in a key position of responsibility. It may be presented to foreign personnel but is not authorized for presentment to civilian personnel. There are four degrees of this decoration that are awarded to foreign personnel only (Chief Commander, Commander, Officer, and Legionnaire). The first two degrees are comparable in rank to the Distinguished Service Medal and are usually awarded to heads of state and to commanders of armed forces, respectively. The last two degrees are comparable in rank to the award of the Legion of Merit to U.S. service members. The Legion of Merit was designed by Colonel Robert Townsend Heard and sculpted by Katharine W. Lane of Boston.

The name and design of the Legion of Merit are strongly influenced by the French Legion of Honor. The medal is a white enameled five-armed cross with ten points, each tipped with a gold ball and bordered in red enamel. In the center of the cross, thirteen stars on a blue field are surrounded by a circle of heraldic clouds. A green enameled laurel wreath circles behind the arms of the cross. Between the wreath and the center of the medal, in between the arms of the cross are two crossed arrows pointing outward. The blue circle with thirteen stars surrounded by clouds is taken from the Great Seal of the United States and is symbolic of a "new constellation," as the signers of the Declaration of Independence called our new republic. The laurel wreath represents achievement, while the arrows represent protection of the nation. The reverse of the cross is a gold colored copy of the front with blank space to be used for engraving The raised inscription, ANNUIT COEPTIS MDCCLXXXII with a bullet separating each word encircles the area to be engraved. The words, UNITED STATES OF AMERICA and ANNUIT COEPTIS (He [God] Has Favored Our Undertaking) come from the Great Seal of the United States and the date MDCCLXXXII (1782) refers to the year General Washington established the Badge of Military Merit. The ribbon is a purple-red called American Beauty Red which is edged in white. The color is a variation of the original color of the Badge of Military Merit.

DISTINGUISHED FLYING CROSS

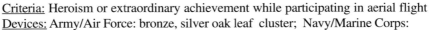

Bronze   Silver   Gold

Silver   Bronze

Service: All Services
Instituted: 1926 (Retroactive to 6 April 1917)
Criteria: Heroism or extraordinary achievement while participating in aerial flight
Devices: Army/Air Force: bronze, silver oak leaf cluster; Navy/Marine Corps: bronze letter "V" (for valor), gold, silver star; Coast Guard: gold, silver star

     Authorized on July 2, 1926 and implemented by an executive order signed by President Calvin Coolidge on January 28, 1927. It is awarded to United States military personnel for heroism or extraordinary achievement that is clearly distinctive involving operations during aerial flight that are not routine. It is the first decoration authorized in identical design and ribbon to all branches of the U.S. Armed Forces. Captain Charles A. Lindbergh was the first recipient of the Distinguished Flying Cross for his solo flight across the Atlantic. The Wright Brothers were awarded the DFC by an Act of Congress for their first manned flight at Kitty Hawk, North Carolina in 1903. Amelia Earhart became the only female civilian to be awarded the DFC when it was presented to her by the United States Army Air Corps for her aerial exploits. Such awards to civilians were prohibited on March 1, 1927 by Executive Order 4601.

     While the Distinguished Flying Cross was never intended to be an automatic award, the Army Air Force did use it in that capacity many times during World War II by awarding DFCs for specific number of sorties and flying hours in a combat theater.

     The front of the medal is a four-bladed propeller contained within a bronze cross suspended from a straight bar attached to the medal drape. The reverse is blank and provides space for the recipient's name and date of the award. The ribbon is blue, with a narrow stripe of red bordered by white in the center. The ribbon edges are outlined with bands of white inside blue. Additional awards are denoted by bronze and silver oak leaf clusters or gold and silver stars depending on the recipient's Service Branch.

SOLDIER'S MEDAL

Silver   Bronze

Service: Army
Instituted: 1926
Criteria: Heroism not involving actual conflict with an armed enemy of the United States
Devices: Bronze, silver oak leaf cluster

     Authorized by Congress on July 2, 1926 to any member of the Army, National Guard or Reserves for heroism not involving actual conflict with an armed enemy.

     The bronze octagonal medal has, as its central feature, a North American bald eagle with raised wings representing the United States. The eagle grasps an ancient Roman fasces symbolizing the State's lawful authority and conveys the concept that the award is to a soldier from the Government. There are seven stars on the eagle's left side and six stars and a spray of leaves to its right. The octagonal shape distinguishes the Soldier's Medal from other decorations. The stars represent the thirteen original colonies that formed the United States. The laurel spray balances the groups of stars and represents achievement. The reverse has a U.S. shield with sprays of laurel and oak leaves representing achievement and strength in front of a scroll. The words: SOLDIER'S MEDAL and: FOR VALOR are inscribed on the reverse.

     The ribbon contains thirteen alternating stripes of white (seven) and red (six) in the center, bordered by blue and are taken from the United States flag. The thirteen red and white stripes are arranged in the same manner as the thirteen vertical stripes in the U.S. Coat of Arms shield and also represent the thirteen original colonies.

     Gaetano Cecere designed and sculpted the Soldier's Medal (the art deco influence of the 1930s can certainly be seen in this medal more than in any other Army award.) The Soldier's Medal is one of four decorations for which an enlisted soldier may increased his retirement by ten percent. The increase is not automatic, however; recipients of the Soldier's Medal must petition the Army Decorations Board for the bonus. Additional awards are denoted by oak leaf clusters.

NAVY AND MARINE CORPS MEDAL

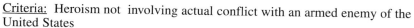

Silver   Gold

Instituted: 1942

Criteria: Heroism not involving actual conflict with an armed enemy of the United States

Devices: Gold, silver star

Notes: For acts of life-saving, action must be at great risk to one's own life

     For heroism that involves the voluntary risk of life under conditions other than those of conflict with an opposing armed force. The Navy and Marine Corps Medal is worn after the Distinguished Flying Cross and before the Bronze Star Medal.

     The Navy and Marine Corps Medal was established by an Act of Congress and approved on 7 August 1942. The medal was established to recognize non-combat heroism. For acts of lifesaving, or attempted lifesaving, it is required that the action be performed at the risk of one's own life. The Navy and Marine Corps Medal is prized above many combat decorations by Marines who have received it.

     The Navy and Marine Corps Medal was designed by Lt. Commander McClelland Barclay, USNR. The medal is a bronze octagon with an eagle perched upon a fouled anchor. Beneath the anchor is a globe and below that is the inscription HEROISM in raised letters. The reverse of the medal is blank to allow for engraving the recipient's name. The ribbon consists of three equal stripes of Navy blue, gold and scarlet- the blue-gold representing the Navy and the scarlet-gold being the Marine Corps' official colors. Additional awards are denoted by five-sixteenth inch gold stars.

AIRMAN'S MEDAL

Bronze

Service: Air Force

Instituted: 1960

Criteria: Heroism involving voluntary risk of life under conditions other than those of actual conflict with an armed enemy

Devices: Bronze, silver oak leaf cluster

Notes: Derived from original design of the Air Force Distinguished Service Medal

     Authorized on August 10, 1956 and instituted on July 6, 1960, the authorizing directive was an amendment to the same order which created the Soldier's Medal (prior to that time, USAF personnel qualifying for such an award were awarded the Soldier's Medal). The medal's name is also fashioned as a carryover from the Soldier's Medal but does not make the casual observer aware of the medal's significance and the acts required to earn the decoration. The Airman's Medal is awarded for actions involving voluntary risk of life under conditions other than combat. A successful voluntary heroic act or the saving of a life is not essential to the award of this decoration. The first Airman's Medal was awarded to Captain John Burger on July 21, 1960 at McDill Air Force Base, Florida for saving a fellow airman's life by removing a live power line that laid across his body after having been severely shocked. Another example of the heroism required for the award was the bravery exhibited by Senior Airman Joe Sampson of Charleston Air Force Base, South Carolina when he saved an Army jumpmaster's life at the risk of his own aboard a C-141 aircraft carrying Army paratroopers. When the jumpmaster's reserve parachute inadvertently deployed and threatened to pull him out of the aircraft, Sr. Airman Sampson, without hesitation, grabbed the jumpmaster and his chute and pulled him back into the aircraft despite the tremendous forces of the airstream. The American bald eagle is depicted on the face of the medal along with the Greek god Hermes, herald and messenger of other gods. Around the edge of the medal is the curved inscription: AIRMAN'S on the left and MEDAL on the right. The reverse contains space for engraving just below the inscription: FOR VALOR. Additional awards of the Airman's Medal are denoted by oakleaf clusters.

COAST GUARD MEDAL

Gold

Service: Coast Guard

Instituted: 1958

Criteria: Heroism not involving actual conflict with an armed enemy of the United States.

Devices: Gold, silver star

    The Coast Guard's search and rescue mission makes it inevitable that personnel of that service will occasionally be faced with extremely hazardous situations. After World War II, to provide a parallel Coast Guard decoration to the Navy and Marine Corps Medal, the Coast Guard sought legislation for an appropriate counterpart decoration. Authority for the new decoration, known as the Coast Guard Medal, was accordingly granted by Act of Congress on August 4, 1949 but it was not designed and struck until 1958. The Coast Guard Medal is awarded to any person who, while serving in any capacity with the Coast Guard, distinguishes himself by heroism not involving actual combat with an enemy. To justify the Coast Guard Medal, the individual must have performed a voluntary act of heroism in the face of great danger which also extended beyond that normally been expected of the individual. For lifesaving, the individual must have displayed heroism at the risk of his life. It was first awarded in June of 1958. The first recipients were Engineman Third Class Earl A. Leyda and Boatswain's Mate Third Class Raymond A. Johnson, both of whom received the medal for their attempted rescue of workers trapped 5,800 feet below Lake Ontario after a tunnel explosion at Oswego, New York. The Coast Guard Medal was designed and sculpted by Thomas Hudson Jones of the Army's Institute of Heraldry and is a bronze octagon. On its obverse it bears the Coast Guard Seal enclosed within a circle of continuous cable. The reverse is plain except for the inscription FOR HEROISM in raised letters. The ribbon is medium blue in the center and at the edges, with two sets of alternating white and red stripes (four white and three red). An additional award is denoted by a five-sixteenth inch dia. gold star.

GOLD LIFE-SAVING MEDAL

Gold

Service: All Services and Civilians

Instituted: 1874 (modified 1882 and 1946)

Criteria: Heroic conduct at the risk of life during the rescue or attempted rescue of a victim of drowning or shipwreck.

Devices: Coast Guard: gold star

Notes: Normally a "Non-Military Decoration" but considered a personal decoration by the Coast Guard. Originally a "table" (non-wearable) medal, then worn with a 2" wide ribbon.

    The Gold Lifesaving Medal may be awarded to any person who rescues or endeavors to rescue another person from drowning, shipwreck or other peril of the water. The rescue or attempted rescue must take place in waters within the United States or, if the rescue or attempted rescue takes place outside of such waters, one of the parties must be a citizen of the United States or from a vessel or aircraft owned or operated by citizens of the United States. To qualify for the Gold Lifesaving Medal, the rescue or attempted rescue must be made at the risk of one's own life and must evince extreme and heroic daring. The medal was designed by Anthony C. Paquet, Chief Engraver of the Philadelphia Mint. The original Gold Lifesaving Medal was not intended to be worn; it was a so-called "table" medal, one and three-fourths inches in circumference showing three men in a boat in a heavy sea attempting to help a fourth figure, a mariner in distress. The whole is surrounded by the words, LIFESAVING MEDAL OF THE FIRST CLASS in the upper half and, UNITED STATES OF AMERICA in the lower half. The reverse contains an American eagle with spread wings perched atop a monument. To its left is the figure of a woman holding an oak wreath in her left hand. Under the monument, in two lines, are the words, ACT OF CONGRESS JUNE 20th 1874. The whole is surrounded by the words, IN TESTIMONY OF HEROIC DEEDS IN SAVING LIFE FROM THE PERILS OF THE SEA. On June 18, 1878, some minor changes were made when the words, LIFESAVING MEDAL OF THE FIRST CLASS were removed from the upper half of the obverse and replaced with UNITED STATES OF AMERICA, taken from the lower half, which was in turn replaced by ACT OF CONGRESS JUNE 20, 1874, which was removed from the reverse of the medal. The Gold Lifesaving Medal was again modified in May 4, 1882, when it was fitted with a red, 2 inch wide ribbon and a suspension device, a gold eagle's head and outstretched wings. On March 13, 1946, several changes were made to the lifesaving medals. The ribbons were changed to avoid confusion with the ribbons to other medals and the size of the medals was reduced to standardize their appearance when worn on the uniform with other medals and ribbon. The only other change to the medal is an inscription change on the lower obverse to ACT OF CONGRESS AUGUST 4, 1949. The ribbon was changed to one and three-eighths inches in width and consists of a center stripe of gold bordered on either side by a stripe of white and edged with a stripe of red.

BRONZE STAR MEDAL

Bronze   Silver   Gold   Silver   Bronze

Service: All Services

Instituted: 1944 retroactive to December 7, 1941.

Criteria: The Bronze Star Medal is awarded to individuals who, while serving in the United States Armed Forces in a combat theater, distinguish themselves by heroism, outstanding achievement, or by meritorious service not involving aerial flight.

Devices: All Services: bronze letter "V" (for Valor) Army/Air Force bronze, silver oak leaf cluster; Navy/Marine Corps/Coast Guard: gold, silver star

Notes: Awarded for meritorious service to WW II holders of Army Combat Infantryman or Combat Medical Badge

Authorized on February 4, 1944, retroactive to December 7, 1941. It is awarded to individuals who, while serving in the United States Armed Forces in a combat theater, distinguish themselves by heroism, outstanding achievement, or by meritorious service not involving aerial flight.

The Bronze Star was originally conceived by the U.S. Navy as a junior decoration comparable to the Air Medal for heroic or meritorious actions by ground and surface personnel. The level of required service would not be sufficient to warrant the Silver Star if awarded for heroism or the Legion of Merit if awarded for meritorious achievement. In a strange twist of fate, the Bronze Star Medal did not reach fruition until championed by General George C. Marshall, the Army Chief of Staff during World War II. Marshall was seeking a decoration that would reward front line troops, particularly infantrymen, whose ranks suffered the heaviest casualties and were forced to endure the greatest danger and hardships during the conflict. Once established, the Bronze Star Medal virtually became the sole province of the Army in terms of the number of medals awarded.

Although Marshall wanted the Bronze Star Medal to be awarded with the same freedom as the Air Medal, it never came close to the vast numbers of Air Medals distributed during the war. The only exception was the award of the Bronze Star Medal to every soldier of the 101st Airborne Division who had fought in the Normandy invasion, Operation Market Garden in Holland and the Battle of the Bulge or were wounded.

After the war, when the ratio of Air Medals to airmen was compared to the numbers of Bronze Star Medals awarded to combat soldiers, it became clear that a huge disparity existed and many troops who deserved the award for their service had not received it. Therefore, in September 1947, the Bronze Star Medal was authorized for all personnel who had received either the Combat Infantryman's Badge (CIB) or the Combat Medical Badge (CMB) between December 7, 1941 to September 2, 1945. In addition, personnel who had participated in the defense of the Philippine Islands between December 7, 1941 and May 10, 1942 were awarded the Bronze Star Medal if their service was on the island of Luzon, the Bataan Peninsula or the harbor defenses on Corregidor Island and they had been awarded the Philippine Presidential Unit Citation. The Bronze Star Medal also replaced some awards of the Purple Heart from early in World War II when that medal was awarded for meritorious or essential service rather than for wounds.

Recipients of the Bronze Star Medal are entitled to wear a "V" device on the ribbon bar and suspension ribbon if the Medal is awarded for heroism in combat. The "V" device was approved in 1945 to clearly distinguish between awards of the medal for heroism in combat or for meritorious service. Additional awards are denoted by bronze and silver oak leaf clusters or gold and silver stars, depending on the recipient's Service Branch.

The Bronze Star Medal is a five-pointed bronze star with a smaller star in the center (similar in design to the Silver Star Medal); the reverse contains the inscription: HEROIC OR MERITORIOUS ACHIEVEMENT in a circular pattern. The ribbon is red with a white-edged blue band in the center and white edge stripes. The Bronze Star Medal was designed by Rudolf Freund of Bailey, Banks and Biddle.

PURPLE HEART

Silver

Gold

Silver

Bronze

Service: All Services (originally Army only)

Instituted: 1932; The Purple Heart is retroactive to April 5, 1917; however, awards for qualifying prior to that date have been made.

Criteria: Awarded to any member of the Armed Forces of the United States or to any civilian national of the United States who, while serving under competent authority in any capacity with one of the U.S. Armed Forces, since April 5, 1917 has been wounded, killed, or who has died or may die of wounds received from an opposing enemy force while in armed combat or as a result of an act of international terrorism or being a Prisoner of War..

Devices: Army/Air Force: bronze, silver oak leaf cluster; Navy/ Marine Corps/Coast Guard: gold, silver star

Notes: A Wound Ribbon appeared briefly in 1917 but was ultimately rescinded. (The Army used wound chevrons during World War I)

The Purple Heart is America's oldest military decoration. It was originally established on August 7, 1782 by General George Washington who designed the original medal called the "Badge of Military Merit." The Badge of Military Merit was awarded for singularly meritorious action to a deserving hero of the Revolutionary War. There were only three recipients of the award, all of whom were noncommissioned officers of the Continental Army. The Badge of Military Merit was intended by Washington to be a permanent decoration but was never used again after the three initial presentations until it was reestablished as the Purple Heart Medal on February 22, 1932 (the 200th anniversary of Washington's birth) by the Army War Department.

During the First World War, War Department General Order No.134 of October 12, 1917 authorized a red ribbon with a narrow white center stripe to be worn on the right breast for wounds received in action. However, the order was rescinded 32 days later and the ribbon never became a reality. Instead the Army authorized wound chevrons which were worn on the lower right sleeve of the tunic.

On July 21, 1932, General Douglas MacArthur, who was a key figure in its revival, received the first Purple Heart after it was reestablished. President Franklin D. Roosevelt signed an executive order on December 3, 1942 that expanded the award to members of the Navy, Marine Corps, and Coast Guard as well. Although the Purple Heart was awarded for meritorious service between 1932 and 1943, the primary purpose of the award has always been to recognize those who received wounds while in the service of the United States military.

Later Presidential Executive Orders extended eligibility for the Purple Heart to military and civilian personnel who received wounds from a terrorist attack or while performing peace keeping duties. Currently, it is awarded for wounds received while serving in any capacity with one of the U.S. Armed Forces after April 5, 1917; it may be awarded to civilians as well as military personnel. The wounds may have been received while in combat against an enemy, while a member of a peacekeeping force, while a Prisoner of War, as a result of a terrorist attack, or as a result of a friendly fire incident in hostile territory. The 1996 Defense Authorization Act extended eligibility for the Purple Heart to prisoners of war before April 25, 1962; previous legislation had only authorized the medal to POWs after April 25, 1962. Wounds that qualify must have required treatment by a medical officer and must be a matter of official record.

The Purple Heart was originally last in precedence of all other personal decorations but was elevated in 1985 to a position just behind the Bronze Star by an act of Congress.

The medal is a heart-shaped, gold-rimmed medallion with a profile of George Washington on a purple enameled base. Above Washington's profile is the shield from his family's coat of arms. FOR MILITARY MERIT is inscribed on the reverse. The ribbon is a dark purple with narrow white edges. The original Badge of Military Merit was a satin purple heart edged in white. The format may have been used since the strongest wood available for gun carriages and weapons during the Revolution was called "Purpleheart", a very strong smooth grain wood from Latin America that was stronger than the famous English oak. Here was an American wood that was stronger, more resistant to rot and termites than any other known wood. Perhaps General Washington chose the American Purpleheart wood as a symbol of strength and resistance over the British hearts of English Oak (a popular English military song of the time).

Additional awards of the Purple Heart are denoted by bronze and silver oak leaf clusters or gold and silver stars, depending on the recipient's Service Branch.

1782 Badge of Military Merit

DEFENSE MERITORIOUS SERVICE MEDAL

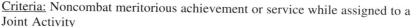

Service: All Services (by Secretary of Defense)
Instituted: November 3, 1977.
Criteria: Noncombat meritorious achievement or service while assigned to a Joint Activity
Devices: All Services: bronze, silver oak leaf cluster

Silver   Bronze

Authorized on November 3, 1977. Awarded to any active member of the U.S. Armed Forces who distinguishes him/herself by noncombat meritorious achievement or service while serving in a Joint Activity after November 3, 1977. Examples of Joint assignments that may allow qualification for this medal are: Office of the Secretary of Defense, Office of the Joint Chiefs of Staff, Unified or Specified Commands, Joint billets in NATO or NORAD, Defense Agencies, National Defense University, National War College, Industrial College of the Armed Forces and Armed Forces Staff College and the Joint Strategic Target Planning Staff.

The bronze medal has an eagle with spread wings in the center superimposed on a pentagon in the center of a laurel wreath. The reverse is inscribed with the words: DEFENSE MERITORIOUS SERVICE and UNITED STATES OF AMERICA. The ribbon has a wide white center stripe with three light blue stripes in the middle. The white stripe is flanked by ruby red and white. The ruby red and white are copied from the ribbon of the Meritorious Service Medal with the blue stripes representing the Department of Defense. Subsequent awards are denoted by bronze and silver oak leaf clusters. The Defense Meritorious Service Medal was designed by Lewis J. King, Jr. of the Army's Institute of Heraldry.

MERITORIOUS SERVICE MEDAL

Service: All Services
Instituted: January 16, 1969
Criteria: Outstanding noncombat meritorious achievement or service to the United States
Devices: Army/Air Force: bronze, silver oak leaf cluster; Navy/ Marine Corps: gold, silver star; Coast Guard: silver letter "O", gold, silver star

Silver   Gold   Silver   Bronze   Silver

Authorized on January 16, 1969 and awarded to members of the Armed Forces for noncombat meritorious achievement or meritorious service after that date. The Meritorious Service Medal evolved from an initial recommendation in 1918 by General John J. Pershing, the Commander of the American Expeditionary Forces during World War I. He suggested that an award for meritorious service be created to provide special recognition to deserving individuals by the U.S. government. Although the request by General Pershing was disapproved, it was revisited several more times during World War II and afterwards. During the Vietnam War the proposal to create the medal received significant attention and was eventually approved when President Lyndon B. Johnson signed the executive order on January 16, 1969. The Meritorious Service Medal cannot be awarded for service in a combat theater. It has often been the decoration of choice for both end of tour and retirement recognition for field grade officers and senior enlisted personnel.

The MSM is a bronze medal with six rays rising from the top of a five-pointed star with beveled edges with two smaller stars outlined within. On the lower part of the medal in front of the star there is an eagle with its wings spread. It is standing on two curving laurel branches tied between the eagle's talons. The eagle, symbol of the nation, holds laurel branches representing achievement. The star represents military service with the rays symbolizing individual efforts to achieve excellence. The reverse of the medal has the inscription UNITED STATES OF AMERICA at the top and MERITORIOUS SERVICE at the bottom; the space inside the circle formed by the text is to be used for engraving the recipient's name.. The ribbon is ruby red with two white stripes and is a variation of the Legion of Merit ribbon. Jay Morris and Lewis J. King of the Army's Institute of Heraldry designed and sculpted the Meritorious Service Medal. Additional awards are indicated by bronze and silver oak leaf clusters or gold and silver stars depending on the recipient's Service Branch.

AIR MEDAL

Silver   Bronze   Bronze   Bronze   Bronze   Silver   Gold

Service: All Services   Instituted: 1942 retroactive to September 8, 1939.
Criteria: Heroic actions or meritorious service while participating in aerial flight, but not of a degree that would justify an award of the Distinguished Flying Cross.
Devices: Army: bronze letter "V" (for valor) effective February 29, 1964, bronze numeral; Air Force: bronze, silver oak leaf cluster; Navy/Marine Corps: bronze letter "V" (for valor), bronze numeral, bronze star , gold, silver star ; Coast Guard: gold, silver star
Note: During World War II, the Army Air Corps and US Army Air Forces employed bronze and silver oak leaf clusters as additional award devices on all decorations including the Air Medal. The same devices were used by the Army until the establishment of the bronze numeral as its unique additional award device for the Air Medal during the Vietnam War.

Authorized on May 11, 1942, the Air Medal is awarded for single acts of achievement after September 8, 1939 to any member of the U.S. Armed Forces who distinguishes him/herself by heroism, outstanding achievement, or by meritorious service while participating in aerial flight. During World War II, the Air Medal was to be awarded for a lesser degree of heroism or achievement than required for the Distinguished Flying Cross. However, many Army Air Force units begin to award the Air Medal on a quota basis, (e.g.: 20 missions equaled one Air Medal or an Air Medal for every enemy aircraft shot down). Some commands carried this to extremes by awarding a DFC for every five Air Medals. By the end of the war, over a million Air Medals were awarded (many of which were, of course, oak leaf clusters). While this might appear extreme, the generous award of the Air Medal provided combat aircrews a visible sign that their devotion and determination were appreciated by the country. The Air Medal helped keep morale up in a force that suffered the highest casualty rate of the war after the Infantry.

Although the Naval Services were authorized to award the Air Medal during World War II, the numbers never approached those received by the Army Air Force amidst the European bombing campaigns. Subsequent to World War II, however, with the increased role of the Navy in joint operations, the use of the Air Medal was subtly redefined. The Air Medal was still awarded for single acts of outstanding achievement which involve superior airmanship but of a lesser degree than would justify an award of a Distinguished Flying Cross. However, during the Korean, Vietnam and Gulf conflicts, awards for meritorious service were made for sustained distinction in the performance of duties involving regular and frequent participation in aerial flight operations. These operations include "strikes" (sorties which deliver ordnance against the enemy; those which land or evacuate personnel in an assault; or, those which involve search and rescue operations which encounter enemy opposition), "flights" (sorties which involve the same kinds of operations as strikes but which do not encounter enemy opposition) or "direct combat support" (sorties which include such activities as reconnaissance, combat air patrol, electronic countermeasures support, psychological warfare, coastal surveillance, etc.). In addition, the Air Medal was awarded for noncombat aerial achievement, such as, to air weather crews who gather major storm data by flying into hurricanes. The Air Force ceased all noncombat awards of the Air Medal with the institution of the Aerial Achievement Medal in 1988 but without a comparable peacetime medal, the other Services still award the Air Medal under circumstances not involving actual combat.

The Air Medal was designed and sculpted by Walker Hancock and is a bronze sixteen point compass rose suspended by a fleur-de-lis. In the center there is an diving eagle carrying a lighting bolt in each talon. The compass rose represents the global capacity of American air power, . The lightning bolts show the United States' ability to wage war from the air and the Fleur-de-lis, the French symbol of nobility, represents the high ideals of American airmen. The reverse of the compass rose is plain with an area for engraving the recipient's name. The ribbon is ultramarine blue with two golden orange stripes, representing the original colors of the Army Air Force.

Placement of Devices on the Air Medal Ribbon

No. of Awards	Army	Navy and Marine Corps Individual	Navy and Marine Corps Strike/Flight	Air Force
1		★		
2	2	★		🍃
3	3	★ ★	3	🍃 🍃
4	4	★ ★ ★	4	🍃 🍃 🍃
5	5	★ ★ ★ ★	5	🍃 🍃 🍃 🍃

Army: 25

Navy and Coast Guard: ★ V 5

Marine Corps: ★ V

Air Force: 🍃🍃🍃🍃

Legend:
★ = 5/16" dia. Gold Star
★ = 3/16" dia. Bronze Star
1,2 etc. = Bronze Block Numerals
🍃 = Bronze Oak Leaf Cluster

SILVER LIFE-SAVING MEDAL

★
Gold

<u>Service:</u> All Services and Civilians

<u>Instituted:</u> 1874 (modified 1882 and 1946)

<u>Criteria:</u> Heroic conduct during rescue or attempted rescue of a victim of drowning or shipwreck.

<u>Devices:</u> Coast Guard: gold star (66)

<u>Notes:</u> Normally a "Non-Military Decoration" but considered a personal decoration by the Coast Guard. Originally a "table" (non-wearable) medal then worn with a 2" wide ribbon.

The Silver Lifesaving Medal is awarded under the same conditions as the Gold Lifesaving Medal, except that the act need not involve the degree of heroism and risk called for in the case of the Gold Medal. The Silver Lifesaving Medal, like the Gold Lifesaving Medal, was designed by Anthony C. Paquet, and, was also originally a table medal. It was one and three-fourths inches in diameter and showed a man struggling in a heavy sea; hovering above him is the figure of a woman who is offering him one end of a long scarf. The whole is encircled by the words, LIFESAVING MEDAL OF THE SECOND CLASS in the upper half, and UNITED STATES OF AMERICA in the lower half. The reverse contains a large wreath of laurel knotted at the bottom with a flowing ribbon. Within the wreath at the top are the words, ACT OF CONGRESS JUNE 20th 1874. The whole is encircled by the words, IN TESTIMONY OF HEROIC DEEDS IN SAVING LIFE FROM THE PERILS OF THE SEA. There is a small decorative scroll at the bottom of the medal.

The Act of Congress on June 18, 1878, which modified the Gold Lifesaving Medal also modified the Silver Lifesaving Medal. The obverse was altered to replace the words, LIFESAVING MEDAL OF THE SECOND CLASS with UNITED STATES OF AMERICA, taken from the lower half. The latter was replaced with ACT OF CONGRESS JUNE 20th 1874, which was removed from the reverse of the medal. In 1882 the Silver Lifesaving Medal was again modified, this time to add a silver suspension bar (of the same design as that of the Gold Lifesaving Medal) and to add a light blue two-inch wide ribbon. The final modification of the Silver Lifesaving Medal occurred in 1949 at the same time and under the same circumstances that the Gold Lifesaving Medal was changed. The current Silver Lifesaving Medal was reduced in size to one and seven-sixteenths of an inch in diameter, the date on the obverse was changed to AUGUST 4, 1949 and the ribbon reduced in width to one and three-eighths inches. The ribbon is composed of a center stripe of silver-gray, bordered by a stripe of white and edged with a stripe of blue. Additional awards of a Gold or Silver Lifesaving Medal are denoted by ornate bars which are inscribed with the recipient's name. A gold star denotes an additional award on the ribbon bar.

AERIAL ACHIEVEMENT MEDAL

Silver   Bronze

<u>Service:</u> Air Force

<u>Instituted:</u> 1988

<u>Criteria:</u> Sustained meritorious achievement while participating in aerial flight

<u>Devices:</u> Bronze, silver oak leaf cluster

<u>Notes:</u> Considered on a par with the Air Medal but more likely to be awarded for peacetime actions

The Aerial Achievement Medal was established on February 3, 1988 and has been in effect since January 1, 1990. It is awarded to U.S. Air Force personnel for sustained meritorious achievement while participating in aerial flight. It is not awarded for single event flights. In contrast to the normal procedure for award of all other military decorations, the individual performance which may qualify for the Aerial Achievement Medal can vary based on the requirements and criteria established by each Major Air Force Command. This is due to the many variations posed by each Command's location, mission, environment, available aircraft types, local political conditions and the general world situation.

The American bald eagle is depicted on the front of the Aerial Achievement Medal just below 13 stars symbolic of the original colonies and in front of two intercepting arcs symbolic of flight paths. The eagle is clutching six lightning bolts which represent the U.S. Air Force. The reverse contains the words FOR MILITARY MERIT surrounding a space for engraving the awardee's name. Additional awards of the Aerial Achievement Medal are denoted by bronze and silver oak leaf clusters.

JOINT SERVICE COMMENDATION MEDAL

<u>Service:</u> All Services (by Secretary of Defense)
<u>Instituted:</u> June 25, 1963
<u>Criteria:</u> Meritorious service or achievement while assigned to a Joint Activity
<u>Devices:</u> All Services: bronze letter "V" (for valor), bronze, silver oak leaf cluster;

 Bronze   Silver   Bronze

Authorized on June 25, 1963, this was the first medal specifically authorized for members of a Joint Service organization. Awarded to members of the Armed Forces for meritorious achievement or service while serving in a Joint Activity after January 1, 1963. The "V" device is authorized if the award is made for direct participation in combat operations.

The medal consists of four conjoined green enameled hexagons edged in gold which represent the unity of the Armed Forces. The top hexagon has thirteen gold five-pointed stars (representing the thirteen original colonies) and the lower hexagon has a gold stylized heraldic device (for land, air and sea). An eagle with spread wings and a shield on its breast is in the center of the hexagons. The eagle is grasping three arrows in its talons. The hexagons are encircled by a laurel wreath bound with gold bands (representing achievement). On the reverse there is a plaque for engraving the recipient's name. Above the plaque are the raised words, FOR MILITARY and below , MERIT with a laurel spray below . The words and laurel spray are derived from the Army and Navy Commendation Medals. The ribbon is a center stripe of green flanked by white, green, white, and light blue stripes. The green and white are from the Army and Navy Commendation ribbons and the light blue represents the Department of Defense.

The Joint Service Commendation Medal was designed by the Army's Institute of Heraldry's Stafford F. Potter. Oak leaf clusters denote additional awards.

ARMY COMMENDATION MEDAL

<u>Service:</u> Army
<u>Instituted:</u> 1945 (retroactive to 1941)
<u>Criteria:</u> Heroism, meritorious achievement or meritorious service
<u>Devices:</u> Bronze letter "V" (for valor), bronze, silver oak leaf cluster
<u>Notes:</u> Originally a ribbon-only award then designated "Army Commendation Ribbon with Metal Pendant". Redesignated: "Army Commendation Medal" in 1960

 Bronze   Silver   Bronze

Authorized on December 18, 1945 as a commendation ribbon and awarded to members of the Army for heroism, meritorious achievement or meritorious service after December 6, 1941. It was meant for award where the Bronze Star Medal was not appropriate, i.e.: outside of operational areas.

The Army Commendation Medal, commonly called the ARCOM, is unique as it is the first and only Army award that started as a ribbon-only award and then became a medal. After World War II, it became the only award created for the express purpose of peacetime and wartime meritorious service as well as the only award designed expressly for presentation to junior officers and enlisted personnel. In short, the ARCOM became the peacetime version of the Bronze Star Medal to recognize outstanding performance and boost morale. Subsequent to World War II, retroactive awards of the Commendation Ribbon were authorized for any individual who had received a Letter of Commendation from a Major General or higher before January 1, 1946.

In 1947 the rules were changed allowing the ARCOM to be awarded in connection with military operations for which the level of service did not meet the requirements for the Bronze Star or Air Medal. In 1949 the change from a ribbon-only award to a pendant was approved. Anyone who received the ribbon could exchange it for the new medal. The Army redesignated the Commendation Ribbon With Metal Pendant as the Army Commendation Medal in 1960. In 1962, it was authorized for award to a member of the Armed Forces of a friendly nation for the same level of achievement or service which was mutually beneficial to that nation and the United States. The next big change occurred on February 29, 1964 with the approval of the "V" device to denote combat heroism of a degree less than that required for the Bronze Star Medal. Additionally, the ARCOM continued to be awarded for acts of courage not qualifying for the Soldier's Medal.

The medal, a bronze hexagon, depicts the American bald eagle with spread wings on the face. The eagle has the U.S. shield on its breast and is grasping three crossed arrows in its talons. On the reverse of the medal are inscriptions FOR MILITARY and MERIT with a plaque for engraving the recipient's name between the two inscriptions. A spray of laurel, representing achievement is at the bottom. The ribbon is a field of Myrtle Green with five white stripes in the center and white edges. The Army Commendation Medal was designed and sculpted by Thomas Hudson Jones of the Army's Institute of Heraldry.

NAVY AND MARINE CORPS COMMENDATION MEDAL

Bronze

Silver

Gold

<u>Instituted:</u> 1944/1950

<u>Criteria:</u> Meritorious service or achievement in a combat or noncombat situation based on sustained performance of a superlative nature

<u>Devices:</u> Bronze letter "V" (for valor), gold, silver star

<u>Notes:</u> Originally a ribbon-only award: "Secretary of the Navy Commendation for Achievement Award with Ribbon". Changed to present name in 1994.

For heroic and meritorious achievement or service. The Navy and Marine Corps Commendation is worn after the Joint Service Commendation Medal and before the Joint Service Achievement Medal.

The Navy and Marine Corps Commendation Medal was originally established as a ribbon-only award on 11 January 1944. The current medal was authorized by the Secretary of the Navy on 22 March 1950. The medal is awarded for both heroism and meritorious achievement. To be awarded for heroism, the act must be worthy of recognition, but to a lesser degree than required for the Bronze Star Medal in combat or the Navy and Marine Corps Medal in a noncombat situation. To be awarded for meritorious achievement, the act must be outstanding and worthy of special recognition, but to a lesser degree than required for the Bronze Star Medal in combat or the Meritorious Service Medal or Air Medal when in a noncombat situation.

The Navy and Marine Corps Commendation Medal was designed by the Army's Institute of Heraldry. The medal is a bronze hexagon with the eagle from the Seal of the Department of Defense in the center. The reverse of the medal has a plaque for inscribing the recipient's name and the raised words, FOR MILITARY (above the plaque) and MERIT (below the plaque). The ribbon is dark green with a narrow stripe of white near each edge. Additional awards of the Navy and Marine Corps Commendation Medal are denoted by five-sixteenth inch gold stars. A Combat Distinguishing Device (Bronze letter "V") may be authorized.

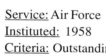

AIR FORCE COMMENDATION MEDAL

<u>Service:</u> Air Force

<u>Instituted:</u> 1958

<u>Criteria:</u> Outstanding achievement or meritorious service rendered on behalf of the United States Air Force

<u>Devices:</u> Bronze, silver oak leaf cluster, bronze letter "V"

Bronze Silver Bronze

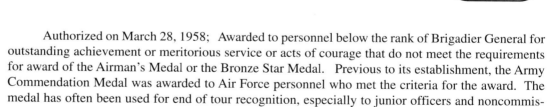

Authorized on March 28, 1958; Awarded to personnel below the rank of Brigadier General for outstanding achievement or meritorious service or acts of courage that do not meet the requirements for award of the Airman's Medal or the Bronze Star Medal.   Previous to its establishment, the Army Commendation Medal was awarded to Air Force personnel who met the criteria for the award. The medal has often been used for end of tour recognition, especially to junior officers and noncommissioned officers. In 1996, the Secretary of the Air Force authorized the award of a bronze letter "V" with this medal, retroactive to January 11, 1996, if the award's recipient distinguishes him/herself while under attack or during a hazardous situation resulting from hostilities,. The "V" may be awarded for actions taken during single acts of terrorism and isolated combat incidents. The first instances of the "V" device being awarded with this medal occurred during the terrorist bombing in Saudi Arabia in 1996. The front of the medal contains an American eagle with outstretched wings in front of a cloud formation and perched above the Air Force Coat of Arms. The reverse contains the words FOR MILITARY MERIT above a blank area which may be used to engrave the recipient's name.

COAST GUARD COMMENDATION MEDAL

Bronze Gold Silver

Service: Coast Guard

Instituted: 1947

Criteria: 1. Heroic or meritorious achievement or service. 2. Meritorious service resulting in unusual or outstanding achievement.

Devices: Silver letter "O", bronze letter "V", gold, silver star

Notes: Originally "Commendation Ribbon with Metal Pendant". Redesignated: "Coast Guard Commendation Medal" in 1959.

Following the lead of the other Services, the Coast Guard Commendation Ribbon with Metal Pendant was established on August 26, 1947. This award was to be granted to members of the Armed Forces of the United States, serving in any capacity with the Coast Guard, for meritorious service resulting in unusual and outstanding achievement rendered while the Coast Guard is serving under Treasury Department jurisdiction. On October 2, 1959, it was redesignated as the Coast Guard Commendation Medal by order of the Commandant of the Coast Guard. To merit this decoration, the outstanding achievement or meritorious service must have been accomplished in a manner above that normally expected and be sufficient to distinguish the individual from those of comparable grade or ratings performing similar acts or services. The heroism, outstanding achievement or meritorious service must be worthy of special recognition, but not of a level which would justify a higher award (e.g.: Bronze Star Medal, etc.) yet more than that required for award of the Coast Guard Achievement Medal. The Coast Guard Commendation Medal has gone through two designs (both executed by the Army's Institute of Heraldry). The first was designed and sculpted by Frank Gasparro. The second version was designed by Jay Morris and sculpted by Lewis J. King, Jr. The first design was employed while the Coast Guard was under the jurisdiction of the Treasury Department and the second was adopted when it was placed under the Department of Transportation. The first design was a bronze hexagon, point up. In the center of the obverse is the former Coast Guard Seal which embodied elements of the Treasury Department Seal, the whole being encircled by a continuous cable. There is a blank plaque in the center of the reverse, which is encircled by a laurel wreath. Above the plaque, in two lines, are the words FOR OUTSTANDING and below it, the word SERVICE. The plaque, words, and wreath are encircled by a continuous cable. The second design, which was approved by the Commandant on June 11, 1968, is very similar to the first and also employs a bronze hexagon, point up. In the center of the obverse is the current Coast Guard Seal. The continuous cable used in the first design is deleted from the second. The reverse contains an annulet consisting of the word AWARDED at the top and, separated by stylized laurel leaves, the words OUTSTANDING SERVICE in the bottom. In the center are the words TO and FOR, separated by space for engraving the recipient's name.

JOINT SERVICE ACHIEVEMENT MEDAL

Silver Bronze

Instituted: 1983

Criteria: Meritorious service or achievement while serving with a Joint Activity

Devices: Bronze, silver oak leaf cluster

The Joint Service Achievement Medal was established in 1983 specifically to complete the Department of Defense awards hierarchy and thereby provide a system of decorations for meritorious achievement comparable to those of the separate services. In so doing, the integrity of the more senior Joint Service medals was protected and the opportunity to earn recognition while assigned to a Joint Activity was provided.

It is awarded for meritorious service or achievement while serving in a Joint Activity after August 3, 1983 to members below the rank of colonel. Oak leaf clusters denote additional awards .

The medal features an American eagle with the United States coat of arms on its breast holding three arrows in the center of the bronze medal which consists of a star of twelve points chosen to make it distinctive. The eagle was taken from the Seal designed for the National Military Establishment in 1947 by the President and the arrows were adapted from the seal of the Department of Defense. This is the same design seen on the Army and Navy Commendation Medals.

The reverse of the medal contains the inscriptions JOINT SERVICE and ACHIEVEMENT AWARD in a circle. There is space in the center for inscribing the recipient's name. The ribbon consists of a center stripe of red flanked on either side by stripes of light blue, white, green, white, and blue.

The Joint Service Achievement Medal was designed by Jay Morris and sculpted by Donald Borja, both of the Army's Institute of Heraldry .

ARMY ACHIEVEMENT MEDAL

Silver   Bronze

Service: Army

Instituted: August 1, 1981

Criteria: Awarded to members of the Armed Forces below the rank of colonel who, while serving in any capacity with the Army in a noncombat area, distinguish themselves by outstanding achievement or meritorious service, but not of a nature that would warrant the award of an Army Commendation Medal.

Devices : Bronze, silver oak leaf clusters.

Key elements of the Department of the Army Seal are centered in a bronze octagon one and a half inches in diameter . The medal shape was chosen to distinguish it from other Army decorations. The Army Seal represents the authority under which the award is given. On the reverse are three lines in the upper half, reading FOR MILITARY ACHIEVEMENT. At the bottom of the medal there is a double spray of laurel which represents achievement. The ribbon has a central stripe of blue with a white center stripe. The blue is bordered by white, green, white and is edged in green.

The Army Achievement Medal states is awarded for significant achievement deserving recognition but not considered adequate to qualify for an award of the Army Commendation Medal. Award authority rest with commanders in the grade of Lieut. Colonel and above. The Army Achievement Medal is limited to noncombat achievement and that members of other branches of the Armed Forces may be eligible for it under certain circumstances.

At the same time the Secretary of the Army approved the Army Achievement medal he also approve the Overseas Service Ribbon, the NCO Academy Ribbon (renamed the NCO Professional Development Ribbon) and the Army Service Ribbon. Additional awards of the Army Achievement Medal are denoted by oak leaf clusters. The Army Achievement Medal was designed by Jay Morris and sculpted by Donald Borja of the Army Institute of Heraldry.

NAVY AND MARINE CORPS ACHIEVEMENT MEDAL

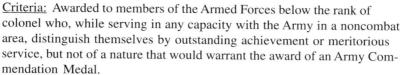

Bronze   Silver   Gold

Instituted: 1961/1967

Criteria: Meritorious service or achievement in a combat or noncombat situation based on sustained performance of a superlative nature

Devices: Bronze letter "V" (for valor), gold, silver star

Notes: Originally a ribbon-only award: "Secretary of the Navy Commendation for Achievement Award with Ribbon"

For junior officers and enlisted personnel whose professional and/or leadership achievements on or after 1 May 1961 are clearly of a superlative nature. The Navy and Marine Corps Achievement Medal is worn after the Joint Service Achievement Medal and before the Combat Action Ribbon.

The Navy and Marine Corps Achievement Medal was originally established as a ribbon-only award on 1 May 1961. The current medal was authorized by the Secretary of the Navy on 17 July 1967. The medal is awarded for both professional and leadership achievement. To be awarded for professional achievement, the act must clearly exceed that which is normally required or expected, and must be an important contribution to benefit the United States Naval Service. To be recognized for leadership achievement, the act must be noteworthy and contribute to the individual's unit mission.

The Navy and Marine Corps Achievement Medal was designed by the Army's Institute of Heraldry. The medal is a bronze square (having clipped corners) with a fouled anchor in the center. There is a star in each of the four corners. The reverse of the medal is blank to allow for engraving the recipient's name. The ribbon is myrtle green with stripes of orange near each edge. Additional awards of the Navy and Marine Corps Achievement Medal are denoted by five-sixteenth inch gold stars. A Combat Distinguishing Device (Combat "V") may be authorized.

AIR FORCE ACHIEVEMENT MEDAL

Bronze   Silver   Bronze

Service: Air Force

Instituted: 1980

Criteria: Outstanding achievement or meritorious service not warranting award of the Air Force Commendation Medal

Devices: Bronze, silver oak leaf cluster, bronze letter "V"

The Air Force Achievement Medal was established by the Secretary of the Air Force on October 12, 1980 and may be awarded to U.S. military personnel below the rank of colonel for meritorious service or outstanding achievement. This medal is the first decoration established for Air Force personnel under Air Force authority. The primary use of the medal has been to recognize specific individual achievements or accomplishments rather than continuing periods of service such as might be associated with a change in permanent assignment, although it has been used for end of tour recognition for some junior ranking personnel. A bronze letter "V" was authorized retroactive to January 11, 1996 for those receiving the award for actions during combat conditions, hostile acts, or single acts of terrorism. The first instances of the "V" device being awarded with the medal were to airmen who received the medal for actions during the 1996 terrorist bombing of an Air Force dormitory in Saudi Arabia. The front of the medal has eleven cog-like shapes on the outer border; within the medal are a set of wings with four thunderbolts crossing through them. The reverse of the medal bears the circular inscription, AIR FORCE MERITORIOUS ACHIEVEMENT around its outer edge.

COAST GUARD ACHIEVEMENT MEDAL

Silver   Bronze   Gold

Service: Coast Guard   Instituted: 1968

Criteria: Professional and/or leadership achievement in a combat or non-combat situation.

Devices: Silver letter "O" (14), bronze letter "V" (for valor) (17), gold, silver star (66, 70)

Notes: Originally a ribbon-only award. Present configuration was adopted in 1968.

Following the lead of the "Secretary of the Navy Commendation for Achievement with Ribbon" in 1961, (subsequently designated the Navy Achievement Medal), the Secretary of the Treasury established a similar ribbon for Coast Guard personnel on January 29, 1964. The ribbon was formally redesignated as the Coast Guard Achievement Medal on June 11, 1968.

The Coast Guard Achievement Medal may be awarded to all members of the Coast Guard, including reserves, as well as to members of other branches of the Armed Forces when serving with Coast Guard units. It is given for professional or leadership achievement in either peacetime or combat situations. It may be awarded based on sustained performance or for specific achieve-ment of a superlative nature, but not of a level which would justify award of a Commendation Medal

The Coast Guard Achievement Medal was designed by Irving Lyons and sculpted by Lewis J. King, Jr., both of the Army's Institute of Heraldry. It is a bronze disc in the center of which is the Coast Guard Seal surrounded by a laurel wreath, which is in turn surrounded by a border of cable. The reverse bears the inscription (in raised letters), AWARDED TO in the upper portion and FOR ACHIEVEMENT in the lower. The ribbon is the same as that of the Navy Achievement Medal except that it has a narrow pinstripe of white in the center of the ribbon.

Symbolically, the laurel wreath represents achievement and the continuous cable stands for fidelity of the seaman in support of the Coast Guard, which is represented by the Coast Guard Seal.

COMMANDANT'S LETTER OF COMMENDATION RIBBON

Silver   Gold

Service: Coast Guard   Instituted: 1979

Criteria: Receipt of a letter of commendation for an act or service resulting in unusual and/or outstanding achievement.

Devices: Silver letter "O" (14), gold, silver star (66, 70)

With the establishment of the Coast Guard Commandant's Letter of Commendation Ribbon in 1979, the Coast Guard formalized one of its oldest awards. Like the Navy's Letter of Commendation, the award had previously existed only as a paper certificate and an entry into the Coast Guardsman's service record before its appearance as a tangible, wearable part of the uniform. It is awarded to any member of the Armed Forces of the United States who, while serving in any capacity with the Coast Guard, is awarded a Letter of Commendation by the Coast Guard Commandant. The service for which the ribbon is awarded must be of a degree less than that required for award of the Coast Guard Achievement Medal.

COMBAT ACTION RIBBON

Services: Navy, Marine Corps

Silver

Gold

Instituted: 1969 retroactive to March 1961. In 1999, it was made retroactive to 6 Dec 1941

Criteria: Active participation in ground or air combat during specifically listed military operations

Devices: Gold, silver star

Notes: This is the only Navy and Marine Corps personal decoration which has no associated medal (a "ribbon-only" award).

For active participation in ground or surface combat subsequent to 6 December 1941, while in the grade of Colonel or below. The Combat Action Ribbon is worn after the Navy and Marine Corps Achievement Medal and before the Navy Presidential Unit Citation in a ribbon display. It is worn as the senior ribbon on the right breast when full-sized medals are worn on the left breast.

The Combat Action Ribbon was authorized by the Secretary of the Navy on 17 February 1969 and recently made retroactive to 6 December 1941. The principal requirement is that the individual was engaged in combat during specifically listed military operations at which time he/she was under enemy fire and that his/her performance was satisfactory.

The Combat Action Ribbon is a ribbon-only award. The ribbon is gold with thin center stripes of red, white and blue and border stripes of dark blue on the left and red on the right. Additional awards are authorized for each separate conflict/war and are represented by five-sixteenth inch gold stars.

PRISONER OF WAR MEDAL

Instituted: 1985

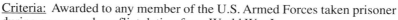
Silver   Bronze

Criteria: Awarded to any member of the U.S. Armed Forces taken prisoner during any armed conflict dating from World War I

Devices: Bronze, silver star

The Prisoner of War Medal is awarded to any person who was taken prisoner of war and held captive after 5 April 1917. It was authorized by Public Law Number 99-145 in 1985 and may be awarded to any person who was taken prisoner or held captive while engaged in an action against an enemy of the United States, while engaged in military operations involving conflict with an opposing armed force or while serving with friendly forces engaged in armed conflict against an opposing armed force in which the United States is not a belligerent party. The recipient's conduct while a prisoner must have been honorable.

The Prisoner of War Medal is worn after all unit awards (after personal decorations in the case of the Army) and before the various Armed Service Good Conduct Medals (before the Combat Readiness Medal in the case of the Air Force).

The Prisoner of War Medal was designed by the Army's Institute of Heraldry. The medal is a circular bronze disc with an American eagle centered and completely surrounded by a ring of barbed wire and bayonet points. The reverse of the medal has a raised inscription: AWARDED TO with a space for the recipient's name and: FOR HONORABLE SERVICE WHILE A PRISONER OF WAR set in three lines. Below this is the shield of the United States and the words: UNITED STATES OF AMERICA. The ribbon is black with thin border stripes of white, blue, white and red. Additional awards are denoted by three-sixteenth inch bronze stars.

COMBAT READINESS MEDAL

Service: Air Force   Instituted: 1964

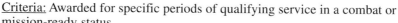
Silver   Bronze

Criteria: Awarded for specific periods of qualifying service in a combat or mission-ready status

Devices: Bronze, silver oak leaf cluster

Authorized on March 9, 1964. Awarded for periods of qualifying service in a combat or mission ready status for direct weapon system employment. Direct weapon system employment is defined as: (1) An aircrew whose wartime mission places them into enemy territory or in the threat envelope of ground enemy defenses, (2) A missile operation which could employ weapons to destroy enemy targets and (3) Individuals who directly control in-flight manned aircraft whose wartime mission is to seek and destroy enemy targets. An individual must be a member of a unit subject to combat readiness reporting under Joint Chiefs of Staff requirements, must have completed all prerequisite training and be certified as combat or mission ready in performing the unit's mission and must be subject to a continuous individual positional evaluation program. In previous regulations, eligibility was extended to Air Force members on special duty with another U.S. military service provided they were certified as combat ready in that service and the combat ready status closely correlated to that of the Air Force. Originally an individual was required to be combat ready for three years to earn this award. Currently, individuals must have 24 months of sustained combat ready status to receive the award. Eligibility for the award is certified by the individual's unit commander and is filed in the unit's personnel records group. An oak leaf cluster attachment is awarded for each additional 24 months of combat ready status provided there is no break greater than 120 days. The front of the medal has a border of concentric rays encircling a ring of stylized cloud forms with two intersecting triangles on a compass rose that has small triangles at his points. The reverse of the medal contains the inscription, FOR COMBAT READINESS-AIR FORCE.

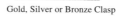

ARMY GOOD CONDUCT MEDAL

Service: Army   Instituted: 1941

Gold, Silver or Bronze Clasp

Criteria: Exemplary conduct, efficiency and fidelity during three years of active enlisted service with the U.S. Army (1 year during wartime)

Devices: Bronze, silver, gold knotted clasp

Authorized on June 28, 1941 for exemplary conduct, efficiency and fidelity and awarded to Army personnel who, on or after August 27, 1940, had honorably completed three years of active Federal military service. The medal could also be awarded for one year of service after December 7, 1941 while the U.S. was at war. The medal was not automatic and required certification by a commanding officer (usually a Battalion commander or higher).

The Army Good Conduct Medal was designed by Joseph Kiselewski with an eagle perched on Roman sword atop a closed book. Around the outside are the words EFFICIENCY, HONOR, FIDELITY. The reverse of the medal has a five pointed star just above center with a blank scroll for engraving the soldier's name. Above the star are the words: FOR GOOD and below the scroll is the word CONDUCT. A wreath of half laurel leaves, denoting accomplishment and half oak leaves, denoting bravery) surrounds the reverse design.

The ribbon was designed by Arthur E. DuBois, the legendary Director of the Army Institute of Heraldry, and is scarlet with three narrow white stripes on each side. The ribbon is divided by the white stripes so as to form thirteen stripes representing the thirteen original colonies of the United States. During the Revolutionary War, the color scarlet symbolized the mother country and the white stripe symbolized the virgin land separated by force from the mother country.

Unlike other additional award devices (e.g.: oak leaf clusters), bronze, silver, or gold clasps with knots (or loops) are used to indicate the *total* number of awards of the Army Good Conduct Medal. For instance, two awards of the medal are indicated by two bronze knots, three by three, etc. Six total awards are indicated by one silver knot, seven by two silver knots, etc. Eleven total awards are indicated by one gold knot, twelve by two gold knots, etc. While all regulations since World War II only authorize a clasp to be worn after the second award or higher; it is not unusual to see veterans with a clasp having a single bronze knot on their Army Good Conduct Medal or ribbon; this may have indicated either a single or second award and seems to have been an accepted practice.

Although the Good Conduct Medal was officially instituted by executive order in 1941 it really goes back to the American Revolution. When General George Washington established the Badge of Military Merit in 1782 he also created an award called the Honorary Badge of Distinction. This was the first good conduct award since it was to be conferred on veteran noncommissioned officers and soldiers of the Army who served more than three years with bravery, fidelity, and good conduct. General Washington directed that the good conduct badge be made of cloth and each soldier who received it sew a narrow piece of white cloth on the left arm of his uniform jacket. Soldiers with more than six years service were to be distinguished by 2 pieces of cloth set parallel to each other. General Washington went on to express that this good conduct badge was a high honor and those who received it should be treated with particular confidence and consideration. However just as the Badge of Military Merit disappeared after the Revolution so did the Honorary Badge of Distinction (our first good conduct award).

When President Roosevelt signed executive order 9323 on 31 March 1943 he officially changed the policy that the Army Good Conduct Medal could be awarded after one year. It should be understood, however, that additional awards of the Good Conduct Medal cannot be given for each additional year service in World War II but required completion of a subsequent additional three-year period.

During the Korean War President Eisenhower approved a first award only which could be presented for service after 27 June 1950 with less than three years but more than one year service.

The Air Force ceased using the Army Good Conduct Medal 1 June 1963. Qualifying airmen were then awarded the Air Force Good Conduct Medal which differed from the Army Good Conduct Medal only in design of the ribbon. The medal remained the same. Personnel who earned the Army Good Conduct medal before earning the Air Force Good Conduct Medal can wear both with the Air Force Good Conduct Medal coming first.

There is often some discussion if the Army Good Conduct Medal is a decoration or service medal. Historically going back to World War II the Good Conduct Medal was considered a decoration and was one of a few medals to be manufactured throughout the war when service medal production was restricted due to the need to divert metal to the arms industry. Today however, it is considered a service award.

There was no certificate to denote the award of the Army Good Conduct Medal until 1981 when the Army began issuing an 8" x 10" paper certificate. The army regulations covering the issue of the paper certificate prohibited the issue of the certificate of those awarded the Good Conduct Medal prior to 1 Jan. 1981.

The Army has changed policy on official engraving of a Good Conduct Medal several times during its history. Currently the Army authorizes engraving at the government's expense by the U.S. Army Support Activity in Philadelphia PA.

The Good Conduct Medal is especially interesting in that it is the last United States Army award established prior to World War II. It was also last medal that the War Department attempted to issue with a serial number (a practice dropped in WW II). It is the only United States Army medal awarded which specifically excludes officers from eligibility and is only authorized enlisted personnel.

RESERVE SPECIAL COMMENDATION RIBBON

No Devices
Authorized

Service: Navy/Marine Corps

Instituted: 1946

Criteria: Awarded to Reserve Officers with 4 years of successful command and a total Reserve service of at least 10 years

Devices: None

The Reserve Special Commendation Ribbon was established by the Secretary of the Navy on 16 April 1946. The ribbon was awarded to those officers of the Naval Reserve or Organized Marine Corps Reserve who had commanded at the battalion, squadron, or separate division level in a meritorious manner for a period of 4 years between 1 January 1930 and 7 December 1941 and had a total service in the Reserve of at least 10 years. The period of command need not have been continuous, but the officer must have been regularly assigned to command such units for a total of four years within a ten year period of time. Owing to the date of promulgation of the award, it was obsolete the day it was authorized and, as a result, no device was ever authorized.

NAVY GOOD CONDUCT MEDAL

Silver

Bronze

Service: Navy   Instituted: 1884

Criteria: Outstanding performance and conduct during three years of continuous active enlisted service in the U.S Navy

Devices: Bronze, silver star

Current

World War II

The Navy Good Conduct Medal was authorized on 21 November 1884. The medal is awarded to enlisted personnel of the United States Navy and Naval Reserve (active duty) for creditable, above average professional performance, military behavior, leadership, military appearance and adaptability based on good conduct and faithful service for three-year periods of continuous active service.

Those receiving the award must have had no convictions by court martial and no nonjudicial punishment during the three year period (there was a time from November 1963 to January 1996 when the period was four years). For the first award the medal may be awarded to the next-of-kin in those cases where the individual is missing in action or dies of wounds received in combat. Naval personnel may also receive the medal if separated from the service as a result of wounds incurred in combat.

The Navy Good Conduct Medal is a circular bronze disc with a raised anchor and anchor chain circling a depiction of the *U.S.S. Constitution* and the words: CONSTITUTION and UNITED STATES NAVY. The reverse side of the medal has the raised inscription FIDELITY - ZEAL - OBEDIENCE around the border with space provided in the center to stamp the recipient's name. The medal is suspended from a plain bronze suspender and is worn after the Prisoner of War Medal and before the Naval Reserve Meritorious Service Medal. The ribbon of the Navy Good Conduct Medal is maroon. Additional awards are denoted by three-sixteenth inch dia. bronze and silver stars.

The forerunner of the Navy Good Conduct Medal was the Navy Good Conduct Badge which was established in 1868 by the Secretary of the Navy, making it our Country's second oldest award. The badge, in use from 1868 to 1884, was awarded to men holding a Continuous Service Certificate awarded upon the successful completion of a term of enlistment. In those early days, any seaman who qualified for three awards was promoted to petty officer.

The Good Conduct Badge was a Maltese Cross with a circular medallion in the center. The medallion was bordered with a border inscribed around the edge with the words FIDELITY - ZEAL - OBEDIENCE and U.S.A. in the center. The cross was suspended from a 1/2 inch wide red, white and blue ribbon.

In 1880 the Navy redesigned the Good Conduct Badge. The new medallion was proposed by Commodore Winfield Scott Schley from the design used on the letterhead of the Navy Department's Bureau of Equipment and Recruiting. This new medallion was suspended from a 1-5/8 inch wide red ribbon with thin border stripes of white and blue.

In 1884 the medal was redesigned and in 1896, the award period was changed to three years of continuous active service. This new medal maintained the 1880 design but was suspended from a maroon ribbon by a straight bar clasp. Subsequent awards were recognized by the addition of clasps placed on the suspension ribbon between the top of the ribbon and the medallion. These clasps were bordered with rope and were engraved with the recipient's ship or duty station. During World War I, medals were impressed with rim numbers but many were issued without engraving. In the 1930's, the ship or duty station name on the clasps was replaced by the recipient's enlistment discharge date. In 1942, all engraved clasps were replaced with generic clasps having SECOND AWARD, THIRD AWARD, etc. in raised letters. Finally, subsequent to World War II, the Navy discontinued the clasps, began stamping the recipient's information on the medal's reverse and authorized the use of three-sixteenth bronze stars to denote additional awards.

Current

WW II

MARINE CORPS GOOD CONDUCT MEDAL

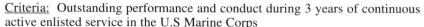

Silver   Bronze

Instituted: 1896

Criteria: Outstanding performance and conduct during 3 years of continuous active enlisted service in the U.S Marine Corps

Devices: Bronze, silver star

Notes: Earlier ribbon was 1 1/4" wide

    The Marine Corps Good Conduct Medal is awarded for outstanding performance, based on good conduct and faithful service for three-year periods of continuous active enlisted service. The Marine Corps Good Conduct Medal is worn after the Prisoner of War Medal and before the Selected Marine Corps Reserve Medal.

    The Marine Corps Good Conduct Medal was established by the Secretary of the Navy on 20 July 1896. The medal is awarded to an enlisted Marine for obedience, sobriety, military proficiency, neatness, and intelligence during three years of continuous active service. The Marine receiving the award must have had no convictions by court martial and no more than one nonjudicial punishment during the three-year period. For the first award, the medal may be awarded to the next of kin in those cases where the individual is missing in action or dies of wounds received in combat. A Marine may also receive the medal if separated from the service as a result of wounds incurred in combat.

    The Marine Good Conduct Medal was designed by Major General Charles Heywood, the ninth Commandant of the Marine Corps. The medal is a circular bronze disc with an anchor and anchor chain circling an enlisted Marine in the uniform of the late nineteenth century. The Marine is holding the lanyard of a naval rifle (gun) and below this is a scroll with the motto of the Corps: SEMPER FIDELIS. In the space between the Marine and the anchor chain is the raised inscription: UNITED STATES MARINE CORPS. The reverse side of the medal has the raised inscription: FIDELITY - ZEAL - OBEDIENCE centered in-between two concentric raised circles and with room in the center to inscribe the recipient's name.

    The medal has undergone several design modification since its inception. The original medal incorporated an upper bronze suspension bar bearing the raised inscription: U.S. MARINES. Number clasps, placed on the suspension ribbon between the upper suspension bar and the medallion were used on the original medal to indicate additional awards. Prior to World War I, medals were engraved with the recipient's name, service number and date span. During World War I, medals were impressed with rim numbers and many were issued without engraving. Following World War II, the Marine Corps changed its practice of engraving to stamping the recipient's information on the medal's reverse. The practice of using a suspension bar and clasps was also eliminated during this period.

    The ribbon of the Marine Corps Good Conduct Medal is dark red with a dark blue stripe in the center. The medal is suspended from the ribbon by a bronze rifle pointing to the right. Additional awards are denoted by three-sixteenth bronze stars.

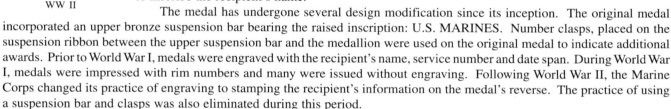

AIR FORCE GOOD CONDUCT MEDAL

Bronze   Silver

Service: Air Force

Instituted: 1963

Criteria: Exemplary conduct, efficiency and fidelity during three years of active enlisted service with the U.S. Air Force

Devices: Bronze, silver oak leaf cluster

    Authorized on June 1, 1963. Awarded to Air Force personnel in an enlisted status upon recommendation of the unit commander for exemplary conduct while in active military service on or after June 1, 1963 after 3 years of continuous service (1 year in wartime- this was rarely done). The U. S. Air Force used the Army Good Conduct Medal to recognize deserving service by enlisted personnel from 1947 to 1963, when the Air Force Good Conduct Medal was created. As with the Army Good Conduct Medal, the award was never automatic and required commander certification prior to being awarded. Commanders usually receive notification from their personnel center that an individual is eligible for this award. The commander then reviews the individual's record and affixes his/her signature to the personnel document verifying that the person is eligible and deserving of the award. The absence of an award of the Air Force Good Conduct medal to an individual having a qualifying period of enlistment would be noteworthy to supervisory personnel.   The front of the medal bears the inscription, "EFFICIENCY, HONOR, FIDELITY," surrounding the American eagle which stands on a closed book and sword. On the reverse is a five-pointed star above a blank scroll; the words, FOR GOOD are above the star and below the scroll is the word, CONDUCT. Bronze and silver oak leaf attachments denote additional awards of the medal.

COAST GUARD GOOD CONDUCT MEDAL

Current

WW II

Service: Coast Guard   **Instituted:** 1923

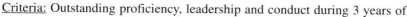
Silver   Bronze

Criteria: Outstanding proficiency, leadership and conduct during 3 years of enlisted service

Devices: Bronze, silver star

Notes: Originally suspended from a 1 1/2" wide ribbon and a square lower suspender bar.

    The Coast Guard Good Conduct Medal was first authorized on 12 December 1923 to recognize superior performance of duty by enlisted Coast Guardsmen during a four year period of service. The time requirement was changed in 1934 to conform to the three year requirement then in effect for the Navy and Marine Corps Good Conduct Medals. Originally, the Coast Guard Good Conduct Medal was attached to a 1 1/2 inch wide ribbon suspended from a rectangular top bar having the inscription: U.S. COAST GUARD. The metal pendant was 1 7/16 inches in diameter with the likeness of a cutter in the center surrounded by the Coast Guard's motto SEMPER PARATUS (Always Prepared). The pendant is suspended from a straight crossbar looped through the bottom of the suspension ribbon. Subsequent awards were indicated by the addition of bronze Good Conduct Bars. These bars were attached to the suspension ribbon with the recipient's ship or duty station engraved on the front and the date of award on the reverse. Both the suspension top bar and the Good Conduct Bars were discontinued following the Korean War.

    The current Coast Guard Good Conduct Medal is suspended from a 1 3/8th inch wide ribbon and the planchet has been reduced to 1 1/4 inches. The new planchet also replaces the small ship in the center with the seal of the U.S. Coast Guard. The reverses of both versions are quite similar with a blank center disk surrounded by an outer ring upon which are inscribed the words: FIDELITY ZEAL OBEDIENCE.

    The current medal also does not use the "square" suspension and bottom crossbar but is attached directly to the ribbon by means of a suspension ring. The ribbon is maroon with a central stripe of white. Additional awards are denoted by bronze and silver stars.

ARMY RESERVE COMPONENTS ACHIEVEMENT MEDAL

Service: Army National Guard and Army Reserve Forces

Instituted: 3 March 1972

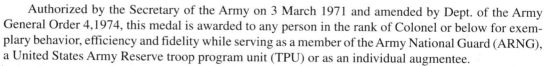
Bronze   Silver

Criteria: Since 3 March 1972 the medal has been authorized on completion of four years service. As of 25 Feb. 1995, the length of qualifying service was reduced to three years.

Devices: Bronze and silver oak leaf clusters

Notes: The medal has different reverses for National Guard and Army Reserve recipients

    Authorized by the Secretary of the Army on 3 March 1971 and amended by Dept. of the Army General Order 4,1974, this medal is awarded to any person in the rank of Colonel or below for exemplary behavior, efficiency and fidelity while serving as a member of the Army National Guard (ARNG), a United States Army Reserve troop program unit (TPU) or as an individual augmentee.

    The medal is 1 1/4 inches in diameter. In the center is a flaming torch symbolizing the vigilance of the Guard and the Reserve and their readiness to come to the Nation's aid. Two crossed swords in front of and behind the torch represent the history of the Guard and Reserve forged in combat. Left and right of the torch are five pointed stars and the entire design is surrounded by a laurel wreath symbolizing accomplishment. Around these symbols is a twelve pointed star superimposed over a smaller twelve-pointed star indicating the Guard and Reserve's ability to travel where needed in the United States or the World. In between the points of the larger star are laurel leaves and a berry representing achievement.

    On the reverse side of the medal in the upper center is a miniature breast plate taken from the Army seal. Above this, the outside edge of the medal is inscribed either: UNITED STATES ARMY RESERVE or ARMY NATIONAL GUARD. Along the bottom edge of the medal are the words: FOR ACHIEVEMENT.

    The ribbon has a wide center stripe of red flanked by narrow stripes of white and blue, reflecting our national colors and patriotism. The outside gold stripes are symbolic of merit. Additional awards are denoted by bronze and silver oak leaf clusters

NAVAL RESERVE MERITORIOUS SERVICE MEDAL

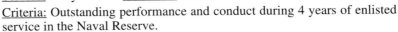

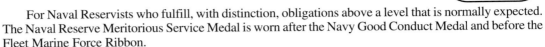

Service: Navy   Instituted: 1964

Silver   Bronze

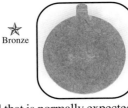

Criteria: Outstanding performance and conduct during 4 years of enlisted service in the Naval Reserve.

Devices: Bronze, silver star   Notes: Originally a ribbon-only award.

For Naval Reservists who fulfill, with distinction, obligations above a level that is normally expected. The Naval Reserve Meritorious Service Medal is worn after the Navy Good Conduct Medal and before the Fleet Marine Force Ribbon.

The Naval Reserve Meritorious Service Medal was authorized on 12 September 1959 originally as a ribbon-only award. The medal was authorized on 22 June 1962 with eligibility backdated to 1 July 1958. The award is made on a selected basis to U. S. Navy Reservists who fulfill, with distinction, the obligations of an inactive Reservists at a higher level than normally expected. The obligations pertain to attendance and performance.

The Naval Reserve Meritorious Service Medal is a circular bronze disc showing an fouled anchor covered with a scroll with the raised words : MERITORIOUS SERVICE. The words: UNITED STATES NAVAL RESERVE encircle the anchor. The reverse of the medal is blank. The ribbon is red with a blue center stripe and thin border stripes of gold and blue. Additional awards are denoted by three-sixteenth bronze stars.

SELECTED MARINE CORPS RESERVE MEDAL

Instituted: 1939

Silver   Bronze

Criteria: Outstanding performance and conduct during 4 years of service in the Marine Corps Selected Reserve

Devices: Bronze, silver star

Notes: Formerly "Organized Marine Corps Reserve Medal"

Awarded for four consecutive years service in the Selected Marine Corps Reserve. The Selected Marine Corps Reserve Medal is worn after the Marine Corps Good Conduct Medal and before the Marine Corps Expeditionary Medal.

The Selected Marine Corps Reserve Medal was established by the Secretary of the Navy on 19 February 1939 as the Fleet Marine Corps Reserve Medal. Later the name was changed to the Organized Marine Corps Reserve Medal and finally to its current designation in the late 1980's. The medal is awarded to members of the Marine Corps Reserve who, subsequent to 1 July 1925, and prior to 24 April 1961, attended 80 percent of all scheduled drills during a four year period. Since 24 April 1961 the attendance criteria was raised to 90 percent.

The Selected Marine Corps Reserve Medal was designed by the United States Mint. The medal is a circular bronze disc with two walking figures. The figure in the foreground is wearing a pre-World War II uniform, and the other is wearing civilian clothes. Above the figures is the raised circular inscription: MARINE CORPS RESERVE and below the figures is the inscription: FOR SERVICE. The reverse of the medal is identical to the that of the Marine Corps Good Conduct Medal with the raised inscription: FIDELITY - ZEAL - OBEDIENCE centered in-between two concentric raised circles and with room in the center to inscribe the recipient's name. The ribbon is gold and has a red center stripe with narrow border stripes of blue, white and red. Additional awards are denoted by three-sixteenth bronze stars.

AIR RESERVE FORCES MERITORIOUS SERVICE MEDAL

Service: Air Force   Instituted: 1964

Criteria: Exemplary behavior, efficiency and fidelity during three years of active enlisted service with the Air Force Reserve

Silver   Bronze

Devices: Bronze, silver oak leaf cluster

Authorized on April 1, 1964 as a ribbon-only award, the medal was created in 1973. Awarded on specific recommendation of the unit commander to enlisted members of the Air Reserve Forces for exemplary behavior, efficiency, and fidelity for a period of four continuous years service prior to July 1, 1972 and for 3 years on/after July 1, 1972. Creditable service ends when the Reservist is called to active duty or is appointed a commissioned officer. The front of the medal has the American eagle perched atop a small circle containing a five-pointed star. A banner sits above the eagle and contains the words: MERITORIOUS SERVICE. On the outer edge of the medal are the words: AIR RESERVE FORCES. On the reverse is a cloud design with thunderbolts and wings with the word, TO inscribed below it with space to engrave the recipient's name. Along the circular outer edge, the words: EXEMPLARY BEHAVIOR are in raised letters on the upper half of the ring and EFFICIENCY-FIDELITY appear on the lower half.

The ribbon has a wide, light blue center with stripes of, reading outward from the center on each side, dark blue-yellow-dark blue, white and light blue selvedges. Additional awards are denoted by bronze and silver oak leaf clusters

COAST GUARD RESERVE GOOD CONDUCT MEDAL

Silver

Bronze

Service: Coast Guard   Instituted: 1963

Criteria: Outstanding proficiency, leadership and conduct during 3 years of enlisted service in the Coast Guard Reserve

Devices: Bronze, silver star (55, 61)

Notes: Originally a ribbon-only award- "Coast Guard Reserve Meritorious Service Ribbon".

On 1 February 1963, the Commandant of the Coast Guard established a ribbon-only award known as the Coast Guard Reserve Meritorious Service Ribbon to recognize enlisted members of the active reserve in much the same manner as the Coast Guard Good Conduct Medal recognizes active duty enlisted personnel. It recognizes outstanding proficiency, leadership and conduct during 3 years of enlisted service in the Coast Guard Reserve. It was renamed and reauthorized in its present form as the Coast Guard Reserve Good Conduct Medal on 3 Sept. 1981. The medal is a circular bronze planchet containing the Coast Guard seal in the center. Surrounding the seal at the edge of the medal is the circular inscription: UNITED STATES COAST GUARD RESERVE. The reverse is contains the raised inscription: GOOD CONDUCT with no other adornment.

The ribbon of the Coast Guard Reserve Good Conduct Medal is identical to that of the Naval Reserve Meritorious Service Medal with addition of a thin white stripe in the center. Additional awards of the Coast Guard Reserve Good Conduct Medal are denoted by three-sixteenth inch dia. bronze and silver stars.

FLEET MARINE FORCE RIBBON

No Devices Authorized

Service: Navy   Instituted: 1984

Criteria: Active participation by professionally skilled Navy personnel with the Fleet Marine Force.

Devices: None

Traditionally, the U.S. Marine Corps has relied upon the Navy to provide trained personnel in specific areas not covered by the USMC's table of organization (e.g.: Chaplains, Medical Personnel, etc.). The Navy Fleet Marine Force Ribbon was authorized by the Secretary of the Navy on 1 September 1984 to recognize the service of these Navy officers and enlisted personnel who serve with the Fleet Marine Force. Qualification for the Navy Fleet Marine Force Ribbon signifies acquisition of specific professional skills, knowledge and military experience that result in qualifications above those normally required of Navy personnel serving with the Fleet Marine Force (FMF). A recipient may qualify only once for the Fleet Marine Force Ribbon, therefore, there are no additional award devices.

OUTSTANDING AIRMAN OF THE YEAR RIBBON

Bronze Silver Bronze

Service: Air Force   Instituted: 1968

Criteria: Awarded to airmen for selection to the "12 Outstanding Airmen of the Year" Competition Program

Devices: Bronze, silver oak leaf cluster, bronze star

Authorized on February 21, 1968. Awarded to those 12 airmen chosen from nominees throughout the Air Force, field operation agencies, the Air Force Reserve and Air National Guard in the 12 Outstanding Airmen of the Year Program. The award of the ribbon is retroactive to include those selected for this program as of June 1970. The 12 current designees wear a bronze service star and multiple winners wear oak leaf clusters to denote additional awards.

AIR FORCE RECOGNITION RIBBON

Silver Bronze

Service: Air Force   Instituted: 1980

Criteria: Awarded to individual recipients of Air Force-level special trophies and awards

Devices: Bronze, silver oak leaf cluster

Authorized on October 12, 1980 and effective January 1, 1981. Awarded to individual recipients of Air Force level special trophies and awards, as listed in appropriate Air Force regulations, except the 12 Outstanding Airmen of the Year nominees. It is not awarded to individuals of a unit which receives a special award. The ribbon is not awarded retroactively. Oak leaf clusters are used to denote additional awards. The Ribbon design is patterned after the Air Force Cross ribbon with a red stripe in the center. Bronze and silver oak leaf clusters are used to note additional awards.

NAVY EXPEDITIONARY MEDAL

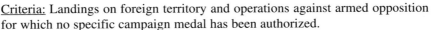

Silver | Silver | Bronze

WAKE ISLAND

<u>Service:</u> Navy   <u>Instituted:</u> 1936

<u>Dates:</u> 1936 to Present (retroactive to 1874)

<u>Criteria:</u> Landings on foreign territory and operations against armed opposition for which no specific campaign medal has been authorized.

<u>Devices:</u> Silver letter "W" (denotes bar below), bronze, silver star

<u>Bars:</u> "Wake Island" (see page 128)

     The Navy Expeditionary Medal was authorized on 5 August 1936. The medal is awarded to members of the Navy who have engaged in operations against armed opposition in foreign territory, or have served in situations warranting special recognition where no other campaign medal was awarded. Many operations have qualified for the award, beginning (retroactively) with operations by Navy and Marine Corps personnel in Honolulu, Hawaii in 1874 and culminating in the rescue operations and civilian evacuation efforts in Liberia and Rwanda in the mid-90's.

     The Navy Expeditionary Medal is a circular bronze disc depicting a sailor beaching a boat containing an officer and Marines with a flag of the United States and the word: EXPEDITIONS. The reverse of the medal shows an American eagle perched atop an anchor and laurel branches. On either side of the eagle are the words: FOR SERVICE. Above, in a semicircle is a raised inscription UNITED STATES NAVY. The ribbon is Navy blue and gold, the official colors of the Navy. The ribbon has a wide blue center stripe flanked by gold with narrow blue edges. Additional awards are denoted by three-sixteenth inch dia. bronze stars. For those who served in the defense of Wake Island in December, 1941, a one-quarter inch silver "W" is worn on the ribbon bar and a bronze clasp bearing the inscription WAKE ISLAND is affixed to the suspension ribbon of the medal. This represents the last time in the 20th century that a named bar has been issued by any Service to commemorate a specific battle or engagement. The Navy Expeditionary Medal is worn after the Navy Fleet Marine Force Ribbon and before all other service and campaign awards.

MARINE CORPS EXPEDITIONARY MEDAL

W | Silver | Bronze

Silver | Silver | Bronze

WAKE ISLAND

<u>Instituted:</u>   1919/1921

<u>Dates:</u> 1919 to present (retroactive to 1874)

<u>Criteria:</u> Landings on foreign territory and operations against armed opposition for which no specific campaign medal has been authorized

<u>Devices:</u> Silver letter "W", bronze, silver star

<u>Notes:</u> Originally a "ribbon-only" award

<u>Bar:</u> "Wake Island"

     For opposed landing on a foreign territory or operations deserving special recognition. The Marine Corps Expeditionary Medal is worn after the Selected Marine Corps Reserve Medal and before the China Service Medal.

     The Marine Corps Expeditionary Ribbon was authorized by Marine Corps General Order on 8 May 1919. The medal pendant was added on 28 July 1921 by Executive Order 3524. The medal is awarded to members of the Marine Corps who have engaged in operations against armed opposition in foreign territory, or have served in situations warranting special recognition where no other campaign medal was awarded. To date more than sixty operations have qualified for the award, the first (retroactively) being operations by Navy and Marine Corps personnel in Honolulu, Hawaii in 1874 and the latest being rescue and evacuation operations in Liberia and Rwanda. The Navy had actually planned to discontinue the medal after World War II (it was awarded only three times in twenty years) in favor of the Navy Expeditionary Medal but the concept was never implemented.

     The Marine Corps Expeditionary Medal was designed by Walter Hancock. The medal is a circular bronze disc showing a Marine charging from the sea (depicted by wave scrolls at his feet). The Marine is in a uniform of the post World War I period with a full pack and fixed bayonet. Above, in a semicircle, is a raised inscription: EXPEDITIONS. The reverse of the medal shows an American eagle perched on an anchor and laurel branches. On either side of the eagle are the words FOR SERVICE. Above, in a semicircle is a raised inscription UNITED STATES MARINE CORPS. The ribbon is cardinal red and gold, the official colors of the Corps. The ribbon has a wide red center stripe flanked by gold (sometimes mistaken for khaki) with narrow red edges. Additional awards are denoted by three-sixteenth inch dia. bronze stars. For those who served in the defense of Wake Island in December, 1941, a one-quarter inch silver "W" is worn on the ribbon bar and a bronze clasp bearing the inscription WAKE ISLAND is affixed to the suspension ribbon of the medal.

CHINA SERVICE MEDAL

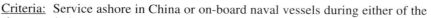

Bronze

Instituted: 1940

Dates: 1937-39, 1945-57

Criteria: Service ashore in China or on-board naval vessels during either of the above periods

Devices: Bronze star

Notes: Medal was reinstituted in 1947 for extended service during dates shown above

For service in China during the periods just prior to and just following World War II. The China Service Medal is worn after the Navy or Marine Corps Expeditionary Medal and before the American Defense Service Medal.

The China Service Medal was authorized by the Department of the Navy on 23 August 1940 for members of the Navy and Marine Corps who served in China or were attached to ships in the area during the period 7 July 1937 to 7 September 1939. The second period was for those who were present for duty during operations in China, Taiwan, and the Formosa Straits during the period 2 September 1947 to 1 April 1957.

The China Service Medal was designed by George Snowden. The medal is a circular bronze disc showing a Chinese junk under full sail with the raised inscribed words: CHINA above and SERVICE below. The reverse of the medal shows an American eagle perched on an anchor and laurel branches. On either side of the eagle are the words: FOR SERVICE. Above, in a semicircle is a raised inscription: UNITED STATES NAVY or UNITED STATES MARINE CORPS depending on the recipient's Service Branch. The ribbon is yellow with a narrow red stripe near each edge. If an individual served during both periods, a bronze three-sixteenth inch star is worn.

AMERICAN DEFENSE SERVICE MEDAL

Bronze   Bronze

Service: All Services

Instituted: 1941

Dates: 1939-41

Criteria: Army: 12 months of active duty service during the above period;

Devices: All Services: bronze star (denotes bars above), bronze letter "A";

Bars: Army: FOREIGN SERVICE for service outside the continental United States (CONUS); Navy/Marine Corps: FLEET for service on the high seas and BASE for service at bases outside CONUS; Coast Guard: SEA for service on the high seas

Navy

Navy

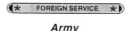
Army

Coast Guard

Authorized on June 28, 1941 for military service during the limited emergency proclaimed by President Roosevelt on Sept. 8, 1939 or during the unlimited emergency proclaimed on May 27, 1941 until December 7, 1941 if under orders to active duty for 12 months or longer. In addition to the bars depicted above, a bronze star is worn on the service ribbon to denote of any of the above bars. The Navy also authorized the wear of a bronze letter "A" if the recipient served with the Atlantic Fleet during the period of the national emergency. The bronze star was not worn if the letter "A" was awarded.

On the front of the medal is the Grecian figure, Columbia, representing America or Liberty, holding a shield and sword while standing on an oak branch, symbolic of strength. The oak leaves represent the strength of the Army, Navy, Marine Corps, and Coast Guard. The inscription, AMERICAN DEFENSE, is around the outside upper edge. The reverse of the medal carries the inscription: FOR SERVICE DURING THE LIMITED EMERGENCY PROCLAIMED BY THE PRESIDENT ON SEPTEMBER 8, 1939 OR DURING THE UNLIMITED EMERGENCY PROCLAIMED BY THE PRESIDENT ON MAY 27, 1941.

The golden yellow color of the ribbon symbolizes the golden opportunity of United States youth to serve the nation, represented by the blue, white, and red stripes on both sides of the ribbon.

WOMEN'S ARMY CORPS SERVICE MEDAL

Service: Army
Instituted: 1943
Dates: 1941-46
Criteria: Service with both the Women's Army Auxiliary Corps and Women's Army Corps during the above period
Devices: None
Notes: Only U.S. award authorized for women only.

Authorized on July 29, 1943 for service in both the Women's Army Auxiliary Corps (WAAC) between July 10, 1942 and August 31, 1943 and the Women's Army Corps (WAC) between September 1, 1943 and September 2, 1945. After 1945, members of the WAC received the same medals as other members of the Army. No attachments are authorized for the medal.

The front of the medal contains the head of Pallas Athena, goddess of victory and wisdom, superimposed on a sword crossed with oak leaves and a palm branch. The sword represents military might; the oak leaves represent strength and the palm branch represents peace. The reverse contains thirteen stars, an eagle and a scroll along with the words, FOR SERVICE IN THE WOMEN'S ARMY AUXILIARY CORPS, and the dates 1942-1943. The dates on the medal, 1942-1943, remained the same even after the WAAC became the WAC. The ribbon is moss green with old gold edges, the branch colors of the Women's Army Corps. Green indicates merit and gold refers to achievement.

Fewer than 100,000 women in World War II qualified for the Women's Army Corps Service Medal; over 40,000 WAC were assigned to the U.S. Army Air Force by 1945. This is the only U.S, service medal specifically created and authorized for women in the military.

AMERICAN CAMPAIGN MEDAL

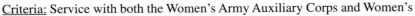

☆
Bronze

Instituted: 1942
Dates: 1941-46
Criteria: Service outside the U.S. in the American theater for 30 days, or within the continental United States (CONUS) for one year.
Devices: All Services: Bronze star

For service during World War II within the American Theater of Operations. The American Campaign Medal was established by Executive Order on 6 November 1942 and amended on 15 March 1946, which established a closing date. The medal is awarded to any member of the Armed Forces who served in the American Theater of Operations during the period from 7 December 1941 to 2 March 1946, or was awarded a combat decoration while in combat against the enemy. The service must have been an aggregate of one year within the continental United States, or thirty consecutive days outside the continental United States, or sixty nonconsecutive days outside the continental United States, but within the American Theater of Operations. Maps of the three theaters of operations during World War II were drawn on 6 November 1942 to include the American Theater, European- African- Middle Eastern Theater and Asiatic-Pacific Theater.

The American Campaign Medal was designed by the Army's Institute of Heraldry. The medal is a circular bronze disc showing a Navy cruiser, a B-24 bomber and a sinking enemy submarine above three waves. Shown in the background are some buildings representing the United States. Above is the raised inscription AMERICAN CAMPAIGN. The reverse of the medal shows an American eagle standing on a rock. On the left of the eagle are the raised inscribed dates: 1941- 1945 and on the right: UNITED STATES OF AMERICA. The ribbon is azure blue with three narrow stripes of red, white and blue (United States) in the center, and four stripes of white, red (Japan), black and white (Germany) near the edges. Three-sixteenth inch bronze stars indicated participation in specialized antisubmarine, escort or special operations. The American Campaign Medal is worn after the Women's Army Corps Service Medal by Army & Air Force personnel and after the American Defense Service Medal by the Naval Services.

ASIATIC - PACIFIC CAMPAIGN MEDAL

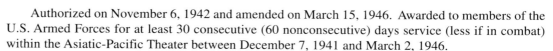

Silver   Bronze   Bronze

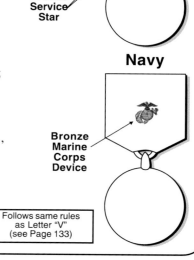

Service: All Services
Instituted: 1942
Dates: 7 December 1941 to 2 March 1946
Criteria: Service in the Asiatic-Pacific theater for 30 days or receipt of any combat decoration
Devices: All Services: bronze, silver star; Army/Air Force: bronze arrowhead; Navy: bronze Marine Corps device

Authorized on November 6, 1942 and amended on March 15, 1946. Awarded to members of the U.S. Armed Forces for at least 30 consecutive (60 nonconsecutive) days service (less if in combat) within the Asiatic-Pacific Theater between December 7, 1941 and March 2, 1946.

The front of the medal shows a palm tree amidst troops with an aircraft overhead and an aircraft carrier, battleship, and submarine in the background. The reverse has the American eagle, symbolizing power, on a rock, symbolizing stability, with the inscription, UNITED STATES OF AMERICA on the eagle's back. The orange yellow of the ribbon represents Asia while the white-red stripes toward each edge represent Japan. The center blue, white, and red thin stripes are taken from the American Defense Service Medal, referring to America's continued defense preparedness after Pearl Harbor. A bronze star denoted participation in a campaign. A silver star attachment is used to represent five bronze stars. An arrowhead attachment is authorized by the Army and Air Force for participation in a combat parachute jump, combat glider landing, or amphibious assault landing (only one arrowhead may be worn on the medal/ribbon despite the number of qualification events). The ribbon is worn with the center blue stripe on the wearer's right. Designated Army & AAF campaigns for the Asiatic-Pacific Campaign Medal are:

Burma, 1941-1942	Air Offensive, Japan, 1942-1945	Luzon, 1944-1945
Philippine Islands, 1941-1942	China Defensive, 1942-1945	Western Pacific , 1944-1945
Central Pacific, 1941-1943	India-Burma, 1942-1945	Central Burma, 1945
East Indies, 1942	Bismark Archipelago, 1943-1944	China Offensive, 1945
Aleutian Islands, 1942-1943	New Guinea, 1943-1944	Ryukyus, 1945
Guadalcanal, 1942-1943	Northern Solomons, 1943-1944	Southern Philippines, 1945
Papua, 1942-1943	Eastern Mandates (Air), 1943-1944	Air Combat, 1941-1945
	Eastern Mandates (Ground), 1944	Antisubmarine, 1941-1945
	Leyte, 1944-1945	Ground Combat, 1941-1945

Designated Navy and Marine Corps campaigns for the Asiatic-Pacific Campaign Medal are:

Pearl Harbor-Midway, 1941	Pacific raids, 1943
Wake Island, 1941	Treasury-Bougainville operation, 1943
Philippine Islands operation, 1941-1942	Gilbert Island operation, 1943
Netherlands East Indies, 1942	Marshall Islands operation, 1943-1944
Pacific raids, 1942	Asiatic-Pacific raids, 1944
Coral Sea, 1942	Western New Guinea, 1944-1945
Midway, 1942	Marianas operation, 1944
Guadalcanal,-Tulagi landings, 1942	Western Caroline Islands, 1944
Capture and defense of Guadalcanal, 1942-1943	Leyte operation, 1944
Makin Raid, 1942	Luzon operation, 1944-1945
Eastern Solomons (Stewart Island), 1942	Iwo Jima operation, 1945
Buin-Faisi-Tonolai raid, 1942	Okinawa Gunto operation, 1945
Cape Esperance (Second Savo), 1942	Third Fleet operations against Japan, 1945
Santa Cruz Islands, 1942	Kurile Islands operation, 1944-1945
Guadalcanal (Third Savo), 1942	Borneo operation, 1945
Tassafaronga (Fourth Savo), 1942	Tinian capture and occupation, 1944
Eastern New Guinea, 1942-1944	Consolidation of Southern Philippines, 1945
Rennel Island operation, 1943	Hollandia operation, 1944
Solomon Islands consolidation, 1943-1945	Manila Bay-Bicol operation, 1945
Aleutians operations, 1943	Escort, antisubmarine, etc, 1942-1945
New Georgia Group operation, 1943	Minesweeping operations, 1945-1946
Bismarck Archipelago, 1943-1944	Submarine war patrols, 1941-1945

Army

Bronze Arrowhead

Silver Service Star

Bronze Service Star

Navy

Bronze Marine Corps Device

Follows same rules as Letter "V" (see Page 133)

EUROPEAN-AFRICAN-MIDDLE EASTERN CAMPAIGN MEDAL

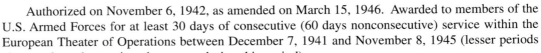

Silver Bronze Bronze

Service: All Services   Instituted: 1942
Dates: 7 December 1941 to 2 March 1946
Criteria: Service in the European-African-Middle Eastern theater for 30 days
or receipt of any combat decoration
Devices: All Services: bronze, silver star; Army/Air Force: bronze arrowhead; Navy: bronze
Marine Corps device

Authorized on November 6, 1942, as amended on March 15, 1946. Awarded to members of the U.S. Armed Forces for at least 30 days of consecutive (60 days nonconsecutive) service within the European Theater of Operations between December 7, 1941 and November 8, 1945 (lesser periods qualify if individual was in actual combat against the enemy during this period).

The front of the bronze medal shows a Landing Ship, Tank (LST) unloading troops while under fire with an airplane overhead. The reverse has the American eagle, symbol of power, standing on a rock, symbol of stability, with the inscription UNITED STATES OF AMERICA and dates, 1941-1945.

Three-sixteenth inch dia. bronze and silver stars denoted participation in the specific campaigns described below. A bronze arrowhead indicated participation in a combat parachute jump, combat glider landing, or amphibious assault landing. The ribbon's central blue, white, and red stripes represent the United States. The wide green stripes represent the green fields of Europe, the brown edges represent the African desert sands, the thin green, white, and red stripes represent Italy and the thin black and white stripes represent Germany.

Designated Army (& AAF) campaigns for the European-African-Middle Eastern Campaign Medal are as follows:

Algeria-French Morocco, 1942
Egypt-Libya, 1942-1943
Tunisia, 1942-1943
Air Offensive, Europe, 1942-1944
Sicily, 1943
Naples-Foggia, 1943-1944
Anzio, 1944
Rome-Arno, 1944
Normandy, 1944
Northern France, 1944

Southern France, 1944
North Apennines, 1944-1945
Rhineland, 1944-1945
Ardennes-Alsace, 1944-1945
Central Europe, 1945
Po Valley, 1945
Air Combat, 1941-1945
Antisubmarine, 1941-1945
Ground Combat, 1941-1945

Army

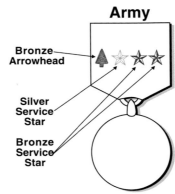

Bronze Arrowhead
Silver Service Star
Bronze Service Star

Designated Navy and Marine Corps campaigns for the European-African-Middle Eastern Campaign Medal are as follows:

Reinforcement of Malta, 1942
North African occupation, 1942-1943
Sicilian Occupation, 1943
Salerno landings, 1943
West Coast of Italy Operations, 1944
Invasion of Normandy, 1944
Northeast Greenland Operation, 1944
Invasion of Southern France, 1944
Escort, antisubmarine, armed guard, special
    operations, 1941-1944

Navy

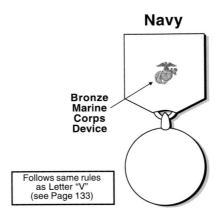

Bronze Marine Corps Device

Follows same rules
as Letter "V"
(see Page 133)

WORLD WAR II VICTORY MEDAL

Service: All Services   Instituted: 1945
Dates: 7 December 1941 to 31 December 1946
Criteria: Awarded for service in the U.S. Armed Forces during the above period
Devices: None

Authorized by an Act of Congress on July 6, 1945 and awarded to all members of the Armed Forces who served at least one day of honorable, active federal service between December 7, 1941 and December 31, 1946, inclusive.

The front of the medal depicts the Liberty figure resting her right foot on a war god's helmet with the hilt of a broken sword in her right hand and the broken blade in her left hand. The reverse contains the words, FREEDOM FROM FEAR AND WANT, FREEDOM OF SPEECH AND RELIGION, and UNITED STATES OF AMERICA 1941-1945. The red center stripe of the ribbon is symbolic of Mars, the God of War, representing both courage and fortitude. The twin rainbow stripes, suggested by the World War I Victory Medal, allude to the peace following a storm. A narrow white stripe separates the center red stripe from each rainbow pattern on both sides of the ribbon. The World War II Victory Medal provides deserving recognition to all of America's veterans who served during World War II.

No attachments are authorized although some veterans received the medal with an affixed bronze star which, according to rumors at the time, was to distinguish those who served in combat from those who did not. However, no official documentation has ever been found to support this supposition.   Although eligible for its award, many World War II veterans never actually received the medal since many were discharged prior to the medal's institution.

U. S. ANTARCTIC EXPEDITION MEDAL

Service: Navy/Coast Guard   Instituted: 1945
Dates: 1939-41

Criteria: Awarded in gold, silver and bronze to members of the U.S. Antarctic Expedition of 1939-41.

Devices: None

The U.S. Antarctic Expedition Medal was created by an Act of Congress on 24 September 1945 and was awarded in gold, silver, and bronze to the participants. 160 medals were authorized, with 60 minted in gold and 50 each in silver and bronze. Rear Admiral Richard E. Byrd, who headed the endeavor, received one of the medals in gold. Unlike previous expeditions headed by Admiral Byrd, this effort was not named for him as it was an official undertaking of the United States Government rather than a privately-funded enterprise.

The 1939-1941 expedition was envisioned as the first of a long series of efforts to explore the South Pole but the advent of World War II forced all such plans to be shelved indefinitely.

The medal was designed by John R. Sinnock. The lower half of the obverse shows a partial map with the engraved names: SOUTH PACIFIC OCEAN, LITTLE AMERICA, SOUTH POLE, ANTARCTICA, AND PALMERLAND. Above this is a three-part scroll inscribed, SCIENCE, PIONEERING, EXPLORATION. Around the edge is the inscription: THE UNITED STATES ANTARCTIC EXPEDITION 1939 1941. On the reverse, the inscription: BY ACT OF CONGRESS OF THE UNITED STATES OF AMERICA TO is set in four lines over a blank space for the recipient's name. Below is the inscription: IN RECOGNITION OF INVALUABLE SERVICE TO THIS NATION BY COURAGEOUS PIONEERING IN POLAR EXPLORATION WHICH RE-SULTED IN IMPORTANT GEOGRAPHICAL AND SCIENTIFIC DISCOVERIES, in seven lines.

The ribbon has three equal stripes - ice blue, white, ice blue - and the white center stripe has two narrow dark red stripes near each edge.

ARMY OF OCCUPATION MEDAL

Service: Army/Air Force   Instituted: 1946

Dates: 1945-55 (Berlin: 1945-90)

Criteria: 30 consecutive days of service in occupied territories of former enemies during above period

Devices: Gold airplane

Bars: "Germany", "Japan"

Gold Airplane

GERMANY — Germany Clasp

JAPAN — Japan Clasp

Authorized on June 7, 1946 and awarded to both Army, and Army Air Force personnel for at least 30 consecutive days of service in formerly held enemy territories, including Germany (1945-1955), Berlin (1945-1990), Austria (1945-1955), Italy (1945-1947), Japan (1945-1952) and Korea (1945-1949).

The front of the medal depicts the Remagen Bridge on the Rhine River with the inscription: ARMY OF OCCUPATION at the top. The reverse depicts Mount Fujiyama in Japan with two Japanese junks in front of the mountain. Although not specifically authorized by regulations, many veterans received Occupation Medals with reversed medallions, apparently to indicate the theater of occupation service (i.e. if occupation service was in Japan, the reverse side showing Mount Fujiyama became the front of the medal). The white and black colors of the ribbon represent Germany and the white and red colors represent Japan.

A gold-colored C-54 airplane device is authorized to denote participation in the Berlin airlift. Medal clasps inscribed: GERMANY and JAPAN are authorized for the suspension ribbon of the medal for occupation service in those respective territories. An individual who performed occupational service in both areas is authorized to wear both clasps with the upper clasp representing the area where occupation was first performed. However, regardless of the clasp configuration, no attachment is authorized for the ribbon bar.

Berlin Airlift Device

GERMANY

Occupation Area Clasp

WWII Occupation Medals

NAVY OCCUPATION SERVICE MEDAL

Service: Navy, Marine Corps, Coast Guard

Instituted: 1948

Dates: 1945-55 (Berlin: 1945-90)

Criteria: 30 consecutive days of service in occupied territories of former enemies during above period

Devices: Gold airplane

Bars: "Europe", "Asia"

Gold Airplane

EUROPE — Europe Clasp

ASIA — Asia Clasp

For thirty consecutive days of service in occupied zones following World War II. The Navy Occupation Service Medal is worn after the World War II Victory Medal and before the Medal for Humane Action.

The Navy Occupation Service Medal was authorized by ALNAV 24 on 22 January 1947 and Navy Department GO on 28 January 1948. The medal was awarded for occupation duty in Japan and Korea from 2 September 1945 to 27 April 1952. The medal was also awarded for occupation service in Germany, Italy, Trieste and Austria.

The Navy Occupation Service Medal was designed by the Army's Institute of Heraldry. The medal is a circular bronze disc showing Neptune, god of the sea, riding a sea serpent with the head and front legs of a horse. Neptune is holding a trident in his right hand and is pointing to an image of land, at the left of the medal, with his left hand. The lower front of the medal depicts the ocean with the words: OCCUPATION SERVICE in two lines. The reverse of the medal shows an American eagle perched on an anchor and laurel branches. On either side of the eagle are the words: FOR SERVICE. Above, in a semicircle is a raised inscription: UNITED STATES NAVY or UNITED STATES MARINE CORPS. The ribbon has two wide stripes of red and black in the center with border stripes of white. Clasps, similar to those used on the World War I Victory Medal, are used to denote service in EUROPE and ASIA, which are authorized for wear with the medal. There are no devices to represent these clasps authorized for wear on the ribbon bar. In addition, Navy and Marine personnel who served 90 consecutive days in support of the Berlin Airlift (1948-1949) are authorized to wear the Berlin Airlift device, a three-eighths inch gold C-54 airplane, on the ribbon bar and suspension ribbon.

MEDAL FOR HUMANE ACTION

No devices
Authorized

Instituted: 1949

Dates: 1948-49

Criteria: 120 consecutive days of service participating in, or in support of the Berlin Airlift

Devices: None

Authorized for members of the U.S. Armed Forces on July 20, 1949 for at least 120 days of service while participating in or providing direct support for the Berlin Airlift during the period June 26, 1948 and September 30, 1949. The prescribed boundaries for qualifying service include the area between the north latitudes of the 54th and the 48th parallels and between the 14th east longitude and the 5th west longitude meridians. Posthumous award may be made to any person who lost his/her life while, or as a direct result of, participating in the Berlin airlift, without regard to the length of such service.

The front of the medal depicts the C-54 aircraft, which served as the primary aircraft used during the airlift, above the coat of arms of Berlin which lies in the center of a wreath of wheat. The reverse has the American eagle with shield and arrows and bears the inscriptions, FOR HUMANE ACTION and TO SUPPLY NECESSITIES OF LIFE TO THE PEOPLE OF BERLIN GERMANY.

On the ribbon the black and white colors of Prussia refer to Berlin , capital of Prussia and Germany. Blue alludes to the sky, and red represents the fortitude and zeal of the personnel who participated in the airlift.

No attachments are authorized. However, instances have been noted where the gold, C-54 airplane device was incorrectly placed on this award rather than its proper usage, the Occupation Medal.

NATIONAL DEFENSE SERVICE MEDAL

Bronze

Instituted: 1953

Dates: 1950-54, 1961-74, 1990-95

Criteria: Any honorable active duty service during any of the above periods

Devices: Bronze star

Notes: Reinstituted in 1966 and 1991 for Vietnam and Southwest Asia (Gulf War) actions respectively

Initially authorized by executive order on April 22, 1953. It is awarded to members of the U.S. Armed Forces for any honorable active federal service during the Korean War (June 27, 1950 - July 27, 1954), Vietnam War (January 1, 1961- August 14, 1974) and/or Desert Shield/Desert Storm (August 2, 1990- November 30, 1995). President Bush issued an Executive Order 12776 on 8 October 1991 authorizing award of the medal to all members of the Reserve forces whether or not on active duty during the designated period of the Gulf War. Today, there are probably more people authorized this medal than any other award in U.S. history. Circumstances not qualifying as active duty for the purpose of this medal include: (1) Members of the Guard and Reserve on short tours of active duty to fulfill training obligations; (2) Service members on active duty to serve on boards, courts, commissions, and like organizations; (3) Service members on active duty for the sole purpose of undergoing a physical examination; and (4) Service members on active duty for purposes other than extended active duty. Reserve personnel who have received the Armed Forces Expeditionary Medal or the Vietnam Service Medal are eligible for this medal. The National Defense Service Medal is also authorized to those individuals serving as cadets or midshipmen at the Air Force, Army, or Naval Academies. The front of the medal shows the American bald eagle with inverted wings standing on a sword and palm branch and contains the words NATIONAL DEFENSE; the reverse has the United States shield amidst an oak leaf and laurel spray. Symbolically, the Eagle is the national emblem of the United States, the sword represents the Armed Forces and the palm is symbolic of victory. The reverse contains the shield from the great seal of the United States flanked by a wreath of laurel and oak representing achievement and strength. The ribbon has a broad center stripe of yellow representing high ideals. The red, white and blue stripes represent the national flag. Red for hardiness and valor, white for purity of purpose and blue for perseverance and justice. No more than one medal is awarded to a single individual but a three-sixteenth inch dia. bronze star denotes additional awards of the medal.

KOREAN SERVICE MEDAL

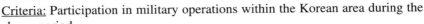

Silver   Bronze   Bronze

Instituted: 1950   Dates: 1950-54

Criteria: Participation in military operations within the Korean area during the above period

Devices: All Services: bronze, silver star, Army, Air Force: bronze arrowhead, Navy: bronze Marine Corps emblem

Authorized by executive order on November 8, 1950 and awarded for service between June 27, 1950 and July 27, 1954 in the Korean theater of operations. Members of the U.S. Armed Forces must have participated in combat or served with a combat or service unit in the Korean Theater for 30 consecutive or 60 nonconsecutive days during the designated period. Personnel who served with a unit or headquarters stationed outside the theater but in direct support of Korean military operations are also entitled to this medal. The combat zone designated for qualification for the medal encompassed both North and South Korea, Korean waters, and the airspace over these areas. The first campaign began when North Korea first invaded South Korea and the last campaign ended when the Korean Armistice cease-fire became effective. The period of Korean service was extended by one year from the cease fire by the Secretary of Defense; individuals could qualify for the medal during this period if stationed in Korea but would not receive any campaign credit. An award of this medal qualifies personnel for award of the United Nations (Korean) Service Medal and the Republic of Korea War Service Medal (approved 1999).

A Korean gateway is depicted on the front of the medal along with the inscription: KOREAN SERVICE and on the reverse are the "Taeguk" symbol from the Korean flag that represents unity and the inscription: UNITED STATES OF AMERICA. A spray of oak and laurel line the bottom edge. The suspension ribbon and ribbon bar are both blue and white representing the United Nations. Bronze and silver stars are affixed to the suspension drape and ribbon bar to indicate participation in any of the 10 designated campaigns in the Korean War (see next page). Army and Air Force personnel who participated in an amphibious assault landing are entitled to wear the arrowhead attachment.

Campaigns designated by the Army and Air Force for the Korea Service Medal are:

UN Defensive, 27 June - 15 Sept, 1950

UN Offensive, 16 Sept - 2 Nov, 1950

CCF Intervention, 3 Nov, 1950 - 24 Jan, 1951

1st UN Counteroffensive, 25 Jan - 21 Apr, 1951

CCF Spring Offensive, 22 Apr - 8 July, 1951

UN Summer-Fall Offensive, 9 July - 27 Nov, 1951

Second Korean Winter, 28 Nov, 1951 - 30 Apr, 1952

Korea, Summer-Fall, 1 May - 30 Nov, 1953

Third Korean Winter, 1 Dec, 1952 - 30 Apr, 1953

Korea, Summer, 1 May - 27 July, 1953

Army

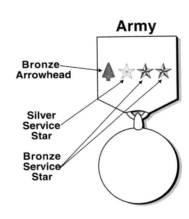

Bronze Arrowhead

Silver Service Star

Bronze Service Star

The ten Navy & Marine Corps campaign designations for the Korean Service Medal are:

North Korean aggression, 27 June - 2 Nov 1950

Communist China aggression, 3 Nov 1950 - 24 Jan 1951

Inchon Landing, 13 September - 17 Sept 1950

1st United Nations counteroffensive, 25 Jan - 21 Apr 1951

Communist China spring offensive, 22 Apr - 8 July 1951

United Nations summer-fall offensive, 9 July - 27 Nov 1951

2nd Korean winter, 28 November 1951 - 30 Apr 1952

Korean defensive, summer-fall 1952, 1 May - 30 Nov 1952

3rd Korean winter, 1 December 1952 - 30 Apr 1953

Korean summer 1953, 1 May - 27 July 1953

Navy

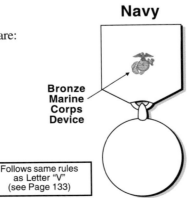

Bronze Marine Corps Device

Follows same rules as Letter "V" (see Page 133)

ANTARCTICA SERVICE MEDAL

Service: All Services
Instituted: July 7, 1960
Dates: 1946 to Present
Criteria: 30 calendar days of service on the Antarctic Continent
Devices: All Services: bronze, gold, silver disks (denote bars below)
Bars: "Wintered Over" in bronze, gold, silver

Bronze, Gold, or Silver

Authorized on July 7, 1960 and awarded to any member of the Armed Forces who, from January 2, 1946, as a member of a U.S. Antarctic expedition, participates in, or performs services in direct support of, scientific or exploratory operations on the Antarctic Continent. Qualifying service includes personnel who participate in flights or naval operations supporting operations in Antarctica. The medal may also be awarded to any U.S. citizen who participates in Antarctic expeditions under the same conditions as Service personnel.

The front of the medal depicts a figure appropriately-clothed in cold weather gear with his hood thrown back, arms extended and legs spread, symbolizing stability, determination, courage and devotion. The reverse depicts a map of the Antarctic continent in polar projection across which are three centered lines containing the inscription: COURAGE SACRIFICE DEVOTION.

A clasp containing the raised inscription: WINTERED OVER is worn on the medal and a disc of the same metal, containing the outline of the Antarctic Continent is worn on the ribbon bar if the individual remains on the continent during the winter months. For the first stay, the disc and bar are made of bronze, for the second stay, they are gold-colored and for the third and all subsequent winter tours, the devices are silver.

ARCTIC SERVICE MEDAL

Service: Coast Guard
Instituted: 1976
Dates: 1946 to Present
Criteria: Awarded for 21 days of service on vessels operating in polar waters north of the Arctic Circle.
Devices: For all deployments after 1 January 1989: bronze, silver star

Silver   Bronze

The Coast Guard Arctic Service Medal was authorized by the Coast Guard Commandant on 20 May 1976 and made retroactive to 1 Jan 1946. It is awarded for 21 days consecutive service aboard a Coast Guard vessel in Polar waters north of the Arctic Circle from 1 May through 31 October or 21 days consecutive service north of latitude 60 degrees N from 1 November through 30 April. Personnel who serve at any of the following Coast Guard Stations for the required 21 days also qualify for the medal:

- Loran Station, Cape Atholl, Greenland
- Loran Station, Cape Christian, Baffin Island, Canada
- Loran Station, Port Clarence, Alaska
- Radio Station, Barrow, Alaska
- Loran Station, Bo, Norway
- Loran Station, Jan Mayen Island, Norway

The front of the medal depicts a polar bear on the Arctic tundra beneath a stylized Polar star. Above this, on the medal's edge is the curved inscription: ARCTIC SERVICE. The reverse contains the Coast Guard Shield in the center of an otherwise unadorned planchet. Although no devices were initially authorized, the regulations now specify three-sixteenths inch dia. bronze and silver stars to denote additional awards for all deployments subsequent to 1 January 1989.

ARMED FORCES EXPEDITIONARY MEDAL

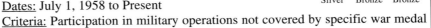

Silver   Bronze   Bronze

Service: All Services   Instituted: 1961
Dates: July 1, 1958 to Present
Criteria: Participation in military operations not covered by specific war medal
Devices: All Services: bronze, silver star; Army: bronze arrowhead; Navy: bronze Marine Corps device
Notes: Authorized for service in Vietnam until establishment of Vietnam Service Medal. The bronze arrowhead was approved for Grenada parachute jump (Army personnel only).

President John F. Kennedy characterized the post World War II period as: " a twilight that is neither peace nor war." During the period commonly referred to as the Cold War, the Armed Services agreed to one medal that would be necessary to recognize major actions not otherwise covered by a specific campaign medal.

Armed Forces Expeditionary Medal was authorized on December 4, 1961 to any member of the United States Armed Forces for US military operations, US operations in direct support of the United Nations, and US operations of assistance to friendly foreign nations after July 1, 1958. Operations that qualify for this medal are authorized in specific orders. Participating personnel must have served at least 30 consecutive (60 nonconsecutive) days in the qualifying operation or less if the operation was less than 30 days in length. The medal may also be authorized for individuals who do not meet the basic criteria but who do merit special recognition for their service in the designated operation.

The first qualifying operation was Operation Blue Bat, a peacekeeping mission in Lebanon from July 1 to November 1, 1958. This medal was initially awarded for Vietnam service between July 1, 1958 and July 3, 1965; an individual awarded the medal for this period of Vietnam service may elect to keep the award or request the Vietnam Service Medal in its place. However, both awards may not be retained for the same period of Vietnam service. Many personnel received this medal for continuing service in Cambodia after the Vietnam cease-fire. The medal was also authorized for those serving in the Persian Gulf area who previously would have qualified for the Southwest Asia Service Medal and the National Defense Service Medal whose qualification periods for that area terminated on November 30, 1995. Individuals who qualify for both the Southwest Asia Service Medal and the Armed Forces Expeditionary Medal must elect to receive the Expeditionary medal.

The front of the medal depicts an American eagle with wings raised, perched on a sword. Behind this is a compass rose with rays coming from the angles of the compass points. The words: ARMED FORCES EXPEDITIONARY SERVICE encircle the design. The reverse of the medal depicts the Presidential shield with branches of laurel below and the inscription, UNITED STATES OF AMERICA. The American national colors are located at the center position or honor point of the ribbon. The light blue sections on either side suggest water and overseas service, while various colors representing areas of the world where American troops may be called upon to serve run outward to the edge.

The qualifying campaigns for the Armed Forces Expeditionary Medal are as follows:

Lebanon, 1958
Taiwan Straits, 1958 - 1959
Quemoy & Matsu Islands, 1958 - 1963
Vietnam, 1958 - 1965
Congo, 1960 - 1962
Laos, 1961 - 1962
Berlin, 1961 - 1963
Cuba, 1962 - 1963
Congo, 1964
Dominican Republic, 1965 - 1966
Korea, 1966 - 1974
Cambodia, Thailand, 1973

Cambodia Evacuation, 1975
Mayaguez Operation, 1975
Vietnam Evacuation, 1975
El Salvador, 1981 - 1992
Grenada, 1983
Lebanon, 1983 - 1987
Libya, 1986
Persian Gulf, 1987 - 1990
Panama, 1989 - 1990
Somalia, 1992 - 1995
Haiti, 1994 - 1995

Iraq/Persian Gulf Operations as follows:
  "Southern Watch", 1995 - TBD
  "Vigilant Sentinel", 1995 - 1997
  Maritime Intercept Operations, 1995 - TBD
  "Northern Watch", 1997 - TBD
  "Desert Thunder", 1998
  "Desert Fox", 1998
"Joint Endeavor", 1995 - 1996
"Joint Guard", 1996 - 1998
"Joint Forge", 1998 - TBD

Army

Bronze Arrowhead

Silver Service Star

Bronze Service Star

Follows same rules
as Letter "V"
(see Page 133)

Navy

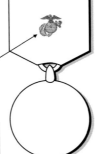

Bronze Marine Corps Device

VIETNAM SERVICE MEDAL

Silver Bronze Bronze

Service: All Services   Instituted: 1965
Dates: 1965-73
Criteria: Service in Vietnam, Laos, Cambodia or Thailand during the above period
Devices: All Services: bronze, silver star; Army: bronze arrowhead; Navy: bronze Marine Corps device

Authorized by executive order on July 8, 1965 for US military personnel serving in the Vietnam Theater of Operations after July 3, 1965 through March 28, 1973. Personnel must have served in Vietnam on temporary duty for at least 30 consecutive/60 nonconsecutive days or have served in combat with a unit directly supporting a military operation in Southeast Asia. Military personnel serving in Laos, Cambodia, or Thailand in direct support of operations in Vietnam are also eligible for this award. The Armed Forces Expeditionary Medal was awarded for earlier service in Vietnam from July 1, 1958 to July 3, 1965, inclusive; personnel receiving that award may be awarded the Vietnam Service Medal but are not authorized both awards for Vietnam service. The front of medal depicts an oriental dragon behind a grove of bamboo trees; below the base of the trees is the inscription: REPUBLIC OF VIETNAM SERVICE. The reverse of the medal depicts a crossbow with a torch through the center and contains the inscription: UNITED STATES OF AMERICA along the bottom edge. The colors of the suspension drape and ribbon suggest the flag of the Republic of Vietnam (the red stripes represent the three ancient Vietnamese empires of Tonkin, Annam, and Cochin China) and the green represents the Vietnamese jungle. Bronze and silver stars are authorized to signify participation in any of the 17 designated campaigns during the inclusive period.

Designated campaigns for the Vietnam Campaign Medal are as follows:

Army and Naval Services
Vietnam (VN) Advisory, 1962 - 1965
VN Defense, 1965 - 1965
VN Counteroffensive Campaign, 1965 - 1966
VN Counteroffensive Campaign Phase II, 1966 -1967
VN Counteroffensive Campaign Phase III, 1967 - 1968
TET Counteroffensive, 1968
VN Counteroffensive Campaign Phase IV, 1968
VN Counteroffensive Campaign Phase V, 1968
VN Counteroffensive Campaign Phase VI, 1968 - 1969
TET69 Counteroffensive, 1969
VN Summer- Fall 1969, 1969
Vietnam Winter- Spring 1970, 1969 - 1970
Sanctuary Counteroffensive, 1970
VN Counteroffensive Campaign Phase VII, 1970 - 1971
Consolidation I, 1971
Consolidation II, 1971 - 1972
Vietnam Cease-Fire Campaign, 1972 - 1973

Air Force:
Vietnam (VN) Advisory, 1961 - 1965
VN Defense, 1965 - 1966
VN Air Campaign, 1966
VN Air Offensive Phase I, 1966 - 1967
VN Air Offensive Phase II, 1967 - 1968
VN Air/Ground Campaign, 1968
VN Air Offensive Phase III, 1968
VN Air Offensive Phase IV, 1968 - 1969
TET 69/Counteroffensive, 1969
VN Summer-Fall, 69, 1969
VN Winter-Spring, 1969 - 1970
Sanctuary Counteroffensive, 1970
Southwest Monsoon, 1970
Commando Hunt V, 1970 - 1971
Commando Hunt VI, 1971
Commando Hunt VII, 1971 - 1972
Vietnam Cease-Fire, 1972 - 1973

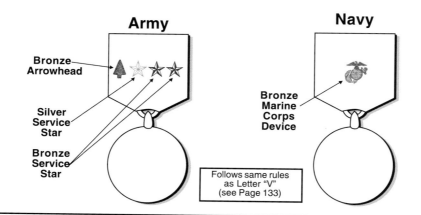

Army

Bronze Arrowhead
Silver Service Star
Bronze Service Star

Follows same rules as Letter "V" (see Page 133)

Navy

Bronze Marine Corps Device

SOUTHWEST ASIA SERVICE MEDAL

Bronze   Bronze

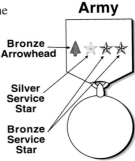

Service: All Services   Instituted: 1992
Dates: 1991 to 1995
Criteria: Active participation in, or support of, Operations Desert Shield, Desert Storm and/or subsequent follow-on operations in southwest Asia.
Devices: All Services: bronze star; Navy: bronze Marine Corps device
Note: Recipients of this medal are usually entitled to the Saudi Arabian Medal for the Liberation of Kuwait and the Emirate of Kuwait Medal for the Liberation of Kuwait.

Army

Bronze Arrowhead

Silver Service Star

Bronze Service Star

Awarded to members of the United States Armed Forces who participated in, or directly supported, military operations in Southwest Asia or in surrounding areas between August 2, 1990 and November 30, 1995 (Operations Desert Shield, Desert Storm and follow-up). The medal was established by an executive order signed by President George Bush on March 15, 1991.

The front of the medal depicts the tools of modern desert warfare (i.e.: aircraft, helicopter, tank, armored personnel carrier, tent and troops, battleship) in both desert and sea settings along with the inscription: SOUTHWEST ASIA SERVICE in the center. The reverse of the medal contains a sword entwined with a palm leaf representing military preparedness and the maintenance of peace and the inscription: UNITED STATES OF AMERICA around the periphery. The ribbon is predominately tan, symbolizing the sands of the desert and contains thin stripes of the U.S. national colors towards each edge. The green and black center stripes and the black edges, along with the red and white, suggest the flag colors of most Arab nations in the region of Southwest Asia.

Navy

Bronze Marine Corps Device

There were three campaign periods designated for the Southwest Asia Service Medal, each being represented by a bronze star. The three campaigns are as follows:

The Defense of Saudi Arabia, August 2, 1990 - January 16, 1991
The Liberation and Defense of Kuwait, January 17, 1991 - April 11, 1991
The Southwest Asia Cease Fire Campaign, April 12, 1991 - November 30, 1995.

Follows same rules as Letter "V" (see Page 133)

KOSOVO CAMPAIGN MEDAL

Bronze

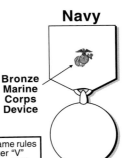

Instituted: 2000
Dates: 1999 to TBD
Criteria: Active participation in, or direct support of, Kosovo operations
Devices: All Services: bronze star; Navy: bronze Marine Corps device

For participation in, or in direct support of Kosovo operations. The Kosovo Campaign Medal is worn after the Southwest Asia Service Medal and before the Armed Forces Service Medal. The Kosovo Campaign Medal was established by Executive Order on 15 May 2000. The medal is awarded to all members of the Armed Forces who participated in or provided direct support to Kosovo operations within established areas of eligibility (AOE) from 24 March 1999 to a date yet to be determined. The service member must have been a member of a unit participating in, or engaged in support of one or more of the following operations for 30 consecutive days or 60 nonconsecutive days:

Allied Force: 24 March - 10 June 1999
Joint Guardian: 11 June 1999- TBD
Allied Harbour: 4 April - 1 Sept 1999
Sustain Hope/Shining Hope: 4 April - 10 July 1999
Noble Anvil: 24 March- 20 July 1999

Task Force Hawk: 5 April - 24 June 1999
Task Force Saber: 31 March - 8 July 1999
Task Force Falcon: 11 June- TBD
Task Force Hunter: 1 April - 1 Nov 1999

The Kosovo Campaign Medal was designed by the Army's Institute of Heraldry. The medal is a circular bronze disk depicting rocky terrain, a fertile valley and sunrise behind a mountain pass in Kosovo. Above the scene, on two lines, are the words: KOSOVO CAMPAIGN. At the lower edge is a stylized wreath of grain reflecting the agricultural nature of the area. The reverse shows an outline of the province of Kosovo with the curved inscription: IN DEFENSE OF HUMANITY across the top. To date, there are two bronze service stars authorized for the Kosovo Campaign Medal as follows:

(1) Kosovo Air Campaign- 24 March 1999 to 10 June 1999
(2) Kosovo Defense Campaign- 11 June 1999 to a date TBD

In addition, Naval personnel who were attached to Marine Corps units are entitled to wear a miniature bronze Marine device on the suspension ribbon and ribbon bar.

ARMED FORCES SERVICE MEDAL

<u>Service:</u> All Services   <u>Instituted:</u> 1995   <u>Dates:</u> 1995 to Present
<u>Criteria:</u> Participation in military operations not covered by a specific war medal or the Armed Forces Expeditionary Medal
<u>Devices:</u> All Services: bronze, silver star

Silver   Bronze

Authorized on January 11, 1996 for U.S. military personnel who, on or after June 1, 1992, participate in a U.S. military operation deemed to be a significant activity in which no foreign armed opposition or imminent hostile action is encountered and for which no previous U.S. service medal is authorized. The medal can be awarded to service members in direct support of the United Nations or North Atlantic Treaty Organization, and for assistance operations to friendly nations. The initial awards of this medal were for operations that have occurred in the Balkans since 1992. Qualifications include at least one day of participation in the designated area. Direct support of the operation and aircraft flights within the area also qualify for award of this medal as long as at least one day is served within the designated area. Recent operations that qualify for the medal are Provide Promise, Joint Endeavor, Able Sentry, Deny Flight, Maritime Monitor, and Sharp Guard.

The front of the medal contains the torch of liberty within its center and contains the inscription: ARMED FORCES SERVICE MEDAL around its periphery. The reverse of the medal depicts the American eagle with the U.S. shield in its chest and spread wings clutching three arrows in its talons encircled by a laurel wreath and the inscription, IN PURSUIT OF DEMOCRACY. Bronze and silver service stars are worn to denote additional awards.

HUMANITARIAN SERVICE MEDAL

Silver   Bronze

<u>Service:</u> All Services   <u>Instituted:</u> 1977   <u>Dates:</u> 1975 to Present
<u>Criteria:</u> Direct participation in specific operations of a humanitarian nature
<u>Devices:</u> All Services: bronze, silver star

Authorized on January 19, 1977 and awarded to Armed Forces personnel (including Reserve components) who, subsequent to April 1, 1975, distinguish themselves by meritorious direct participation in a DOD-approved, significant military act or operation of a humanitarian nature. According to regulations, the participation must be "hands-on" at the site of the operation; personnel assigned to staff functions geographically separated from the operation are not eligible for this medal. Service members must be assigned and/or attached to participating units for specific operations by official orders. Members who were present for duty at specific qualifying locations for the medal but who did not make a direct contribution to the action or operation are specifically excluded from eligibility. It should be noted that some of the earliest recipients of the Humanitarian Service Medal (e.g.: for the evacuations of Laos, Cambodia and Vietnam) would more likely be awarded the Armed Forces Service Medal in today's environment.

The medal was designed by the Army's Institute of Heraldry. The front of the medal depicts a human right hand with open palm within a raised circle. At the top of the medal's reverse is the raised inscription: FOR HUMANITARIAN SERVICE set in three lines. In the center is an oak branch with three acorns and leaves and, below this, is the raised circular inscription: UNITED STATES ARMED FORCES around the lower edge of the medal. The ribbon is medium blue with a wide center stripe of Navy blue. It is edged by a wide stripe of purple which is separated from the light blue field by a narrow white stripe. Bronze and silver stars are authorized for additional awards.

Former Placement of Devices on the Humanitarian Service Medal

No. of Awards	Navy, Marine Corps and Air Force	Army	Coast Guard
2	2	1	★
3	3	2	★ ★
4	4	3	★ ★ ★
5	5	4	★ ★ ★ ★
6	6	5	★

Legend: **1**, **2** etc. = **Bronze Block Numerals**
★ = 3/16" dia. Bronze Star
☆ = 3/16" dia. Silver Star

Note: All branches now use Coast Guard placement of stars.

Navy, Marine Corps and Coast Guard	Army	Air Force
5	4	★ ★ ★ ★

NOTE:
1. When medals overlap, Navy regulations require the wear of all attachments: ...to the wearer's left on suspension ribbons". In practice, the devices are still mounted horizontally and centered on the exposed portion of the suspension ribbon. Marine Corps regulations make no such provision so the devices remain as shown, centered on the suspension ribbon regardless of the degree of overlap.

OUTSTANDING VOLUNTEER SERVICE MEDAL

Service: All Services   Instituted: 1993
Dates: 1993 to Present
Criteria: Awarded for outstanding and sustained voluntary service to the civilian community
Devices: All Services: bronze, silver star

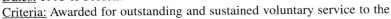

Silver   Bronze

Authorized in 1993 to members of the U.S. Armed Forces and reserve components. Awarded for outstanding and sustained voluntary service to the civilian community after December 31, 1992. It may be awarded to active duty and reserve members who perform outstanding volunteer service over time as opposed to a single event. The service performed must have been to the civilian community and must be strictly voluntary and not duty-related. The volunteerism must be of a sustained and direct nature and must be significant and produce tangible results while reflecting favorably on the Armed Forces and the Department of Defense. There are no specific time requirements as to how many hours must be spent on the volunteer activity, but the activity should consist of significant action and involvement rather than, for example, simply attending meetings as a member of a community service group. An individual would normally be considered for only one award during an assignment. Group-level commanders, including commanders of provisional and composite groups, have approval authority for the medal.

The front of the bronze medal has a five-pointed star with a circular ring over each point; the star, a symbol of the military and representing outstanding service, is encircled by a laurel wreath which represents honor and achievement. The reverse has an oak leaf branch, symbolic of strength and potential, with three oak leaves and two acorns along with the inscriptions, OUTSTANDING VOLUNTEER SERVICE, and UNITED STATES ARMED FORCES. Bronze and silver stars are authorized to denote additional awards.

ARMED FORCES RESERVE MEDAL

Service: All Services   Instituted: 1950
Dates: 1949 to Present
Criteria: 10 years of honorable service in any reserve component of the United States Armed Forces Reserve or award of "M" device
Devices: Bronze, silver and gold hourglass, bronze letter "M", bronze numeral

Bronze, Silver, Gold   Bronze   Bronze

Authorized in 1950 for 10 years of honorable and satisfactory service within a 12 year period as a member of one or more of the Reserve Components of the Armed Forces of the United States.

An Executive Order of Aug 8, 1996 authorized the award of a bronze letter "M" mobilization device to U.S. reserve component members who were called to active-duty service in support of designated operations on or after August 1, 1990 (the M device was not authorized for any operations prior to August 1, 1990 although it had been previously proposed). Units called up in support of Operations Desert Storm/ Desert Shield were the first units to be authorized the "M" device. If an "M" is authorized, the medal is awarded even though service might be less than 10 years. Previous to this change, only bronze hourglasses were awarded at each successive 10 year point (first hourglass at the 20 year point).

The front of the medal depicts a flaming torch placed vertically between a crossed bugle and powder horn; thirteen stars and thirteen rays surround the design. The front of the medal is the same for all services; only the reverse design is different (see designs below). Bronze numerals beginning with "2" are worn to the right of the bronze "M" on the ribbon bar and below the "M" on the medal, indicating the total number of times the individual was mobilized. Bronze, silver and gold hourglasses are awarded for 10, 20, 30 years service, respectively.

The medal reverses are as follows:

Army	**Navy**	**Marine Corps**	**Air Force**	**Coast Guard**	**Air Force National Guard**
has a Minuteman in front of a circle with 13 stars representing the original colonies	has a sailing ship with an anchor on its front with an eagle with wings spread superimposed upon it	has the USMC emblem, eagle, globe, and anchor	has an eagle with wings spread in front of a circle with clouds and includes the inscription: 768ub ARMED FORCES RESERVE.	has the Coast Guard emblem, crossed anchor with the Coast Guard shield in the center	has the National Guard insignia on the reverse eagle with crossed cannons in its center.

NAVAL RESERVE MEDAL (Obsolete)

★
Bronze

Service: Navy   Instituted: 1938   Dates: 1938 to 1958

Criteria: Awarded for 10 years of honorable service in the U.S. Naval Reserve

Devices: Bronze star

Notes: ; The earlier ribbon version was a deep reddish-purple shade (the so-called: "plum" version). The medal was superseded by the Armed Forces Reserve Medal

This medal was authorized on September 12, 1938, and awarded to officers and enlisted men of the Naval Reserve who had completed ten years of satisfactory federal service in the U.S. Naval Reserve. Eligibility ceased during a time of war or national emergency if called to active duty. After the establishment of the Armed Forces Reserve Medal in 1950, a Naval Reservist who was eligible for the Naval Reserve Medal and the Armed Forces Reserve Medal could elect which award he was to receive. The Naval Reserve Medal was terminated on September 12, 1958, and now only the Armed Forces Reserve Medal is awarded. The obverse of the Naval Reserve Medal shows an eagle in an attitude of defiance, facing left, with wings raised. The eagle is perched on an anchor, flukes down to the left. The reverse of the medal is flat, with the inscription UNITED STATES NAVAL RESERVE encircling the outer edge. At the bottom is a large star and the words FAITHFUL SERVICE centered in two lines. A bronze star was authorized for each additional ten years of qualifying service. However there is little likelihood that a device was ever earned since a potential recipient would have to spend the total life span of the medal (twenty years) in the Naval Reserve during both World War II and the Korean Conflict.

MARKSMANSHIP MEDALS & RIBBONS

NAVY EXPERT RIFLEMAN MEDAL

Service: Navy

Instituted: 1920

Criteria: Attainment of the minimum qualifying score for the expert level during prescribed shooting exercises.

Devices: None on medal (but see: Navy Rifle Marksmanship Ribbon)

The Navy Expert Rifleman Medal was designed by the U. S. Mint and is awarded to members of the U. S. Navy and Naval Reserve who qualify as Expert with a rifle on a prescribed military rifle course. The medallion is a bronze disc bordered with a rope edge. The ribbon hangs from a smaller disc superimposed at the top containing the figure of an eagle clutching an anchor in its talons, taken from the seal of the U.S. Navy. The larger disc has a raised "bull's eye" (rifle target) in the center. Above the bull's eye is the raised inscription: EXPERT RIFLEMAN and on the lower edge, the curved inscription: UNITED STATES NAVY. The reverse of the medallion is blank for engraving. The ribbon is navy blue with three thin light green stripes. Although originally intended as a single, one class award, the concept was extended during the Vietnam War to provide for two additional levels of achievement with the creation of the Navy Rifle Marksmanship Ribbon (see page 98).

NAVY EXPERT PISTOL SHOT MEDAL

Service: Navy

Established: 1920

Criteria: Attainment of the minimum qualifying score for the expert level during prescribed shooting exercises.

Devices: None on medal (but see Navy Pistol Marksmanship Ribbon)

The Navy Expert Pistol Shot Badge was created at the same time as the Navy Expert Rifleman Badge and is awarded to Naval Personnel who qualify as experts with the pistol on a prescribed military course. The medallion is the same as the Expert Rifleman badge except for the raised inscription EXPERT PISTOL SHOT. The ribbon is navy blue with a narrow light green stripe at each edge. Also like its rifle counterpart, the concept was later extended to provide for two additional levels of achievement with the creation of the Navy Pistol Marksmanship Ribbon (see page 98).

NAVY RIFLE MARKSMANSHIP RIBBON

Bronze   Silver

Service: Navy
Established: 1969
Criteria: Attainment of the minimum qualifying scores during prescribed shooting exercises.
Devices: Bronze letter "S", silver letter "E"

The Navy Rifle Marksmanship Ribbon was established by the Secretary of the Navy on 14 October 1969 to extend the range of marksmanship awards below the Expert level. To create this "ribbon-only" award, the ribbon of the Navy Expert Rifleman Medal was retained and redesignated as the Navy Rifle Marksmanship Ribbon with devices to denote the Marksman and Sharpshooter levels. To indicate the various levels, the ribbon for the Marksman level is unadorned and the Sharpshooter level uses a bronze letter "S". To reward the attainment of the Expert level, the medal is retained unadorned but a silver letter "E," is placed on the ribbon bar. The ribbon is Navy blue with three thin stripes of light green. Attachment letters are affixed to the center of the ribbon. Earlier regulations provided for a bronze letter "E" to denote to first qualification at the Expert level and the silver "E" to indicate the "final" achievement of Expert status but this was soon discontinued in favor of the silver "E".

NAVY PISTOL MARKSMANSHIP RIBBON

Bronze   Silver

Service: Navy   Established: 1969
Criteria: Attainment of the minimum qualifying scores during prescribed shooting exercises.
Devices: Bronze letter "S", silver letter "E"

The Navy Pistol Marksmanship Ribbon was established by the Secretary of the Navy on 14 October 1969 to extend the range of marksmanship awards below the Expert level. To create this "ribbon-only" award, the ribbon of the Navy Expert Pistol Shot Medal was retained and redesignated as the Navy Pistol Marksmanship Ribbon with devices to denote the various levels. To indicate the Marksman level, the ribbon is unadorned while the Sharpshooter level uses a bronze letter "S". To reward the attainment of the Expert level, the medal is retained unadorned but a silver letter "E," is placed on the ribbon bar. The ribbon is Navy blue with two thin stripes of light green. Attachment letters are affixed to the center of the ribbon. Earlier regulations provided for a bronze letter "E" to denote to first qualification at the Expert level and the silver "E" to indicate the "final" achievement of Expert status but this was soon discontinued in favor of the silver "E".

SMALL ARMS EXPERT MARKSMANSHIP RIBBON

Bronze

Service: Air Force   Instituted: 1962
Criteria: Qualification as expert with either the M-16 rifle or standard Air Force issue handgun
Devices: Bronze star

Authorized on August 28, 1962. Awarded to Air Force personnel who, after 1 Jan 1963, qualify as Expert with either the M16 rifle or issue handgun on the Air Force qualification course or on a prescribed course or who completes the Combat Rifle Program. The ribbon is only awarded once regardless of how many times an individual qualifies as "Expert." A bronze star device is added (only once) if the recipient meets the award criteria with both the rifle and handgun.

COAST GUARD EXPERT RIFLEMAN MEDAL

Service: Coast Guard

Criteria: Attainment of the minimum qualifying score for the Expert level during prescribed shooting exercises.

Devices: None on medal (but see Coast Guard Rifle Marksmanship Ribbon)

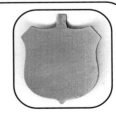

The Coast Guard Expert Rifleman Medal was established to reward outstanding rifle marksmanship and to recognize the attainment of the minimum qualifying score for the Expert level during prescribed shooting exercises. The medal is a bronze pendant in the shape of a shield, the upper portion of which contains the raised inscription: U.S. COAST GUARD EXPERT in two lines. In the center of the medal is a pair of crossed rifles beneath which is a rifle target. The reverse is plain and is suitable for engraving the recipient's name. The ribbon is navy blue with four thin white stripes, two near the center and one each towards the edges. Although originally intended as a single, one class award, the concept was extended during the Vietnam War to provide for two additional levels of achievement with the creation of the Coast Guard Rifle Marksmanship Ribbon (see below).

COAST GUARD EXPERT PISTOL SHOT MEDAL

<u>Service:</u> Coast Guard

<u>Criteria:</u> Attainment of the minimum qualifying score for the Expert level during prescribed shooting exercises.

<u>Devices:</u> None on medal (but see the Coast Guard pistol Marksmanship Ribbon)

The Coast Guard Expert Pistol Shot Medal was established to reward outstanding pistol marksmanship and to recognize the attainment of the minimum qualifying score for the Expert level during prescribed shooting exercises. The medal is a bronze pendant in the shape of a shield, the upper portion of which contains the raised inscription: U.S. COAST GUARD EXPERT in two lines. In the center of the medal is a pair of crossed pistols beneath which is a pistol target. The reverse is plain and is suitable for engraving the recipient's name. The ribbon is navy blue with two thin white stripes, one each towards each edge. Although originally intended as a single, one class award, the concept was extended during the Vietnam War to provide for two additional levels of achievement with the creation of the Coast Guard Pistol Marksmanship Ribbon (see below).

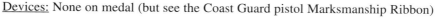

COAST GUARD RIFLE MARKSMANSHIP RIBBON

Silver   Silver   Gold

Bronze, Silver

<u>Service:</u> Coast Guard

<u>Criteria:</u> Attainment of the minimum qualifying score during prescribed shooting exercises.

<u>Devices:</u> Silver letter "E", silver letter "S" , bronze, silver rifle , gold rifle target

The Coast Guard Rifle Marksmanship Ribbon was established to extend the range of marksmanship awards below the Expert level. To create this "ribbon-only" award, the ribbon of the Coast Guard Expert Rifleman Medal was retained and redesignated as the Coast Guard Rifle Marksmanship Ribbon with devices to denote the various levels. To indicate the Marksman level, the ribbon is unadorned while the Sharpshooter level uses a silver letter "S". For the Expert level, the medal is retained unadorned but a silver letter "E" is placed on the ribbon bar. Earlier regulations provided for a bronze letter "E" to denote to first qualification at the Expert level and the silver "E" to indicate the "final" achievement of Expert status but this was soon discontinued in favor of the silver "E". The silver and bronze M14 rifle replicas denote the award of the Silver and Bronze Rifleman Excellence in Competition Badges respectively. The gold replica of a rifle target indicates the award of the Distinguished Marksman Badge. All attachments are affixed to the center of the ribbon.

COAST GUARD PISTOL MARKSMANSHIP RIBBON

Silver   Silver   Gold

Bronze, Silver

<u>Service:</u> Coast Guard

<u>Criteria:</u> Attainment of the minimum qualifying score during prescribed shooting exercises.

<u>Devices:</u> Silver letter "E", silver letter "S" , bronze, silver pistol, gold pistol target

The Coast Guard Pistol Marksmanship Ribbon was established to extend the range of marksmanship awards below the Expert level. To create this "ribbon-only" award, the ribbon of the Coast Guard Expert Pistol Shot Medal was retained and redesignated as the Coast Guard Pistol Marksmanship Ribbon with devices to denote the various levels. To indicate the Marksman level, the ribbon is unadorned while the Sharpshooter level uses a silver letter "S". For the Expert level, the medal is retained unadorned but a silver letter "E" is placed on the ribbon bar. Earlier regulations provided for a bronze letter "E" to denote to first qualification at the Expert level and the silver "E" to indicate the "final" achievement of Expert status but this was soon discontinued in favor of the silver "E". The silver and bronze M1911A1 pistol replicas denote the award of the Silver and Bronze Pistol Shot Excellence in Competition Badges respectively. The gold replica of a pistol target indicates the award of the Distinguished Pistol Shot Badge. All attachments are affixed to the center of the ribbon.

CROIX DE GUERRE

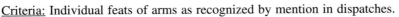

Bronze Bronze Silver Gold

Country: France

Instituted: 1915, Reinstituted: 1939

Criteria: Individual feats of arms as recognized by mention in dispatches.

Devices: Bronze palm similar to (36), bronze, silver, gold stars similar to (73) through (75) denote level of award and additional awards

Notes: Belgium awarded its own Croix de Guerre to selected U.S. personnel.

The French Croix de Guerre was instituted in 1915 and was awarded to soldiers and sailors of all ranks in the French and Allied forces for individual feats of arms mentioned in despatches by the commanding officer of any unit from an Army down to a regiment. The medal is a bronze, straight-armed cross *patte* with crossed swords in the angles. At the center of the cross is the head of the figure of *La Republique,* the traditional figure of France, around which is the raised, circular inscription, REPUBLIQUE FRANCAISE . The reverse contains the dates: 1914-1918. Emblems worn on the ribbon denote the level at which the medal was achieved. For an Army Despatch: a bronze palm or laurel branch (known as *Croix de Guerre avec Palme);* for an Army Corps Despatch: a gilt star; for a Divisional Despatch: a silver star; for a Brigade, Regimental or Unit Despatch: a bronze star. There are no restrictions on the number of devices which may be worn on the ribbon. The Croix de Guerre was reinstituted on 26 September 1939 at the outset of World War II. The new version was identical to the 1915 model with the exception of the date: 1939 on the reverse and a new ribbon 37 mm wide, predominantly green with three central 1.5 mm red stripes, 4 mm apart, and 8 mm red edges.

GALLANTRY CROSS

Bronze Silver Gold Bronze

Country: Republic of Vietnam

Instituted: 1950

Criteria: Deeds of valor and acts of courage/heroism while fighting the enemy.

Devices: Bronze palm similar to (36), bronze, silver, gold stars similar to (73) through (75) denote level of award and additional awards.

Reflecting her French Colonial heritage, Vietnam's Gallantry Cross was the direct equivalent of the French Croix de Guerre and rewarded acts of valor or heroic conduct during a conflict with an armed enemy. Although awarded sparingly during the early years of the Vietnam War, the Gallantry Cross was widely bestowed upon RVN troops as the conflict wore on. As a result, some infantrymen were required to wear a longer-than-usual suspension ribbon on the Gallantry Cross to accommodate the huge number of devices. However, awards to American troops, while quite liberal, never approached the staggering numbers awarded to indigenous personnel. As with the French Croix de Guerre, the emblems worn on the ribbon denoted the level at which the medal was achieved. For an Army or Armed Forces Despatch: a bronze palm*;* for an Army Corps Despatch: a gilt star; for a Divisional Despatch: a silver star; for a Brigade, Regimental or Unit Despatch: a bronze star. There were no restrictions on the number of devices which could be worn on the ribbon. The medal is a bronze, cross *patte* with the four arms interconnected by engravings representing two dragons with two crossed sabres between the arms, handles down. In the center is a disk showing the map of Vietnam with a laurel branch on either side and the ribbon across the map inscribed: REWARD OF THE STATE (in Vietnamese characters). The reverse contains the same design except the disk in the center is plain. The suspension is rectangular in shape and depicts two stylized dragons facing one other.

The Gallantry Cross also appeared in a second configuration, that of a unit citation. In this format, the ribbon was worn encased in a typical U.S. gold unit award frame. When conferred upon a unit, no medal was awarded but personnel of the U.S. Air Force and Naval Services wore a bronze palm on the unit award ribbon. Army recipients were also awarded the unit citation but all four devices described above were utilized to indicate the size of the cited unit. For more detailed information on Republic of Vietnam awards refer to the book *The Decorations and Medals of the Republic of Vietnam and Her Allies, 1950-1975* by Foster/ Sylvester.

ARMED FORCES HONOR MEDAL

Country: Republic of Vietnam

Instituted: 1953

Criteria: For outstanding contributions to the training and development of RVN Armed Forces.

Devices: None for U.S. military personnel.

Notes: 1st Class for officers is shown; the 2nd Class ribbon does not have the yellow edge stripes.

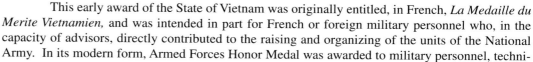

This early award of the State of Vietnam was originally entitled, in French, *La Medaille du Merite Vietnamien,* and was intended in part for French or foreign military personnel who, in the capacity of advisors, directly contributed to the raising and organizing of the units of the National Army. In its modern form, Armed Forces Honor Medal was awarded to military personnel, technicians, government employees or civilians of any nationality who contributed to the formation and organization of the Republic of Vietnam Armed Forces and the training of troops or technical cadres for the various branches. It was intended for noncombat achievements.

The Armed Forces Honor Medal is a cross formee coupled with additional points reflected down the arms and with thin blade points coming between the arms. In the central disk is a coiled dragon encircled by a ribbon inscribed at the top: ARMED FORCES HONOR MEDAL (in Vietnamese characters) and VIETNAM at the bottom. This design is, in turn, encircled by a wreath of oak leaves around the design of the cross arms. The reverse of the medal is plain. The medal is suspended from the ribbon by a laurel wreath design.

The Second Class Medal, which was awarded to NCO's and enlisted men is silver in color and has a ribbon with wide red edges and seven equally-spaced stripes, 4 golden yellow and three red, in the center. The First Class Medal was awarded to officers and fashioned in gold with a ribbon identical to the Second Class Medal except for the addition of a stripe of golden yellow at each edge. Although a device consisting of an eagle and shield was worn on the ribbon bar by indigenous troops, no devices accompanied the medal when conferred upon American officers and men.

CIVIL ACTIONS MEDAL

Country: Republic of Vietnam

Instituted: 1964

Criteria: For outstanding achievements in the field of civil actions.

Devices: Bronze palm (none authorized for Vietnamese personnel)

Notes: 1st Class for officers is shown; the 2nd Class ribbon has no center red stripes.

The Civil Actions Medal was awarded to the Republic of Vietnam Armed Forces and foreign military personnel or units that performed outstanding achievements in the field of civil actions (it could also be awarded posthumously).

The medal is an eight-pointed gold star with the points on the diagonal being smooth and long and the points on the horizontal and vertical being a little shorter and with cut lines. In the center of the star is a brown disk depicting the figures of a soldier, a child and a farmer with a shovel. The disk is, in turn, surrounded by a white ribbon inscribed: CIVIL ACTIONS above and MEDAL below, both in Vietnamese characters) with many short lines in between the inscriptions. The reverse is plain.

The Second Class Medal, which was awarded to NCO's and enlisted men, is silver in color and has a ribbon that is predominately dark green with a red stripe, 5mm wide, near each edge. The First Class Medal was awarded to officers and fashioned in gold with a ribbon identical to the Second Class Medal except for the addition of two thin red stripes in the center.

The Civil Actions award also appeared in a third configuration, that of a unit citation. In this form, the First Class ribbon was worn encased in a typical U.S. gold unit award frame. When conferred upon a unit, no medal was awarded but, in a total reversal of the Armed Forces Honor Medal's device policy, (see above), American military personnel officers and men wore a bronze palm on the unit award ribbon.

PHILIPPINE DEFENSE RIBBON AND MEDAL

★
Bronze

Country: Republic of the Philippines

Instituted: 1945

Criteria: Service in defense of the Philippines between 8 December 1941 and 15 June 1942

Devices: Bronze star

The Philippine Defense Ribbon was instituted by the Philippine Commonwealth (now The Philippine Republic) in 1944 and authorized for wear on the U.S. uniform by the United States Government in 1945. It is awarded for service in the defense of the Philippine Islands from 8 December 1941 to 15 June 1942.

To qualify, the recipient must: (a) have been assigned or stationed in Philippine territory or in Philippine waters for not less than 30 days during the above period and/or (b) participate in any engagement against the enemy on Philippine territory, in Philippine waters or in the air over the Philippines or Philippine waters during the above period.

Participation includes members of the defense garrison of the Bataan Peninsula, or of the fortified islands at the entrance to Manila Bay, or members of and present with a unit actually under enemy fire or air attack, or crew members or passengers in an airplane which was under enemy aerial or ground fire. Individuals eligible under both (a) and (b) above are entitled to wear a bronze star on the ribbon bar.

The Philippine Defense Ribbon is classified as a foreign service award. Although not authorized for wear on the U.S. military uniform, a medal was designed and struck for the Philippine Government by the Manila firm of El Oro and is a circular gold disc with an outer edge of ten scallops. The medal's center depicts a female figure with a sword and shield representing the Philippines. Above the figure are three stars and surrounding it is a green enamel wreath. At the bottom right of the medal is a map of Corregidor and Bataan. The reverse of the medal has the raised inscription: FOR THE DEFENSE OF THE PHILIPPINES in English set in four lines. The ribbon is red with a white stripe near each edge and, repeating the starred motif of the medal, three white five-pointed stars in the center.

PHILIPPINE LIBERATION RIBBON AND MEDAL

★
Bronze

Country: Republic of the Philippines

Instituted: 1945

Criteria: Service in the liberation of the Philippine Islands between 17 October 1944 and 3 September 1945

Devices: Bronze star

Awarded by the Philippine Commonwealth (now The Philippine Republic) for service in the liberation of the Philippine Islands from 17 October 1944 to 3 September 1945. In order to qualify, one of the following provisions must be met:

(a) Participation in the initial landing operation on Leyte and adjoining islands from 17-20 October 1944.
(b) Participation in any engagement against the enemy during the Philippine Liberation Campaign.
(c) Service in the Philippine Islands or in ships in Philippine Waters for not less than 30 days during the period from 17 October 1944, to 2 September 1945.
(Individuals eligible under any two of the foregoing provisions are authorized to wear one bronze star on the ribbon bar.)

Personnel eligible under all three provisions are authorized to wear two bronze stars on the ribbon bar.

The Philippine Liberation Ribbon is classified as a foreign service award. Although not authorized for wear on the U.S. military uniform, a medal was designed and struck by the Manila firm of El Oro for the Philippine Government. The medal is gold with a Philippine sword, point up, superimposed over a white native shield having three gold stars at the top and the word LIBERTY below. Below are vertical stripes of blue, white and red enamel with the sword being in the center of the white stripe. At the sides of the medal and below the shield are gold arched wings. The reverse of the medal has the raised inscription FOR THE LIBERATION OF THE PHILIPPINES set in four lines (all inscriptions are in English). The ribbon is red with a narrow blue stripe and a narrow white stripe in the center.

PHILIPPINE INDEPENDENCE RIBBON AND MEDAL

Country: Republic of the Philippines   Instituted: 1946; Criteria modified: 1954

Criteria: Receipt of both the Philippine Defense and Liberation Medals/Ribbons. Originally awarded to those present for duty in the Philippines on 4 July 1946

Devices: None

    Awarded by the Philippine Commonwealth to those members of the Armed Forces who received both the Philippine Defense Ribbon and the Philippine Liberation Ribbon. The Philippine Independence Ribbon was authorized in 1946 by the United States and the Philippine Commonwealth. It is one of the more unusual awards presented to U.S. Service personnel since it has two independent and totally applicable sets of award criteria. As originally promulgated, the ribbon was presented to those members of the United States Armed Forces who were actually serving in the Philippine Islands or in Philippine territorial waters on 4 July 1946. In 1954, the criteria were changed to grant the ribbon to all those who were previously awarded both the Philippine Defense Ribbon and the Philippine Liberation Ribbon. Although the award qualifications established in 1946 were removed from applicable regulations, no attempt was made to rescind the previous awards made under those earlier criteria. The Philippine Independence Ribbon is classified as a foreign service award. Although not authorized for wear on the U.S. military uniform, a medal was designed and struck for the Philippine Government by the Manila firm of El Oro. The medal is a circular gold disc with a female figure in the center, dressed in native garb and holding the Philippine flag. There are flags on either side of the figure and she is surrounded by a circular border. Inside the border is a raised inscription PHILIPPINE INDEPENDENCE (in English) around the top and JULY 4 1946 at the bottom. The reverse contains the inscription: GRANTED PHILIPPINE INDEPENDENCE BY THE UNITED STATES OF AMERICA set in six lines (also in English). The ribbon is derived from the colors of the Philippine flag and consists of a medium blue base with a narrow white center stripe bordered by thin red stripes. There are thin, golden yellow stripes at each edge.

UNITED NATIONS SERVICE MEDAL (KOREA)

Service: All Services   Instituted: 1951   Devices: None

Criteria: Service on behalf of the United Nations in Korea between 27 June 1950 and 27 July 1954

Notes: Above date denotes when award was authorized for wear by U.S. Armed Forces personnel

    For service on behalf of the United Nations in Korea during the Korean Conflict. The United Nations Service Medal is classified as a foreign service award. It was authorized by the United Nations General Assembly on 12 December 1950 and the Department of Defense approved it for United States Armed Forces on 27 November 1951. The medal was awarded to any member of the United States Armed Forces for service in support of the United Nations Command during the period from 27 June 1950 to 27 July 1954. Individuals who were awarded the Korean Service Medal automatically established eligibility for this decoration.

    The United Nations Service Medal was designed by the United Nations. The medal is a circular bronze disc containing the United Nations emblem (a polar projection of the world taken from the North Pole, encircled by two olive branches). The reverse of the medal has the raised inscription FOR SERVICE IN DEFENCE OF THE PRINCIPLES OF THE CHARTER OF THE UNITED NATIONS set in five lines. The medal is suspended permanently from a bar, similar to British medals, with the raised inscription KOREA. The ribbon passes through the bar and is narrow stripes of alternating light blue ("United Nations Blue") and white. For further information on United Nations medals, see: *United Nations Medals and Missions* by Lawrence H. Borts, Medals of America Press, 1998

INTER-AMERICAN DEFENSE BOARD MEDAL

★
Gold

Service: All Services   Instituted: 1981   Devices: Gold star

Criteria: Service with the Inter-American Defense Board for at least one year

Notes: Above date denotes when award was authorized for wear by U.S. military personnel

    The medal and ribbon were authorized on December 11, 1945 by the Inter-American Defense Board, (IADB) and were approved by the U.S. Department of Defense for wear by U.S. military personnel on May 12, 1981. The IADB Medal is classified as a foreign service award and is awarded for permanent wear to military personnel who have served on the Inter-American Defense Board for at least one year, either as chairman of the board, delegates, advisors, officers of the staff, as officers of the secretariat or officers of the Inter-American Defense College. U.S. Military personnel who have been awarded the medal may wear it when attending meetings, ceremonies or other functions where Latin-American members of the board are present.

    The medal is a golden-bronze circular disk with a representation of the globe of the world in the center depicting the Western Hemisphere. Around the periphery of the globe are the arrayed the flags of the member nations of the IADB. The reverse of the medal is plain. A five-sixteenth inch dia. gold star device is worn on the ribbon bar and the suspension ribbon for each five (5) years of service to the IADB.

UNITED NATIONS MEDAL

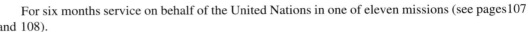

Bronze

Instituted: 1964

Criteria: 6 months service with any U.N. peacekeeping mission

Devices: Bronze star

Notes: Above date denotes when award was authorized for wear by U.S. Armed Forces personnel

For six months service on behalf of the United Nations in one of eleven missions (see pages 107 and 108).

The United Nations Medal is designated as a foreign service award. It was authorized by the United Nations General Assembly on 30 July 1959 and approved for wear on the U.S. military uniform by Executive Order on 11 March 1964. The medal is awarded to any member of the United States Armed Forces for not less than six months service in support of a United Nations mission.

The United Nations Medal was designed by the United Nations. The medal is a bronze disc with the United Nations emblem (a polar projection of the world taken from the North Pole, encircled by two olive branches). Centered above this are the bold letters UN. The reverse of the medal contains the raised inscription: IN THE SERVICE OF PEACE on two lines. The medallion for all UN operations is the same for all authorized operations. The only ribbon originally authorized for wear on the U.S. uniform is United Nations blue with narrow stripes of white near the edges. In recent years, however, U.S. policy was changed to permit the unique ribbon authorized for each United Nations operation to be worn (see page 38). Individuals who have participated in more than one UN operation wear only the first ribbon/medal for which they qualify with a three-sixteenth inch bronze star for each subsequent award. For further information on United Nations medals, see: *United Nations Medals and Missions* by Lawrence H. Borts, Medals of America Press, 1998

NATO MEDAL

Service: All Services

Instituted: Yugoslavia: July 1, 1992; Kosovo: June 7, 2000

Criteria: Service under NATO command and in direct support of NATO operations for (a) 30 days service in or 90 days outside the former Republic of Yugoslavia and the Adriatic Sea or (b) 30 continuous/accumulated days on land, at sea or in the air space of the Province of Kosovo

Devices: Bronze star

Notes: Above dates denote when awards were authorized for wear by U.S. military personnel

FORMER YUGOSLAVIA

NATO MEDAL (KOSOVO)

Awarded to U.S. military personnel for service under the NATO command and in direct support of NATO operations. Recipients, as of this writing, may qualify for two NATO operations:

(1) Former Yugoslavia: 30 days service inside or 90 days outside the former Republic of Yugoslavia after July 1, 1992 to a date to be determined.

(2) Kosovo: 30 continuous/accumulated days in or around the former Yugoslavian province of Kosovo from October 13, 1998 to a date to be determined.

Multiple rotations or tours in either operational area will only qualify for a single award of that medal.

The NATO Medal, like the United Nations Medal, has a common planchet/pendant but comes with unique ribbons for each operation. As in the case of the United Nations, US Service personnel who qualify for both NATO Medals will wear the first medal/ribbon awarded and a bronze service star on the ribbon bar and suspension ribbon to denote the second award. As before however, the two medal clasps which may accompany the medal (i.e.: FORMER YUGOSLAVIA and KOSOVO) may not be worn on the US military uniform.

The medal is a bronze disk featuring the NATO symbol in the center surrounded by olive branches around the periphery. The reverse contains the inscription: NORTH ATLANTIC TREATY ORGANIZATION in English around the top edge and the same wording in French along the lower edge. A horizontal olive branch separates the central area into two areas. Atop this, set in three lines, is the inscription: IN SERVICE OF PEACE AND FREEDOM in English. The same text in French on four lines is inscribed in the lower half.

MULTINATIONAL FORCE & OBSERVERS MEDAL

Service: All Services

Instituted: 1982

3
Bronze

Criteria: Originally 90 days, then 170 days of service with the Multinational Force & Observers peacekeeping force in the Sinai Desert

Devices: Bronze numeral

Notes: Above date denotes when award was authorized for wear by U.S. military personnel

The international peacekeeping force known as The Multinational Force and Observers (MFO) was established following the ratification of the Camp David Accords and the 1979 peace treaty between Israel and Egypt. Its sole purpose was to monitor the withdrawal of Israeli forces from the occupied portions of the Sinai Peninsula and the return of that territory to the sovereignty of Egypt.

The MFO Medal was established by the Director General on March 24, 1982 to recognize those personnel who served at least 90 days with the Multinational Force and Observers after August 3,1981 (the requirement was changed to 170 days after March 15, 1985). Periods of service on behalf of the MFO outside the Sinai are also counted towards medal eligibility.

The medal is a bronze disk depicting a stylized dove of peace surrounded by olive branches in its center. Around the edge of the medallion are the raised inscriptions: MULTINATIONAL FORCE at the top and: & OBSERVERS on the lower half. The reverse is plain with the inscription: UNITED IN SERVICE FOR PEACE set on 5 lines (all inscriptions are in English).

The second and subsequent tours with the MFO are indicated by appropriate bronze numerals affixed to the center of the ribbon bar or suspension ribbon starting with the numeral "2"- the ribbon/medal itself representing the first award.

REPUBLIC OF VIETNAM CAMPAIGN MEDAL

Silver

Country: Republic of Vietnam

Service: All Services   Instituted: 1966

Criteria: 6 months service in the Republic of Vietnam between 1961 and 1973 or if wounded, captured or killed in action during the above period

Devices: Silver date bar

Notes: Bar inscribed "1960" is the only authorized version

The Republic of Vietnam Campaign Medal was established by the Government of the Republic of Vietnam on May 12, 1964 and authorized for award to members of the United States Armed Forces by the Department of Defense on June 20, 1966. To qualify for award personnel must meet one of the following requirements:

(1) Have served in the Republic of Vietnam for 6 months during the period from 1 March 1961 to 28 March 1973,

(2) Have served outside the geographical limits of the Republic of Vietnam and contributed direct combat support to the Republic of Vietnam and Armed Forces for 6 months. Such individuals must meet the criteria established for the Armed Forces Expeditionary Medal (Vietnam) or the Vietnam Service Medal, during .the period of service required to qualify for the Republic of Vietnam Campaign Medal.

(3) Have served for less than 6 months and have been wounded by hostile forces, captured by hostile forces, but later escaped, was rescued or released; or killed in action.

Special eligibility rules were established for personnel assigned in the Republic of Vietnam on 28 January 1973. To be eligible for the medal, an individual must have served a minimum of 60 days in the Republic of Vietnam as of that date or have completed a minimum of 60 days service in the Republic of Vietnam during the period from 28 January 1973 to 28 March 1973, inclusive.

The Republic of Vietnam Campaign Medal is a white six-pointed star with cut lined, broad gold star points between and a central green disk with a map of Vietnam in silver surmounted with three painted flames in red, signifying the three regions of Vietnam. The reverse contains the inscription *VIET-NAM* in a lined circle in the center with the name of the medal inscribed in Vietnamese text at the upper and lower edges separated by many short lines. The device, an integral part of the award, is a silver ribbon 28mm long on the suspension ribbon and 15mm long on the service bar inscribed: "1960- " and was evidently intended to include a terminal date for the hostilities. Many examples of this medal are found with devices inscribed with other dates but the only version authorized for U.S. personnel is the one described herein.

REPUBLIC OF KOREA WAR SERVICE MEDAL

Service: All Services

Country: Republic of Korea

Instituted: 1999

Criteria: 6 months service in the Republic of Korea between 1950 and 1953

Devices: None

Notes: The date above indicates when the award was accepted by the United States Government.

* Some original 1953 medals had a tae-guk in the center of the drape like the ribbon.

The Republic of Korea War Service Medal was established in 1951 by the Government of the Republic of Korea for presentation to the foreign military personnel who served on or over the Korean Peninsula or in its territorial waters between June 27, 1950 and July 27, 1953. To be eligible for this award, US military personnel must have been on permanent assignment or on temporary duty for 30 consecutive days or 60 non-consecutive days. The duty must have been performed within the territorial limits of Korea, in the waters immediately adjacent thereto or in aerial flight over Korea participating in actual combat operations or in support of combat operations. The 48 year interval between establishment and its formal acceptance represents the longest period of time in U.S. history between an event of significant national and military importance and the establishment of an appropriate commemorative medal. This dubious record was formerly held by the Marine Corps Expeditionary Medal (45 years).

The medal is a bronze disk containing a map of the Korean Peninsula at top center over a grid of the world and olive branches on either side of the design. Below the map are two crossed bullets. In the center of the ribbon and earlier medal drapes (1950's), is an ancient oriental symbol called a tae-guk (the top half is red and the bottom half is blue). The reverse contains the inscription: FOR SERVICE IN KOREA in English embossed on two lines with two small blank plaques on which the recipient's name may be engraved.

KUWAIT LIBERATION MEDAL (SAUDI ARABIA)

Gold

Service: All Services

Instituted: 1991

Criteria: Participation in, or support of, Operation Desert Storm (1991)

Devices: Gold palm tree device

Notes: Support must have been performed in theater (e.g.: Persian Gulf, Red Sea, Iraq, Kuwait, Saudi Arabia, Gulf of Oman, etc.)

Established in 1991 by the Government of Saudi Arabia for members of the Coalition Forces who participated in Operation DESERT STORM and the liberation of Kuwait. In the same year, the U.S. Defense Department authorized the acceptance and wearing of the Kuwait Liberation Medal by members of the Armed Forces of the United States.

To be eligible, U.S. military personnel must have served for at least one day in support of operation DESERT STORM between January 17 and February 28, 1991 in The Persian Gulf, Red Sea, Gulf of Oman, portions of the Arabian Sea, The Gulf of Aden or the total land areas of Iraq, Kuwait, Saudi Arabia, Oman, Bahrain, Qatar, and the United Arab Emirates. The recipient must have been attached to or regularly serving for one or more days with an organization participating in ground and/or shore operations, aboard a naval vessel directly supporting military operations, actually participating as a crew member in one or more aerial flights supporting military operations in the areas designated above or serving on temporary duty for 30 consecutive days during this period. That time limitation may be waived for people participating in actual combat operations.

The medal depicts the map of Kuwait in the center with a crown at its top between two encircling palm branches, all of which is fashioned in gold. Above this is a gold palm tree surmounted by two crossed swords. Surrounding the entire design is a representation of an exploding bomb in silver. The reverse is plain. The ribbon bar is issued with a replica of the palm tree with crossed swords found on the medal and is the only authorized attachment.

KUWAIT LIBERATION MEDAL (EMIRATE OF KUWAIT)

Service: All Services   Instituted: 1995

Criteria: Participation in, or support of, Operations Desert Shield and/or Desert Storm (1990-93)

Devices: None

Notes: Above date denotes when award was authorized for wear by U.S. military personnel

Established in July, 1994 by the Government of Kuwait for members of the United States military who participated in Operations DESERT SHIELD and DESERT STORM. On March 16, 1995, the Secretary of Defense authorized the acceptance and wearing of the Kuwait Liberation Medal (Kuwait) by members of the Armed Forces of the United States. To be eligible, U.S. military personnel must have served in support of Operations DESERT SHIELD and DESERT STORM between August 2, 1990 and August 31, 1993, in The Arabian Gulf, Red Sea, Gulf of Oman, portions of the Arabian Sea , The Gulf of Aden or the total land areas of Iraq, Kuwait, Saudi Arabia, Oman, Bahrain, Qatar, and the United Arab Emirates. The recipient must have been attached to or regularly serving for one or more days with an organization participating in ground and/ or shore operations, aboard a naval vessel directly supporting military operations, actually participating as a crew member in one or more aerial flights directly supporting military operations in the areas designated above or serving on temporary duty for 30 consecutive days or 60 nonconsecutive days during this period. That time limitation may be waived for people participating in actual combat operations. The Kuwait Liberation Medal (Kuwait) follows the Kuwait Liberation Medal from the government of Saudi Arabia in the order of precedence. The medal is a bronze disk which depicts the Kuwaiti Coat of Arms with the Arabic inscription: 1991 - LIBERATION MEDAL. The reverse contains a map of Kuwait with a series of rays emanating from the center out to the edge of the medal- all in bas-relief. The ribbon bar may be one of the most unusual ever displayed on the American military uniform. It consists of three equal stripes of red, white and green with a black, trapezoidal-shaped section silk-screened across the entire upper half. No attachments are authorized for the medal or ribbon.

United Nations Missions Participated in by United States Armed Forces Personnel

Until recently, U.S. military personnel serving on or with a United Nations mission were permitted to wear only two UN medals, the United Nations Korean Service Medal and the UNTSO (UN Truce Supervision Organization) Medal.

A change in Department of Defense regulations now authorizes military personnel to wear the ribbon of one of 11 UN missions. Only one UN ribbon may be worn. Subsequent mission awards are denoted by three-sixteenth inch bronze stars on the originally-earned UN ribbon. The United States has participated in 17 UN Missions (as of the date this book was published). To date, U.S. military personnel are permitted to wear medals from 11 of these missions as well as the United Nations Special Service Medal. The authorized medals are shown below:

1. KOREA - UNITED NATIONS KOREAN SERVICE
 COUNTRY/LOCATION: Korea   DATES: June 1950 to July 1953
 COUNTRIES PARTICIPATING: (19) Australia, Belgium, Canada, Colombia, Ethiopia, France, Greece, Luxembourg, Netherlands, New Zealand, Philippines, South Korea, Thailand, Turkey, Union of South Africa, United Kingdom, United States (plus Denmark and Italy which provided medical support)
 MAXIMUM STRENGTH (approx): 1,000,000 (UN & South Korea combined)
 CURRENT STRENGTH: ------FATALITIES (approx): Korea: 415,000, U.S.: 55,000, Other UN: 3,100   CLASP(S): None

2. UNTSO - UNITED NATIONS TRUCE SUPERVISION ORGANIZATION
COUNTRY/LOCATION: Palestine/Israel   DATES: June 1948 to present
COUNTRIES PARTICIPATING: (20) Argentina, Australia, Austria, Belgium, Canada, Chile, China, Denmark, Finland, France, Ireland, Italy, Myanmar, Netherlands, New Zealand, Norway, Sweden, Switzerland, United States, USSR
MAXIMUM STRENGTH: 572 military observers (1948)
CURRENT STRENGTH: 143 (1999)
FATALITIES: 38 (1996)

3. UNMOGIP - UNITED NATIONS MILITARY OBSERVER GROUP IN INDIA AND PAKISTAN
COUNTRY/LOCATION: India, Pakistan (Jammu & Kashmir)
DATES: January 1949 to present
COUNTRIES PARTICIPATING: (15) Australia, Belgium, Canada, Chile, Denmark, Ecuador, Finland, Italy, Korean Republic, Mexico, New Zealand, Norway, Sweden, United States, Uruguay
MAXIMUM STRENGTH: 102 military observers (1965)
CURRENT STRENGTH: 45 (1999)   FATALITIES: 9 (1996)   CLASP(S): None

4. UNSF - United Nations Security Force in West New Guinea (West Irian) UNTEA-United Nations Temporary Executive Authority
COUNTRY/LOCATION: West Irian (West New Guinea)
DATES: October 1962 to April 1963
COUNTRIES PARTICIPATING: (9) Brazil, Canada, Ceylon, India, Ireland, Nigeria, Pakistan, Sweden, United States
MAXIMUM STRENGTH: 1,576 military observers (1963)
STRENGTH AT WITHDRAWAL: 1,576   FATALITIES: None   CLASP(S): None

5. UNIKOM - UNITED NATIONS IRAQ-KUWAIT OBSERVATION MISSION

COUNTRY/LOCATION: Iraq, Kuwait DATES: April 1991 to present
COUNTRIES PARTICIPATING: (36) Argentina, Austria, Bangladesh, Canada, Chile, China, Denmark, Fiji, Finland, France, Germany, Ghana, Greece, Hungary, India, Indonesia, Ireland, Italy, Kenya, Malaysia, Nigeria, Norway, Pakistan, Poland, Romania, Russian Federation, Senegal, Singapore, Sweden, Switzerland, Thailand, Turkey, United Kingdom, United States, Uruguay, Venezuela
MAXIMUM STRENGTH: 1,187 military observers CURRENTSTRENGTH: 1,102 (1999) FATALITIES: 6 (1996)
CLASP(S): None

6.MINURSO - UNITED NATIONS MISSION FOR THE REFERENDUM IN WESTERN SAHARA

COUNTRY/LOCATION: Western Sahara (Morocco) DATES: September 1991 to present
COUNTRIES PARTICIPATING: (36) Argentina, Australia, Austria, Bangladesh, Belgium, Canada, China, Egypt, El Salvador, Finland, France, Germany, Ghana, Greece, Guinea-Bissau, Honduras, Hungary, Ireland, Italy, Kenya, Korean Republic, Malaysia, Nigeria, Norway, Pakistan, Peru, Poland, Portugal, Russian Federation, Switzerland, Togo, Tunisia, United Kingdom, United States, Uruguay, Venezuela
MAXIMUM STRENGTH: 3,000 authorized (1,700 military observers and troops, 300 police officers, approx. 1,000 civilian personnel)
CURRENT STRENGTH: 316 (1999) FATALITIES: 7 (1996) CLASP(S): None

7. UNAMIC - UNITED NATIONS ADVANCE MISSION IN CAMBODIA COUNTRY/LOCATION: CAMBODIA

DATES: November 1991 to March 1992
COUNTRIES PARTICIPATING: (24) Algeria, Argentina, Australia, Austria, Belgium, Canada, China, France, Germany, Ghana, India, Indonesia, Ireland, Malaysia, New Zealand, Pakistan, Poland, Russian Federation, Senegal, Thailand, Tunisia, United Kingdom, United States, Uruguay
MAXIMUM STRENGTH: 1,090 military and civilian personnel (1992)
STRENGTH AT TRANSITION TO UNTAC: 1,090 FATALITIES: None

8. UNPROFOR - UNITED NATIONS PROTECTION FORCE

COUNTRY/LOCATION: Former Yugoslavia (Bosnia, Herzegovina, Croatia, Serbia, Montenegro, Macedonia) DATES: March 1992 to December 1995
COUNTRIES PARTICIPATING: (43) Argentina, Australia, Bangladesh, Belgium, Brazil, Canada, Colombia, Czech Republic, Denmark, Egypt, Finland, France, Germany, Ghana, India, Indonesia, Ireland, Jordan, Kenya, Lithuania, Luxembourg, Malaysia, Nepal, Netherlands, New Zealand, Nigeria, Norway, Pakistan, Poland, Portugal, Russian Federation, Senegal, Slovakia, Spain, Sweden, Switzerland, Thailand, Tunisia, Turkey, Ukraine, United Kingdom, United States, Venezuela
MAXIMUM STRENGTH: 39,922 (38,614 troops and support personnel, 637 military observers, 671 civilian police and 4,058 staff (1994)
STRENGTH AT WITHDRAWAL: 2,675 FATALITIES: 207 CLASP(S): None

9. UNTAC - UNITED NATIONS TRANSITIONAL AUTHORITY IN CAMBODIA

LOCATION: Cambodia DATES: Mar. 1992 to Sept. 1993
COUNTRIES PARTICIPATING: (46) Algeria, Argentina, Australia, Austria, Bangladesh, Belgium, Brunei, Bulgaria, Cameroon, Canada, Chile, China, Colombia, Egypt, Fiji, France, Germany, Ghana, Hungary, India, Indonesia, Ireland, Italy, Japan, Jordan, Kenya, Malaysia, Morocco, Namibia, Nepal, Netherlands, New Zealand, Nigeria, Norway, Pakistan, Philippines, Poland, Russian Federation, Senegal, Singapore, Sweden, Thailand, Tunisia, United Kingdom, United States, Uruguay
MAXIMUM STRENGTH: 19,350 military and civilian personnel (1993)
STRENGTH AT WITHDRAWAL: 2,500 (approx.) FATALITIES: 78 CLASP(S): UNAMIC (later withdrawn)

10. UNOSOM II - UNITED NATIONS OPERATION IN SOMALIA II

COUNTRY/LOCATION: Somalia _____ DATES: May 1993 to March 1995
COUNTRIES PARTICIPATING: (34) Australia, Bangladesh, Belgium, Botswana, Canada, Egypt, France, Germany, Ghana, Greece, India, Indonesia, Ireland, Italy, Korean Republic, Kuwait, Malaysia, Morocco, Nepal, Netherlands, New Zealand, Nigeria, Norway, Pakistan, Philippines, Romania, Saudi Arabia, Sweden, Tunisia, Turkey, United Arab Emirates, United States, Zambia, Zimbabwe
MAXIMUM STRENGTH: 30,800 authorized (28,000 military personnel and approximately 2,800 civilian staff)
STRENGTH AT WITHDRAWAL:14,968 FATALITIES: 147 CLASP(S): None

11.UNMIH - UNITED NATIONS MISSION IN HAITI

COUNTRY/LOCATION: Haiti DATES: Sept 1993 to June 1996
COUNTRIES PARTICIPATING: (34) Algeria, Antigua and Barbuda, Argentina, Austria, Bahamas, Bangladesh, Barbados, Belize, Benin, Canada, Djibouti, France, Guatemala, Guinea-Bissau, Guyana, Honduras, India, Ireland, Jamaica, Jordan, Mali. Nepal, Netherlands, New Zealand, Pakistan, Philippines, Russian Federation, St.Kitts & Nevis, St.Lucia, Suriname, Togo, Trinidad and Tobago, Tunisia, United States
MAXIMUM STRENGTH: 6,065 military personnel and 847 civilian police (1995)
STRENGTH AT TRANSITION TO UNSMIH: 1,200 troops and 300 civilian police FATALITIES: 6 CLASP(S): None

---

UNSSM - UNITED NATIONS SPECIAL SERVICE MEDAL

BACKGROUND: Established in 1994 by the Secretary-General of the United Nations, the United Nations Medal for Special Service is awarded to military and civilian police personnel serving the United Nations in capacities other than established peacekeeping missions or those permanently assigned to United Nations Headquarters. The Medal for Special Service may be awarded to eligible personnel serving for a minimum of ninety (90) consecutive days under the control of the United Nations in operations or offices for which no other United Nations award is authorized. Posthumous awards may be granted to personnel otherwise eligible for the medal who die while serving under the United Nations before completing the required 90 consecutive days of service.
CLASP(S): Clasps engraved with the name of the country or the United Nations organization (e.g., UNHCR, UNSCOM, MINUGUA, etc.) are added to the medal suspension ribbon and ribbon bar.

The "Ribbon Only" Award Syndrome

The next chapter in this review of the totally unique American awards system will deal with the ribbons depicted on the following pages. These items fall into a special class of honors known as "ribbon-only" awards since there is no associated medal. Although the U.S. is not the only country which has employed this variety of award, it has certainly become the world's greatest proponent of the format.

The practice seems to stem from the late 19th century when various German States, among them Baden, Bavaria, Mecklenburg and Prussia, issued "schnalle" or buckles to members of their Landwehr (militia) as a reward for long and faithful service. The award usually consisted of a unicolored ribbon on which the sovereign's initials were embroidered along with other forms of ornamentation (e.g.: Maltese crosses, the class of the award (II), etc). The ribbon was surrounded by a metal frame and affixed to the uniform by a simple pin back, thus giving the impression of a belt buckle (hence the name).

The first such items in the U.S. inventory were the Presidential Unit Citations established by the Army and Navy during World War II, both as a reward to units/ships cited for collective battle honors and as visual recognition of the individuals who served in such units. As an interesting sidelight, it will be noted that all U.S. Army unit awards, whether by design or pure accident, reintroduce the buckle format by surrounding each ribbon with a gold frame containing a design of laurel leaves. The influence of the Senior Service on others may also be seen in the unit awards issued by the Department of Defense, by our wartime allies (The Republics of the Philippines, Korea and Vietnam) and most recently, the Coast Guard, all of which emulate the Army's gold frame arrangement.

The Marine Corps Reserve Ribbon (now obsolete) was the first non-unit award to appear in this form and, as can be seen, was the forerunner of a large number of ribbons having no medallic counterparts. Whether the form was selected because of simplicity, to provide decorations and service medals a higher degree of stature or forced by budgetary considerations, it has certainly become a major element in the U.S. award structure. It may be expected to continue as a major factor in future awards policies.

Bronze

N.C.O. PROFESSIONAL DEVELOPMENT RIBBON

Service: Army
Instituted: 1981
Criteria: Successful completion of designated NCO professional development courses.
Devices: Bronze numeral

The Non-Commissioned Officer Professional Development Ribbon was established by the Secretary of the Army on April 10, 1981 and is awarded to members of the U.S. Army, Army National Guard and Army Reserve who successfully complete designated NCO professional development courses. To indicate completion of specific levels of subsequent courses, a bronze numeral is affixed to the center of the ribbon. The basic ribbon itself represents the Primary Level, the numeral "2" indicates the Basic Level course, the numeral "3" denotes the Advanced Level course and the numeral "4" indicates the Senior Level (Sergeants Major Academy) course. At one time, the numeral "5" signified completion of the Sergeants Major Academy but this was later rescinded.

ARMY SERVICE RIBBON

Service: Army
Instituted: 1981
Criteria: Successful completion of initial entry training.
Devices: None

The Army Service ribbon was established on April 10, 1981 by the Secretary of the Army and is awarded to members of the Army, Army Reserve and Army National Guard for successful completion of initial-entry training. It may also be awarded retroactively to those personnel who completed the required training before August 1, 1981. Officers will be awarded this ribbon upon successful completion of their basic/orientation or higher level course. Enlisted soldiers will be awarded the ribbon upon successful completion of their initial MOS-producing course. Officer or Enlisted personnel assigned to a specialty, special skill identifier or MOS based on civilian or other service acquired skills, will be awarded the ribbon upon honorable completion of four months active service. Since only one award is authorized, no devices are worn with this ribbon.

Bronze

ARMY OVERSEAS SERVICE RIBBON

Service: Army

Instituted: 1981

Criteria: Successful completion of normal overseas tours not recognized by any other service award.

Devices: Bronze numeral

The Army Overseas Service Ribbon was established by the Secretary of the Army on April 10, 1981. Effective August 1, 1981, the Army Overseas Service Ribbon is awarded to all members of the Active Army, Army National Guard, and Army Reserve in an active Reserve status for successful completion of overseas tours if the tour is not recognized by the award of another service or campaign medal. The ribbon may be awarded retroactively to personnel who were credited with a normal overseas tour completion before August 1, 1981, provided they had an Active Army status on or after August 1, 1981. Subsequent tours will be indicated by the use of numerals with the basic ribbon representing the first tour, the bronze numeral "2" denoting the second tour, the numeral "3" the third, etc.

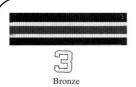
Bronze

ARMY RESERVE COMPONENTS OVERSEAS TRAINING RIBBON

Service: Army   Instituted: 1984

Criteria: Successful completion of annual training or active duty training for 10 consecutive duty days on foreign soil.

Devices: Bronze numeral

The Reserve Components Overseas Training Ribbon was established on July 11, 1984 by the Secretary of the Army and is awarded to members of the Army Reserves or Army National Guard for successful completion of annual training or active duty for training for a period of not less than ten consecutive duty days on foreign soil (outside the 50 states, District of Columbia, and U.S. possessions and territories), in the performance of duties in conjunction with Active Army, Joint Services, or Allied Forces. The ribbon may be awarded retroactively to personnel who successfully completed annual training or active duty for training on foreign soil in a Reserve status prior to July 11, 1984, provided they had an active status in the Reserve Components on or after July 11, 1984. Bronze numerals are used to denote second and subsequent awards.

☆ Silver   ★ Bronze

NAVY SEA SERVICE DEPLOYMENT RIBBON

Service: Navy, Marine Corps   Instituted: 1981 (retroactive to 1974)

Criteria: 12 months active duty on deployed vessels operating away from their home port for extended periods

Devices: Bronze, silver star

The Navy Sea Service Deployment Ribbon was approved by the Secretary of the Navy in 1981 and made retroactive to 15 August 1974. The ribbon was created to recognize the unique and demanding nature of sea service and the arduous duty attendant with such service deployments. The award is made to Navy and Marine Corps personnel for twelve months of accumulated sea duty or duty with the Fleet Marine Force, which includes at least one, ninety day deployment.

The ribbon consists of a wide center stripe of light blue, bordered on either side by a narrow stripe of medium blue and equal stripes of gold, red and navy blue. Additional awards are denoted by three-sixteenth inch bronze stars. The Navy Sea Service Deployment Ribbon is worn after the Outstanding Volunteer Service Medal and before the Navy Arctic Service Ribbon.

NAVY ARCTIC SERVICE RIBBON

Service: Navy, Marine Corps

Instituted: 1986

Criteria: 28 days of service on naval vessels operating above the Arctic Circle

The Navy Arctic Service Ribbon was established by the Secretary of the Navy on 8 May 1986 and authorized for wear on 3 June 1987. The ribbon is awarded to members of the Naval Service who participate in operations in support of the Arctic Warfare Program. To be eligible, the individual must have served 28 days north of, or within 50 miles of the Marginal Ice Zone (MIZ). The MIZ is defined as an area consisting of more than 10% ice concentration. The ribbon is medium blue with a narrow center stripe of navy blue flanked on either side by three thin stripes of gradually lighter shades of blue, a narrow stripe of white, followed again by two thin stripes of gradually darker shades of blue. There are no provisions for additional awards. The Navy Arctic Service Ribbon is worn after the Navy Sea Service Deployment Ribbon and before the Navy and Marine Corps Overseas Service Ribbon.

Silver   Bronze

NAVAL RESERVE SEA SERVICE RIBBON

Service: Navy

Instituted: 1987

Criteria: 24 months of cumulative service embarked on Naval Reserve vessels or an embarked Reserve unit.

Devices: Bronze, silver star

The Naval Reserve Sea Service Ribbon was authorized by the Secretary of the Navy on May 28, 1986. It is awarded to officer and enlisted personnel of the U.S. Navy and Naval Reserve who perform active duty or Selected Reserve service, or any combination of active or Selected Reserve service after 15 August 1974 aboard a Naval Reserve ship or its Reserve unit or an embarked active or Reserve staff, for a cumulative total of 24 months. Qualifying ship duty includes duty in a self-propelled Naval Reserve ship, boat, or craft operated under the operational control of fleet or type commanders. Selected Reserve duty with staffs which regularly embark in such Naval Reserve ships, craft, or boats, is also qualifying provided at least 50 percent of the drills performed for each creditable period have been underway drills. A 3/16 inch bronze star denotes a subsequent award.

Silver   Bronze

NAVY AND MARINE CORPS OVERSEAS SERVICE RIBBON

Service: Navy, Marine Corps

Instituted: 1987

Criteria: 12 months consecutive or accumulated duty at an overseas shore base duty station

Devices: Bronze, silver star

The Navy and Marine Corps Overseas Service Ribbon was approved by the Secretary of the Navy on 3 June 1987 and made retroactive to 15 August 1974. The award is made to active duty members of the Naval Service who serve 12 months consecutive or accumulated active duty at an overseas duty station; or 30 consecutive days or 45 cumulative days of active duty for training or temporary active duty.

The ribbon is intended to recognize individuals who serve overseas, but are not members of ships, squadrons or detachments of the Fleet Marine Force and do not qualify for the Navy Sea Service Deployment Ribbon. An individual cannot be awarded the Navy and Marine Corps Overseas Service Ribbon and the Navy Sea Service Deployment Ribbon for the same period of service. The Navy and Marine Corps Overseas Service Ribbon is worn after the Navy Arctic Service Ribbon and before the Marine Corps Recruiting Ribbon. Additional awards are denoted by three-sixteenth inch bronze stars.

Silver   Bronze

NAVY RECRUITING SERVICE RIBBON

Service: Navy

Instituted: 1986 (retroactive to 1974)

Criteria: For successful completion of three consecutive years of recruiting duty.

Devices: Bronze, silver star

The Navy Recruiting Service Ribbon was established in 1986 (retroactive to 15 August 1974) and is awarded for successful completion of three consecutive years of recruiting duty. The ribbon is gold with Navy blue stripes near the borders and at the center. The blue center stripe has a thin red stripe, and is bordered by stripes of light green on either side. The Navy Recruiting Service Ribbon is worn after the Navy and Marine Corps Overseas Service Ribbon and before the Navy Recruit Training Service Ribbon. Additional awards are denoted by three-sixteenth inch bronze stars.

Silver   Bronze

NAVY RECRUIT TRAINING SERVICE RIBBON

Service: Navy,

Instituted: 1998 (retroactive to 1995)

Criteria: Successful service as a Navy Recruit Division Commander (RDC)

Devices: Bronze, silver star

The Navy Recruit Training Service Ribbon was established in 1998 (retroactive to 1995) and is awarded for successful service as a Navy Recruit Division Commander (RDC) and training at least nine Divisions over a minimum tour of three years. The ribbon has a broad scarlet center with equal-sized blue stripes on either side and gold edges. The Navy Recruit Training Service Ribbon is worn after the Navy Recruiting Service Ribbon and before the Armed Forces Reserve Medal. Additional awards are denoted by three-sixteenth inch bronze stars.

MARINE CORPS RECRUITING RIBBON

Service: Marine Corps   Instituted: 1995 (retroactive to 1973)

Criteria: Successful completion of 3 consecutive years of recruiting duty

Devices: Bronze, silver star

The Marine Corps Recruiting Ribbon was established in 1995 and made retroactive to 1973. The ribbon is awarded to Marines who successfully complete three consecutive years of recruiting duty.

The ribbon is dark blue with a wide red center stripe. The Marine Corps Recruiting Ribbon is worn after the Navy and Marine Corps Overseas Service Ribbon and before the Marine Corps Drill Instructor Ribbon. Additional awards are denoted by three-sixteenth inch bronze stars.

MARINE CORPS DRILL INSTRUCTOR RIBBON

Service: Marine Corps   Instituted: 1997 (retroactive to 1952)

Criteria: Successful completion of a tour of duty as a drill instructor (staff billets require completion of 18 months to be eligible).

Devices: Bronze, silver star

The Marine Corps Drill Instructor Ribbon was established in 1997 (retroactive to 6 October 1952) and is awarded to Marines who serve successfully in a drill instructor assignment. An assignment is defined as a tour of a minimum of 20 months for those who received their 8511 MOS before December 1996 or 30 months thereafter.

The ribbon is also awarded to Marines who have successfully completed assignments of at least 18 cumulative months in the following billets:

Recruit Training Battalion -
Commanding Officer
   Executive Officer
   S-3 Officer
   Sergeant Major

Recruit Training Company - Commanding
Officer (Less Headquarters Company)
   Executive Officer
   First Sergeant
   Series Commander

Officer Candidate Company -
Commanding Officer
   Executive Officer — First Sergeant
   Company Gunnery Sergeant
   Platoon Commanders

The ribbon is dark olive green with a wide khaki tan center stripe. The Marine Corps Drill Instructor Ribbon is worn after the Marine Corps Recruiting Ribbon and before the Marine Security Guard Ribbon. Additional awards are denoted by three-sixteenth inch bronze stars.

MARINE SECURITY GUARD RIBBON

Service: Marine Corps   Instituted: 1997 (retroactive to 1949)

Criteria: Successful completion of 24 months of cumulative security guard duty service at a foreign service establishment.

Devices: Bronze, silver star

The Marine Security Guard Ribbon was established in 1997 and made retroactive to 28 January 1949, the date the first Marine Security Guards departed for overseas assignments. The ribbon is awarded to Marines assigned to Marine Security Guard duty (MOS 8151), who have successfully completed 24 months service at a foreign service establishment. Marines who served successful tours at a lettered company headquarters within MSGBn are also eligible to receive the ribbon upon completion of 24 months service. The ribbon is medium blue with a narrow red center stripe bordered by bands of white. The Marine Security Guard Ribbon is worn after the Marine Corps Drill Instructor Ribbon and before the Armed Forces Reserve Medal. Additional awards are denoted by three-sixteenth inch bronze stars.

MARINE CORPS RESERVE RIBBON (Obsolete)

Service: Marine Corps   Instituted: 1945   Dates: 1945-1965

Criteria: Successful completion of 10 years of honorable service in any class of the Marine Corps Reserve

Devices: Bronze star

The Marine Corps Reserve Ribbon was authorized by the Secretary of the Navy on 17 December 1945 and awarded to members of the Marine Corps Reserve for ten years of honorable service. On 18 December 1965, it was superseded by the Armed Forces Reserve Medal. Service counted in completing the required time for the Selected Marine Corps Reserve Medal or the Armed Forces Reserve Medal was not eligible for this award. A Marine Reservist who was eligible for these three awards could elect which one he or she would receive.

The ribbon is gold with a thin stripe of red at each edge. The Marine Corps Reserve Ribbon is worn after the Armed Forces Reserve Medal and before any foreign awards. A three-sixteenth inch bronze star was authorized for a second, ten-year period of Marine Corps Reserve service. However, the award of a bronze star was highly unlikely since the total life span of the ribbon was exactly twenty years.

Silver   Bronze

AIR FORCE OVERSEAS (SHORT TOUR) RIBBON

Service: Air Force   Instituted: 1980

Criteria: Successful completion of an overseas tour designated as "short term" by appropriate authority

Devices: Bronze, silver oak leaf cluster

Authorized on October 12, 1980 and awarded to Air Force active duty, Reserve, and National Guard personnel who have been awarded credit for a short overseas tour after September 1, 1980. Individual must have been on active status as of the institution date to qualify for this ribbon; an individual who may have earned short tour credit in 1970, for example, would be eligible for this ribbon if he/she were still on active duty in 1980. To receive short tour credit, an individual must spend at least 15 months overseas; short tour credit can also be awarded if the individual accumulates 300 days of temporary duty overseas in an 18 month period. Additional awards are denoted by bronze and silver oak leaf clusters.

Silver   Bronze

AIR FORCE OVERSEAS (LONG TOUR) RIBBON

Service: Air Force   Instituted: 1980

Criteria: Successful completion of an overseas tour designated as "long term" by appropriate authority

Devices: Bronze, silver oak leaf cluster

Authorized on October 12, 1980 and awarded to Air Force active duty, Reserve and National Guard personnel who have been awarded credit for a long overseas tour after September 1, 1980. Individual must have been on active status as of the institution date to qualify for this ribbon. Long tour credit is awarded for an assignment of at least 24 months overseas; credit for a long tour may be also be awarded for accumulating 365 days of temporary duty overseas in a three year period. The ribbon may be awarded retroactively to those personnel who were on active duty as of the institution date. Additional awards are denoted by bronze and silver oak leaf clusters.

Silver   Bronze

AIR FORCE LONGEVITY SERVICE AWARD RIBBON

Service: Air Force   Instituted: 1957

Criteria: Successful completion of an aggregate total of four years of honorable active service

Devices: Bronze, silver oak leaf cluster

Awarded to U.S. Air Force personnel for 4 years honorable active federal military service with any branch of the U.S. Armed Forces or reserve components. Reserve and Guard require 4 years creditable service for retirement. An additional 4 years' of creditable service is denoted by a bronze oak leaf cluster. As an example, an individual who retires after 20 years service would wear 4 bronze oak leaf clusters on the ribbon. Individuals on active duty as of the institution date are authorized to wear the appropriate attachments to properly reflect their service both prior to and after that date. Individuals who served both in the Army Air Force and continued their service into the U.S. Air Force until 1957 or later would be authorized to wear the Longevity Service Award with appropriate oak leaf clusters to properly represent their total service during both periods.

Silver   Bronze

AIR FORCE MILITARY TRAINING INSTRUCTOR RIBBON

Service: Air Force   Instituted: 1998

Criteria: Successful completion of at least 12 months tour of duty as a Military Training Instructor

Devices: Bronze, silver oak leaf cluster

The Secretary of the Air Force established the Air Force Military Training Instructor Ribbon on 7 December 1998 to acknowledge past, present, and future Military Training Instructors (MTI's) who display commitment and dedication to the training of Air Force personnel. This ribbon is intended for MTI's at Air Force Basic Military Training (BMT) and Officer Training School (OTS) (instructors at Technical Training Schools do not qualify). The basic award is presented to Air Force active duty, Reserve, and National Guard personnel upon graduation from Military Training Instructor School. Wear of the ribbon becomes permanent after successful completion of at least 12 months tour of duty as an MTI. Each additional three years of MTI duty following the basic tour entitles the member to an oak leaf cluster. The ribbon is retroactive for any individual who has successfully completed 12 months duty as an MTI and is currently on active duty or a member of a reserve component as of the establishment date (7 Dec 98). The ribbon is worn between the Air Force Longevity Service Ribbon and the Armed Forces Reserve Medal.

N.C.O. PROFESSIONAL MILITARY EDUCATION GRADUATE RIBBON

Service: Air Force   Instituted: 1962

Criteria: Successful completion of a certified NCO professional military education school

Devices: Bronze, silver oak leaf cluster

Silver   Bronze

    The Air Force Non-Commissioned Officer Professional Military Education Graduate Ribbon was authorized by the Secretary of the Air Force on 28 August 1962 and is awarded to graduates of all Air Force-certified NCO PME schools (i.e.: NCO Preparatory Course, Airman Leadership School, NCO Leadership School, NCO Academy and SRNCO Academy.). Graduation from each successive level of PME entitles the member to wear an oak leaf cluster on the ribbon. The ribbon is not, however, awarded to members who only complete the correspondence courses or similar training conducted by other military services except for completion of the U.S. Army Sergeant Major Academy or the Navy Senior Enlisted Academy. This award also has the dubious distinction of bearing the longest name in United States award history.

USAF BASIC MILITARY TRAINING (BMT) HONOR GRADUATE RIBBON

Service: Air Force   Instituted: 1976

Criteria: Demonstration of excellence in all academic and military training phases of basic Air Force entry training

Devices: None

    The Basic Military Training Honor Graduate Ribbon was authorized by the Chief of Staff, U.S. Air Force on April 3, 1976, this ribbon is awarded to honor graduates of Basic Military Training who, after July 29, 1976, have demonstrated excellence in all phases of academic and military training. It is limited to the top 10 percent of the training flight. The USAF BMT Honor Graduate Ribbon was designed by the Institute of Heraldry, and is awarded to basic training graduates only. The ribbon has a wide center stripe of ultramarine blue flanked with equal stripes of yellow, brittany blue and white on either side. Since this is a "one-time only" award, no devices are authorized.

AIR FORCE TRAINING RIBBON

Service: Air Force   Instituted: 1980

Criteria: Successful completion of an Air Force accession training program

Devices: Bronze, silver oak leaf cluster

Silver   Bronze

    The Air Force Training Ribbon was authorized on October 12, 1980 and awarded to Air Force members who complete an Air Force accession training program after August 14, 1974 such as Basic Military Training (BMT), Officer Training School (OTS), Reserve Officer Training Corps (ROTC), USAF Academy, Medical Services, Judge Advocate, Chaplain orientation etc. Also authorized for Guard and Reserve members who complete the appropriate training program. If a member completes two accession training programs, such as BMT and OTS, a bronze oak leaf cluster is worn on the ribbon. The award is retroactive for those personnel on active duty as of the authorization date.

SPECIAL OPERATIONS SERVICE RIBBON

Service: Coast Guard (Inst: 1987)

Criteria: Participation in a Coast Guard special noncombat operation not recognized by another service award.

Devices: Bronze, silver star

Silver   Bronze

    The Coast Guard Special Operations Service Ribbon was authorized by the Commandant of the Coast Guard on July 1, 1987 and is awarded to any member of the U.S. Armed Forces serving in any capacity with the Coast Guard who, after 1 July 1987, participates in a major Coast Guard operation of a special nature, not involving combat, which has not been recognized by another service award for the same operation during the same period of service. Personnel must be attached to a unit and be present for not less than 21 days (consecutive or nonconsecutive) during the period the unit is engaged in the special operation or serve for the full period when an operation is less than 21 days duration. The Coast Guard Special Operations Service Ribbon may also be authorized for multi-unit or multi-service operations such as Coast Guard operations of a special nature involving national security/law enforcement, Coast Guard involvement with foreign governments in all areas of saving life and property at sea and Coast Guard operations of assistance to friendly and/or developing nations. Additional awards of the Special Operations Service Ribbon are denoted by 3/16" dia. bronze and silver stars.

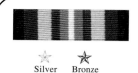

COAST GUARD SEA SERVICE RIBBON

Silver   Bronze

<u>Service:</u> Coast Guard (Inst: 1984)

<u>Criteria:</u> Satisfactory completion of a minimum of 12 months of cumulative sea duty.

<u>Devices:</u> Bronze, silver star

The Coast Guard Sea Service Ribbon was established by the Coast Guard Commandant on March 3rd 1984. It is awarded to active duty members of the Coast Guard and Coast Guard Reserve, inactive duty members of the Coast Guard Reserve or non-Coast Guard personnel who, under temporary or permanent assignment, satisfactorily complete a minimum of 12 months of cumulative sea duty. For the purposes of this award, sea duty is defined as duty performed aboard any Coast Guard cutter 65 feet or more in length in an active status, in commission or in service or while assigned to a Fleet Training Group/Unit (FTG/FTU). A 3/16 inch bronze service star is authorized for each additional 3 years of such sea duty.

RESTRICTED DUTY RIBBON

Silver   Bronze

<u>Service:</u> Coast Guard (Inst: 1984)

<u>Criteria:</u> Successful completion of a tour of duty at remote shore stations (LORAN stations, light ships, etc.) without family.

<u>Devices:</u> Bronze, silver star

The Coast Guard Restricted Duty Ribbon was established by the Coast Guard Commandant on March 3, 1984. It is awarded to all Coast Guard personnel who have completed a permanent change of station (PCS) tour of duty at a remote shore station (such as LORAN stations, light stations, etc.) where no accompanying dependents are permitted. Coast Guard personnel who are assigned on a temporary basis to such a restricted unit are not eligible for this award. A 3/16 inch bronze star is authorized for each subsequent PCS tour of duty at a restricted shore unit.

COAST GUARD BASIC TRAINING HONOR GRADUATE RIBBON

<u>Service:</u> Coast Guard

<u>Instituted:</u> 1984

<u>Criteria:</u> Successful attainment of the top 3 percent of the class during Coast Guard recruit training.

<u>Devices:</u> None

The Coast Guard Basic Training Honor Graduate Ribbon was established by the Commandant of the Coast Guard on 3 March 1984. Effective 1 April 1984, it is awarded to Coast Guard personnel comprising the top 3 percent of each Coast Guard recruit training graduating class. Individuals who graduated from Coast Guard recruit training prior to 1 April 1984 and meet the above criteria and believe themselves eligible for this award may submit a request, with supporting documentation to the Coast Guard Commandant. Prior service personnel who graduated from other than Coast Guard recruit training are not eligible for the award. Since this is a "one-time only" award, no devices are authorized.

COAST GUARD RECRUITING SERVICE RIBBON

Silver   Bronze

<u>Service:</u> Coast Guard

<u>Instituted:</u> 1995 (retroactive to 1980)

<u>Criteria:</u> Successful completion of two consecutive years of recruiting duty.

<u>Devices:</u> Bronze, silver star

The Coast Guard Recruiting Service Ribbon was established on November 2, 1995 by the Commandant of the Coast Guard and made retroactive to Recruiting tours performed subsequent to January 1, 1980. It is awarded for two consecutive duty tours in Coast Guard Recruiting offices. The ribbon is worn after the Coast Guard Basic Training Honor Graduate Ribbon and before the Armed Forces Reserve Medal. Each additional successful two-year tour of duty is signified by a bronze star worn on the ribbon.

ARMY PRESIDENTIAL UNIT CITATION

Silver   Bronze

<u>Service:</u> Army   <u>Instituted:</u> 1942, redesignated 1966
<u>Criteria:</u> Awarded to Army units for extraordinary heroism in action against an armed enemy
<u>Devices:</u> Bronze, silver oak leaf cluster
<u>Notes:</u> Original designation: Distinguished Unit Citation. Redesignated to present name in 1966

The Army Presidential Unit Citation (PUC) was established on February 26, 1942 as the "Distinguished Unit Badge" or the "Distinguished Unit Citation" and redesignated as the Presidential Unit Citation in 1966. It is awarded to Army units that display the same degree of heroism in combat as would warrant the Distinguished Service Cross for an individual. Like all Army unit awards, the PUC is worn above the pocket on the right breast of the uniform. The gold-colored frame around the ribbon is worn with the open end of the "V" of the laurel leaf pattern pointing upward. The badge may only be worn permanently by those individuals who were assigned to the unit for the period for which it was cited. Current members of the unit who were not assigned to the unit for the award period are entitled to wear the ribbon but only for the duration of their assignment with the cited unit. Such personnel must remove it from their uniform upon reassignment. Additional awards of the Army Presidential Unit Citation are denoted by bronze oak leaf clusters.

NAVY PRESIDENTIAL UNIT CITATION

Silver   Bronze

<u>Service:</u> Navy, Marine Corps   <u>Instituted:</u> 1942
<u>Criteria:</u> Awarded to Navy/Marine Corps units for extraordinary heroism in action against an armed enemy.
<u>Devices:</u> Bronze, silver star

The Navy Presidential Unit Citation is awarded in the name of the President for service in a unit with outstanding performance in action. The Navy Presidential Unit Citation was established on 6 February 1942 and amended on 28 June 1943. The citation is conferred on units for displaying extraordinary heroism subsequent to 16 October 1941, the degree of heroism required is the same as that which is required for the award of the Navy Cross to an individual. Unlike the Army, only individuals actually assigned to the unit when the award was granted may wear the ribbon on their uniform. The ribbon consists of three equal horizontal stripes of navy blue (top), gold (middle) and red (bottom) and is worn after the Combat Action Ribbon and before the Joint Meritorious Unit Award. Additional awards of the Navy Presidential Unit Citation are denoted by three-sixteenth inch bronze stars.

AIR FORCE PRESIDENTIAL UNIT CITATION

Silver   Bronze

<u>Service:</u> Air Force   <u>Instituted:</u> 1957
<u>Criteria:</u> Awarded to Air Force units for extraordinary heroism in action against an armed enemy
<u>Devices:</u> Bronze, silver oak leaf cluster
<u>Notes:</u> Original designation: Distinguished Unit Citation. Redesignated to present name in 1957

The Air Force Presidential Unit Citation owes its heritage to the original Army award which was created in Feb. 26, 1942, and modified by Executive Order on Dec. 2, 1943. The order created the Distinguished Unit Citation which was redesignated as the Presidential Unit Citation, on Jan. 10, 1957. It is conferred upon units of the Army and Air Force of the United States for extraordinary heroism in action against an armed enemy on or after Dec. 7, 1941. The unit must display such gallantry, determination and esprit de corps as to set it apart from and above other units participating in the same campaign. The degree of heroism required is the same that which would warrant award of the Distinguished Service Cross or Air Force Cross to an individual. Unlike the Army, the Air Force PUC may only be worn by individuals who are assigned or permanently attached to and also present for duty with a unit in the action for which the Presidential Unit Citation is awarded. Subsequent awards of the Presidential Unit Citation are denoted by bronze oak-leaf clusters.

JOINT MERITORIOUS UNIT AWARD

Silver   Bronze

<u>Service:</u> All Services   <u>Instituted:</u> 1981 (retroactive to 1979)
<u>Criteria:</u> Awarded to Joint Service units for superior meritorious achievement or service
<u>Devices:</u> Bronze, silver oak leaf cluster

The Joint Meritorious Unit Award was authorized by the Secretary of Defense on 10 June 1981 (retroactive to 23 January 1979) and was originally called the Department of Defense Meritorious Unit Award. It is awarded in the name of the Secretary of Defense for meritorious service, superior to that which would normally be expected during combat, a declared national emergency or under extraordinary circumstances that involve national interest. The service performed by the unit would be similar to that performed by an individual awarded the Defense Superior Service Medal. The ribbon is similar to the Defense Superior Service Medal ribbon with a gold metal frame with laurel leaves. Like the Defense Superior Service Medal, the ribbon consists of a central stripe of red flanked on either side by stripes of white, blue and yellow, but with blue edges. Additional awards are denoted by oak leaf clusters.

ARMY VALOROUS UNIT AWARD

Service: Army   Instituted: 1963

Criteria: Awarded to U.S. Army units for outstanding heroism in armed combat against an opposing armed force.

Devices: Bronze, silver oak leaf cluster

Silver   Bronze

The Army Valorous Unit Award was approved and established by the Army Chief of Staff on January 12, 1966. It is awarded to units of the Armed Forces of the United States for extraordinary heroism in action against an armed enemy of the United States while engaged in conflict with an opposing foreign force on or after 3 August 1963. The Valorous Unit Award requires a lesser degree of gallantry than that required for the Presidential Unit Citation. Nevertheless, the unit must have performed with marked distinction under difficult and hazardous conditions so as to set it apart from the other units participating in the same conflict. The degree of heroism required is the same as that which would warrant award of the Silver Star to an individual. This award will normally be earned by units that have participated in single or successive actions covering relatively brief time spans but only on rare occasions will a unit larger than a battalion qualify for this award. Additional awards are denoted by bronze oak leaf clusters

NAVY UNIT COMMENDATION

Service: Navy, Marine Corps

Instituted: 1944

Criteria: Awarded to Navy/Marine Corps units for outstanding heroism in action or extremely meritorious service

Devices: Bronze, silver star

Silver   Bronze

. The Navy Unit Commendation was established by the Secretary of the Navy on 18 December 1944. The Commendation is awarded by the Secretary of the Navy with the approval of the President to units, which, subsequent to 6 December 1941, distinguish themselves by outstanding heroism in action against an enemy, but to a lesser degree than required for the Presidential Unit Citation. The Commendation may also be awarded for extremely meritorious service not involving combat, but in support of military operations, which is outstanding when compared to other units performing similar service. The ribbon is dark green with narrow border stripes of red, gold and blue and is worn after the Joint Meritorious Unit Award and before the Navy Meritorious Unit Commendation. Additional awards are denoted by three-sixteenth inch bronze stars.

AIR FORCE OUTSTANDING UNIT AWARD

Service: Air Force

Instituted: 1954

Bronze   Silver   Bronze

Criteria: Awarded to U.S. Air Force units for exceptionally meritorious achievement or meritorious service

Devices: Bronze letter "V", bronze, silver oak leaf cluster

The Outstanding Unit Award was established on January 6, 1954 and is awarded by the Secretary of the Air Force to units for exceptionally meritorious service or outstanding achievement that clearly sets the unit above and apart from similar units. A unit must clearly perform at a high level for a sustained period of time to receive such recognition as afforded by this award. The exceptionally meritorious service must have been performed for a period of not more than two years and not less than one year. A bronze letter V is worn on the ribbon when awarded for combat or direct combat support actions. Bronze and silver oak leaf clusters are worn to denote additional awards.

DEPT. OF TRANSPORTATION OUTSTANDING UNIT AWARD

Service: Coast Guard (Inst: 1995)

Criteria: Awarded to U.S. Coast Guard units for valorous or extremely meritorious service on behalf of the Transportation Dept.

Devices: Gold, silver star

Gold   Silver

The Department of Transportation Outstanding Unit Award was authorized by the Secretary of Transportation effective November 3, 1994 as an award to Coast Guard units for valorous or extremely meritorious service on behalf of the Transportation Dept. The first (and, thus far, the only) award was presented to all Coast Guard active duty personnel, civilian employees, Reservists, Auxiliarists cadets, U.S. Public Health Service personnel and Dept. of Defense personnel serving with the Coast Guard for any length of honorable service between October 1, 1993 and September 30, 1994. Any additional awards, whether to individual units or Service-wide will be denoted by gold and silver stars.

Silver   Gold   Silver

COAST GUARD UNIT COMMENDATION

Service: Coast Guard   Instituted: 1963

Criteria: Awarded to U.S. Coast Guard units for valorous or extremely meritorious service on behalf of the Transportation Dept.

Devices: Gold, silver star

The Coast Guard Unit Commendation was authorized by the Coast Guard Commandant effective 1 January 1963 for award to any unit which has distinguished itself by valorous or extremely meritorious service not involving combat but in support of Coast Guard operations, which renders the unit outstanding compared to other units performing similar service. This award may also be conferred upon a unit of another branch of the Armed Forces of the United States. To justify this award, the unit must have performed service as a unit of a character comparable to that which would merit the award of the Coast Guard Commendation Medal or higher award to an individual. The silver letter "O" (Operational Distinguishing Device) may be authorized. Additional awards are denoted by 5/16 inch dia. gold and silver stars.

Silver   Bronze

ARMY MERITORIOUS UNIT COMMENDATION

Service: Army   Instituted: 1944

Criteria: Awarded to U.S. Army units for exceptionally meritorious conduct in the performance of outstanding service

Devices: Bronze, silver oak leaf cluster

Notes: Originally a golden wreath worn on the lower sleeve. Authorized in its present form in 1961

The Army Meritorious Unit Commendation is awarded to units for exceptionally meritorious conduct in performance of outstanding services for at least 6 continuous months during the period of military operations against an armed enemy occurring on or after January 1, 1944. Service in a combat zone is not required but must be directly related to the combat effort. Units based within the continental U.S. or outside the area of operation are excluded from this award. The unit must display such outstanding devotion and superior performance of exceptional difficult tasks as to set it apart and above other units with similar missions. The award is usually given to units larger than battalions. The degree of achievement required is the same as that which would warrant award of the Legion of Merit to an individual. It was originally authorized as a wreath emblem that was worn on the lower right sleeve of the Army uniform but was redeveloped in its present form in 1961. As with other unit citations, it has a gold frame surrounding the ribbon; the open end of the "V" shaped design on the frame points upward and is worn with other unit citations on the right side of the uniform. Additional awards are denoted by bronze and silver oak leaf clusters.

Silver   Bronze

NAVY MERITORIOUS UNIT COMMENDATION RIBBON

Service: Navy, Marine Corps   Instituted: 1967

Criteria: Awarded to Navy/Marine Corps units for valorous actions or meritorious achievement (combat or noncombat)

Devices: Bronze, silver star

The Navy Meritorious Unit Commendation was established by the Secretary of the Navy on July 17 1967 and is awarded by the Secretary of the Navy to units which distinguish themselves by either valorous or meritorious achievement considered outstanding, but to a lesser degree than required for the Navy Unit Commendation. The Commendation may be awarded for services in combat or noncombat situations. The ribbon is dark green with a narrow red center stripe flanked on either side by stripes of gold, navy blue and gold. The Meritorious Unit Commendation is worn after the Navy Unit Commendation and before the Navy "E" ribbon. Additional awards are denoted by three-sixteenth inch bronze stars.

Bronze   Silver   Bronze

AIR FORCE ORGANIZATIONAL EXCELLENCE AWARD (AFOEA)

Service: Air Force   Instituted: 1969

Criteria: Same as Outstanding Unit Award but awarded to unique unnumbered organizations performing staff functions

Devices: Bronze letter "V", bronze, silver oak leaf cluster

The Air Force Organizational Excellence Award was established on August 26, 1969 to recognize unique, unnumbered organizations/units that have performed exceptionally meritorious service for a nominated time period of not less than 2 years. It is awarded to recognize the achievements and accomplishments of Air Force organizations or activities that do not meet the eligibility requirements of the Air Force Outstanding Unit Awards such as Headquarters organizations and Air Force Academy units. The letter V is authorized if awarded for combat or direct combat support actions. Additional awards are signified by bronze and silver oak leaf clusters.

COAST GUARD MERITORIOUS UNIT COMMENDATION

Silver   Gold   Silver

Service: Coast Guard   Instituted: 1973

Criteria: Awarded to U.S. Coast Guard units for valorous or meritorious achievement (combat or noncombat).

Devices: Silver letter "O", gold, silver star

    The Coast Guard Meritorious Unit Commendation was authorized by the Coast Guard Commandant effective 13 November 1973 and is awarded to any unit of the Coast Guard which distinguishes itself by either valorous or meritorious achievement or service in support of Coast Guard operations not involving combat which renders the unit outstanding compared to other units performing similar service but not sufficient to justify the award of the Coast Guard Unit Commendation. The service performed as a unit must be of a character comparable to that which would merit the award of the Coast Guard Achievement Medal to an individual. This award may also be conferred by the Commandant upon a unit of other branches of the Armed Forces of the United States. The silver letter "O" (Operational Distinguishing Device) may be authorized. Additional awards are denoted by gold and silver stars.

ARMY SUPERIOR UNIT AWARD

Bronze   Silver

Service: Army   Instituted: 1985

Criteria: Awarded to U.S. Army units for meritorious performance in difficult and challenging peacetime missions.

Devices: Bronze, silver oak leaf cluster

    The Army Superior Unit Award was approved in April, 1985 (modified in July, 1986) and is awarded for outstanding meritorious performance of a unit during peacetime in a difficult and challenging mission under extraordinary circumstances. The unit must display such outstanding devotion and superior performance of exceptionally difficult tasks to set it apart from and above other units with similar missions. For the purpose of this award, peacetime is defined as any period during which wartime or combat awards are not authorized in the geographical area in which the mission was executed. The award may be given for operations of a humanitarian nature. The award is designed for Battalion-size and smaller or comparable units, but, under most circumstances, headquarters type units would not be eligible. Awards to units larger than battalion size would be infrequent. As with other Army unit citations, it has a gold frame surrounding the ribbon; the open end of the "V" shaped design on the frame points upward and is worn with other unit citations on the right side of the uniform. Additional awards are denoted by bronze and silver oak leaf clusters.

COAST GUARD MERITORIOUS TEAM COMMENDATION

Silver   Gold   Silver

Service: Coast Guard   Instituted: 1993

Criteria: Awarded to smaller U.S. Coast Guard groups/teams for outstanding accomplishment of a study, process or mission.

Devices: Silver letter "O" , gold, silver star

    The Coast Guard Meritorious Team Commendation was authorized on December 22, 1993 by the Coast Guard Commandant to recognize outstanding performance by small groups (e.g.: teams, detachments or sub-units) which do not constitute a Coast Guard Unit. To justify the award, the individual members of these groups must perform service which makes a significant contribution to the group's outstanding accomplishment of a study, process, mission, etc. The service performed as a group or team must be of a character comparable to that which would merit the award of the Commandant's Letter of Commendation to an individual. The silver letter "O" (Operational Distinguishing Device) may be authorized. Additional awards are denoted by gold and silver stars.

NAVY "E" RIBBON

Silver   Silver

Service: Navy, Marine Corps

Instituted: 1976

Criteria: Awarded to ships or squadrons which have won battle efficiency competitions

Devices: Silver letter "E", wreathed silver letter "E"

    The Navy "E" Ribbon was established in June 1976 to recognize individuals who, subsequent to 1 July 1974, are permanently assigned to ships or squadrons that win battle efficiency competitions. It may be worn by all personnel who served as permanent members of the ship's company or squadrons winning the Battle Efficiency Award. The Navy "E" Ribbon is worn after the Meritorious Unit Commendation and before the Prisoner of War Medal. The ribbon is navy blue with borders of white and gold and is issued with a silver "E" device in the center denoting the first award. Subsequent awards are signified by additional "E" devices, with the fourth (and final) award indicated by a silver "E" surrounded by a silver wreath.

COAST GUARD "E" RIBBON

Service: Coast Guard (Inst: 1990)

Criteria: Awarded to U.S. Coast Guard ships and cutters which earn the overall operational readiness efficiency award.

Devices: Gold, silver star

Gold   Silver

The Coast Guard "E" Ribbon was authorized by the Coast Guard Commandant on 25 September 1990. It is awarded by area commanders to provide visible recognition for personnel of cutters earning the overall operational readiness "E" award during Refresher Training. All personnel serving aboard their unit for more than 50 percent of the period during which it undergoes Refresher Training are eligible for the "E" Ribbon. Additional awards are denoted by 5/16 inch dia. gold and silver stars.

COAST GUARD BICENTENNIAL UNIT COMMENDATION

Service: Coast Guard   Instituted: 1990

Criteria: Awarded to all Coast Guard personnel serving satisfactorily during their Bicentennial year.

The Coast Guard Bicentennial Unit Commendation was authorized by the Coast Guard Commandant effective 2 January 1990. It was awarded to all Coast Guard members, including selected Reservists, civilians and Auxiliarists, serving satisfactorily during any period from 4 June 1989 to 4 August 1990. Personnel of other Services who were assigned to and served with the Coast Guard during this period were also eligible for this award. Since this was a "one-time only" award, no devices were authorized.

PHILIPPINE REPUBLIC PRESIDENTIAL UNIT CITATION

Country: Republic of the Philippines   Instituted: 1948

Criteria: Awarded to units of the U.S. Armed Forces for service in the war against Japan and/or for 1970 and 1972 disaster relief   Devices: Bronze star

Bronze

The Philippine Republic Presidential Unit Citation was awarded to U.S. Armed Forces personnel for services resulting in the liberation of the Philippines during World War II. The award was made in the name of the President of the Republic of the Philippines. It was also awarded to U.S. Forces who participated in disaster relief operations in 1970 and 1972. The ribbon has three equal stripes of blue, white and red enclosed in a rectangular gold frame with laurel leaves identical to U.S. unit awards. A three-sixteenth inch bronze star denotes receipt of an additional award.

REPUBLIC OF KOREA PRESIDENTIAL UNIT CITATION

Country: Republic of Vietnam   Instituted: 1951

Criteria: Awarded to certain units of the U.S. Armed Forces for services rendered during the Korean War

Notes: Above date denotes when award was authorized for wear by U.S. Armed Forces personnel

Awarded by the Republic of Korea for service in a unit cited in the name of the President of the Republic of Korea for outstanding performance in action. The Republic of Korea Presidential Unit Citation is a foreign award. It was awarded to units of the United Nations Command for service in Korea during the Korean Conflict from 1950 to 1954. The award was made in the name of the President of the Republic of Korea. The ribbon is white bordered with a wide green stripe and thin stripes of white, red, white, red, white and green. In the center is an ancient oriental symbol called a Taeguk (the top half is red and the bottom half is blue). The ribbon is enclosed in a rectangular gold frame with laurel leaves identical to U.S. unit awards. No devices are authorized.

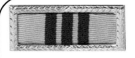

REPUBLIC OF VIETNAM PRESIDENTIAL UNIT CITATION (FRIENDSHIP RIBBON)

Country: Republic of Vietnam   Instituted: 1954

Criteria: Awarded to certain units of the U.S. Armed Forces for humanitarian service in the evacuation of civilians from North and Central Vietnam

Notes: Above date denotes when award was authorized for wear by U.S. Armed Forces personnel

Awarded by the Republic of Vietnam for service in a unit cited in the name of the President of the Republic of Vietnam for outstanding performance in action. The Republic of Vietnam Presidential Unit Citation is a foreign award. Referred to as the "Friendship Ribbon", it was awarded to members of the United States Military Assistance Advisory Group in Indo-China for services rendered during August and September 1954. The ribbon is awarded in the name of the President of the Republic of Vietnam. The ribbon is yellow with three narrow red stripes in the center. The ribbon is enclosed in a rectangular gold frame with laurel leaves identical to U.S. unit awards. No devices are authorized.

Bronze Palm

★ ☆ ☆
Bronze Silver Gold

REPUBLIC OF VIETNAM GALLANTRY CROSS UNIT CITATION

<u>Country:</u> Republic of Vietnam   <u>Instituted:</u> 1966

<u>Dates:</u> March 1, 1961 to March 28, 1974

<u>Criteria:</u> Awarded to certain units of the U.S. Armed Forces for valorous combat achievement during the Vietnam War,

<u>Devices:</u> All Services:bronze palm; Army only:bronze, silver, gold star

<u>Notes:</u> Above date denotes when award was authorized for wear by U.S. Armed Forces personnel

The Republic of Vietnam Gallantry Cross Unit Citation was established on 15 August 1950 and awarded by the Republic of Vietnam to units of the U.S. Armed Forces in recognition of valorous achievement in combat during the Vietnam War. The ribbon was awarded to units by the Republic of Vietnam for the same services as would be required for the Navy Unit Commendation. The Republic of Vietnam Gallantry Cross Unit Citation is a foreign award. The ribbon is red with a very wide yellow center stripe which has eight very thin double red stripes. The ribbon bar is enclosed in a gold frame with laurel leaves identical to U.S. unit awards. For more information on Vietnamese decorations and medals see *The Decorations and Medals of the Republic of Vietnam and Her Allies 1950-1975.*

Bronze Palm

REPUBLIC OF VIETNAM CIVIL ACTIONS UNIT CITATION

<u>Country:</u> Republic of Vietnam   <u>Instituted:</u> 1966

<u>Criteria:</u> Awarded to certain units of the U.S. Armed Forces for meritorious service during the Vietnam War, 1 March 1961 to 28 March 1974

<u>Devices:</u> Bronze palm

Awarded by the Republic of Vietnam to units in recognition of meritorious civil action service. The Republic of Vietnam Civil Actions Unit Citation was widely bestowed on American forces in Vietnam and recognizes outstanding achievements made by units in the field of civil affairs. The Republic of Vietnam Civil Actions Unit Citation is a foreign award. The ribbon is dark green with a very thin double red center stripe narrow red stripes near the edges. The ribbon is enclosed in a rectangular one-sixteenth inch gold frame with laurel leaves identical to U.S. unit awards and is awarded with a bronze laurel leaf palm attachment. For more information on Vietnamese decorations and medals see *The Decorations and Medals of the Republic of Vietnam and Her Allies 1950-1975.*

Commemorative Medals — *225 Years of American Tradition*

The United States Government, State Governments, Veterans Organizations, private mints and individuals have a long tradition of striking Commemorative Medals to recognize and honor specify military victories, historical events and military service to our great Republic. Until the 20th century the United States did not issue military service Medals recognizing service by veterans in the different wars, battles, campaigns or other significant military events.

The tradition of honoring U.S. military heroes began when the Continental Congress awarded gold and silver medals to our triumphant commanders of The Revolutionary War. While these were struck as table display medals General Gates the victor of Saratoga wasted no time hanging his from a neck ribbon and wearing it for his official portrait. Great battles at sea and famous naval heroes also are honored. The first such medal, struck in gold, was awarded to Captain John Paul Jones. These Congressionally authorized medals were the forerunners of modern combat decorations. Some medals commemorate events such as the War with Mexico and the Civil War, with reverse designs depicting famous battle scenes.

Captain John Paul Jones's Commemorative Medal

Grand Army of the Republic Reunion Medal

Aztec Club Medal

During the Mexican war certain states such as South Carolina issued medals to veterans of the state regiment which fought in the war. Other times veterans formed societies and issued medals commemorating their service. Some of the more famous examples are the Grand Army of the Republic reunion medals and Aztec Club medal struck by veterans of the Mexican War. In some cases commanders during the Civil War issued privately commissioned commemorative medals such as the Kearney Cross.

The Mint regularly produces commemorative medals typically to celebrate and honor American people, places, events, including medals honoring military heroes, veterans, and the armed services. For example The Vietnam Veterans National Medal commemorates the courage and dedication of the men and women who served in that conflict. The Missing in Action medal is a 1^{5}/$_{16}$ inch miniature replica of the 3-inch medal authorized for presentation to the next-of-kin of American military and civilian personnel missing or otherwise unaccounted for in Southeast Asia. The 200th anniversaries of the U.S. Army, Navy, Marine Corps, and Coast Guard were also celebrated with the striking of national medals, and the Persian Gulf National Medal honored Persian Gulf War veterans. Only bronze medals are available for sale to the public. For a complete listing of medals available from the U.S. Mint, call (202) 283-2646.

While the federal government issues commemorative Medals from the U.S. mint. State and county governments who were particularly active after World War I used private mints and contractors to issue hundreds of different commemorative medals honoring World War veterans and providing a visible symbol of gratitude to their returning veterans. All of these medals were especially meaningful to both returning veterans and their families. Veteran's associations such as the American Legion, Veterans of Foreign Wars, and even the Daughters of the Confederacy issued commemorative medals. For the past two hundred years these groups coupled with private mints have issued medals honoring historical military events, victories, deeds and service that honor American veterans.

Commemorative Medals reflect typical American ingenuity and spirit, where local government, veterans associations, and private leadership step toward to facilitate honoring service and deeds the federal government fails to recognize. In recent years the 75th Anniversary of World War I and the 50th Anniversary celebration of both World War II and the Korea War were the occasions for well-deserved commemorative medals to honor the veterans of these conflicts. The most recent example is the Cold War Victory Commemorative Medal struck to fill the void created when Congress authorized a Cold War Victory Recognition certificate but never funded a medal.

Cold War Victory Commemorative Medal

Although unofficial in nature and usually struck by private mints or associations, Commemorative Medals provide a very tangible memento to honor all veterans and families for their service and sacrifice. Shown below are examples of commemorative Medals from the last sixty years (1940 — 2000).

The Cold War Victory Commemorative Medal

The Cold War Victory Commemorative medal was inspired by the Cold War Certificate of Recognition created by Congressional Resolution to recognizes "members of the Armed Forces who served during the Cold War."

Congress did not authorize a medal for the cold war, limiting its recognition to the certificate . The Cold War Victory Commemorative medal is intended to recognize citizen-soldiers who served during the cold war between September 2, 1945 and December 26, 1991.

The medal depicts an American Eagle holding arrows in the right claw and the olive branch in the left (war eagle design). Inscription above reads, "Duty, Honor, Country". "Cold War Victory Commemorative" is in raised letters across the top of the medal and 13 raised stars are embossed along the bottom edge.

The ribbon is a cool grey representing the cold dismal pall thrown over the world by the cold war. The center of the ribbon has stripes of red, white and blue, the United States National colors

The Combat Service Commemorative Medal

Struck to honor all Soldiers, Sailors, Marines and Airmen who served in an overseas combat theater or in expeditionary combat operations.

The medal is bronze and is 1^{1}/$_{4}$" in diameter. The front of the medal depicts key symbols representing the four branches of the Armed Forces. The Words "Combat Service" are over the 3 spears representing air, land and sea forces. Beneath the spearheads are pilot wings over body armor with crossed cannon and rifle all held together on the arms and flukes of an anchor. The words "Commemorative" are at the bottom separated from the words "Combat Service" by 13 stars representing the original colonies.

The ribbon is designed to reflect the National colors separated by a broad band of gold symbolizing courage.

Overseas Service Commemorative Medal

Struck to honor all Soldiers, Sailors, Marines, Airmen and Coast Guard personnel who served overseas or in expeditionary operations for 30 days or more.

The Medal depicts an American Eagle with the national shield overlooking two globes showing both sides of the earth. Beneath the globes are five stars representing the branches of the Armed Forces. Around the top of the medal are the words "Overseas Service". The word "Commemorative" is at the bottom separated from the words "Overseas Service" by laurel leaves flanking the globes.

The Overseas Service Commemorative Medal Ribbon is designed to reflect the ocean, sky and land with the national colors running down the center.

Samples of Award Certificates

**Large Size Army Bronze Star Certificate
Awarded in the 1960s**

Current Navy Award Certificate

**Smaller Style Army Certificate Used
Starting in the 70s**

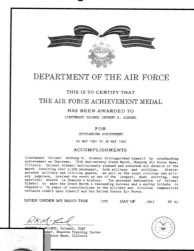

**Vertical Style Air Force
Certificate**

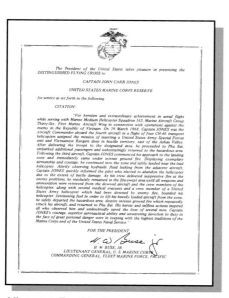

Vietnam Era Marine Award Certificate

**NATO Award Certificate
for Current NATO Medal**

**Saudi Arabian Award Certificate for
Liberation of Kuwait Medal**

Attachments and Devices

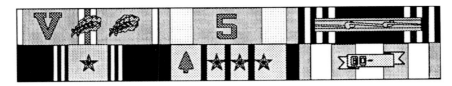

Looking back from the perspective of the late 20th century, it is apparent that early in the history of the U.S. awards program, little attention was paid to the possibility that a medal could be bestowed upon an individual more than once. This was to cause some embarrassment when five individuals (three Army and two Marine Corps) won <u>second</u> awards of the Medal of Honor in the span of years between the Civil War and World War I.

In contrast, the British Empire had recognized this need as far back as 1856 when the Victoria Cross was instituted. The original Royal Warrant authorized the use of an ornate bar affixed to the medal's suspension ribbon to represent the second award of the Cross. The bar, however, was not used universally and had to be authorized on an individual basis as each new medal was introduced or many years thereafter. Also to be noted, the custom of wearing a device directly on the ribbon bar to denote an additional award was still many years away, not finding its way into Victoria Cross regulations until 1916.

Although no one in possession of all his faculties would characterize World War I as an Age of Enlightenment, that certainly describes the era from the standpoint of medal and ribbon devices. By the end of the Great War, the use of ribbon attachments was quite widespread throughout the world and the U.S. had instituted its first four ribbon attachments, thus setting the stage for the many such accessories which would follow.

The best known of these, the oak leaf cluster, was established (although not by that name) at the same time that the Army's Distinguished Service Cross and Distinguished Service Medal came into being. The 1918 regulations provided for "..a bar or other suitable device.." for each succeeding deed or act sufficient to justify a subsequent award".

The same act authorized the use of a silver star device, three-sixteenths of an inch in diameter to denote a citation for gallantry in action. Although the directive seemed quite straightforward, it never made clear the actual ribbon to which the star should be affixed. However, the War Department directed that it be used on the appropriate service medal/ribbon. This led to a large number of retroactive awards, some dating back to the Civil War, but of greater significance, to the establishment of the Silver Star Medal as described earlier in this book. As a footnote to this discussion, the U.S. Navy also adopted the small silver star device but only for wear on the ribbon of the World War I

Victory Medal after the receipt of a letter of commendation for performance of duty not justifying the award of the Medal of Honor, Navy Cross or Distinguished Service Medal (the only decorations in existence at the time).

For the record, the other two ribbon attachments authorized for use just after the Great War were the 3/16" diameter bronze stars representing the battle clasps to the Victory Medal and the bronze scroll numeral (now obsolete) used on the Marine Corps Expeditionary Ribbon (not a Medal yet!) to indicate the number of additional awards of the ribbon. Note that the Navy did not authorize its 5/16" diameter gold star to denote additional awards of a decoration until the early 1920s.

The great number of decorations and awards created during World War II also resulted in a vast increase in the number of available devices. The most significant of these was the silver device used in a five-for-one swap to eliminate the clutter that resulted from the huge number of decorations being awarded at the time. As an example, an Airman could now display 13 awards of the Air Medal with only four oak leaf clusters, 2 bronze and 2 silver, with the ribbon itself representing one award. The Navy's 5/16" silver star and the universally-used 3/16" silver "battle star" also aided in the war on ribbon clutter.

This is not to say that the device situation today is as clear as crystal. The bare fact is that, exclusive of the Merchant Marine, only 9 ribbons authorized since World War II have **no** device associated with their wear on the uniform. More to the point, there are only <u>five</u> ribbons awarded today that fit this category.

The large number of devices employed on the modern ribbon chest might seem excessive but, given the use of awards as a means of managing today's vastly scaled-down military establishment, it makes sense. One need only examine the awards of the former Soviet Union to witness the results of having NO means to represent multiple awards of a medal. The great World War II Russian military leaders, in wearing <u>every</u> medal they possessed, virtually covered every available square inch of their tunics with awards.

Thus, to make some sense of the American system of devices and attachments, the reader is invited to examine the illustrations and tables on the next few pages, noting that the reference number under each device and in the left-hand column of the table is keyed to the earlier text material describing each associated award.

Plate 20. Attachments/Devices Used On American Ribbons

DEVICE	NAME	RIBBON USE	DENOTES
1	Airplane, C-54 Gold	ALL SERVICES- World War II Occupation Medal	Berlin Airlift participation
2	Arrowhead, Bronze	ARMY and AIR FORCE- Campaign awards since World War II	Participation in combat parachute, glider or amphibious assault landing
3	Bar, Date, Silver	ALL SERVICES- Republic of Vietnam Campaign Medal	No significance- worn upon initial issue
4	Bar, Knotted: Bronze .... Silver .... Gold	ARMY- Good Conduct Medal	Additional awards: Nos. 2 - 5 Nos. 6 - 10 Nos. 11 - 15
5	Disk,"Wintered-Over" Bronze .... Gold .... Silver	ALL SERVICES- Antarctica Service Medal	Wintering over on the Antarctic Continent: 1 winter 2 winters 3 winters
6	Globe, Gold	NAVY- Presidential Unit Citation	Service aboard USS Triton during 1st submerged cruise around the world
7	Hourglass, Bronze Bronze .... Silver .... Gold	ALL SERVICES: Armed Forces Reserve Medal	Reserve Service Anniversaries: 10 Years 20 Years 30 Years
8	Letter "A", Bronze	NAVY, MARINE CORPS, COAST GUARD American Defense Service Medal	Atlantic Fleet service prior to World War II
9	Letter "E", Bronze	NAVY and COAST GUARD- Marksmanship awards	Expert- 1st qualification (obsolete)
10	Letter "E", Silver	NAVY and COAST GUARD- Marksmanship awards	Expert qualification
11	" " "	NAVY and MARINE CORPS- Navy "E" Ribbon	One (1) device per award- three (3) maximum
12	Letter "E", Silver, Wreathed	NAVY and MARINE CORPS- Navy "E" Ribbon	4th (final) award
13	Letter "M", Bronze	ALL SERVICES- Armed Forces Reserve Medal	Mobilization Device for Reservists called to active duty
14	Letter "N", Gold	NAVY- Presidential Unit Citation	Service aboard USS Nautilus during first cruise under the north polar ice cap
15	Letter "O", Silver	COAST GUARD- Decorations and unit awards	Operational Distinguishing Device
16	Letter "S", Bronze	NAVY - Marksmanship awards	Sharpshooter qualification
17	Letter "S", Silver	COAST GUARD- Marksmanship awards	Sharpshooter qualification
18	Letter "V", Bronze	ALL SERVICES- Decorations, AIR FORCE- Unit awards	Combat Distinguishing Device
19	Letter "W", Silver	NAVY and MARINE CORPS- Expeditionary Medals	Participation in defense of Wake Island- (1941)

Attachments/Devices Used On American Ribbons

DEVICE		NAME	RIBBON USE	DENOTES
20		Marine Corps Device, Bronze	NAVY and COAST GUARD- Campaign awards since World War II	Combat service by Naval personnel with Marine Corps units
21		Numeral, Block, Bronze	NAVY and MARINE CORPS-Air Medal	Total number of strike/flight awards
22		" " "	ALL SERVICES (except COAST GUARD)- Humanitarian Service Medal	Additional awards (obsolete)
23		" " "	ALL SERVICES- Multinational Force and Observers Medal, ARMY- Air Medal and service awards	Total number of awards
24		" " "	ALL SERVICES- Armed Forces Reserve Medal	Number of times mobilized for active duty service
25		" " "	ARMY- NCO Professional Development Ribbon	Level of professional training attained:

Basic Ribbon .... Primary Level
Numeral "2" .... Basic Level
Numeral "3" .... Advanced Level
Numeral "4" .... Senior Level
Numeral "5" (obsolete) .... Sergeant Major Academy

DEVICE		NAME	RIBBON USE	DENOTES
26		Numeral, Block, Gold	NAVY and MARINE CORPS- Air Medal	Number of individual awards (obsolete)
27		Oak Leaf Cluster, Bronze	AIR FORCE- Achievement awards, ARMY and AIR FORCE- Decorations, service and unit awards, ALL SERVICES- Joint Service decorations	Additional awards
28		" " "	ARMY- National Defense Service Medal	Additional award (obsolete)
29		Oak Leaf Cluster, Silver	AIR FORCE- Achievement awards, ARMY and AIR FORCE- Decorations, service and unit awards, ALL SERVICES- Joint Service decorations	5 additional awards
30		Palm, Bronze	ALL SERVICES- (except ARMY) Republic of Vietnam Gallantry Cross Unit Citation, ALL SERVICES- Republic of Vietnam Civil Actions Unit Citation	No significance- worn upon initial issue
31		Palm, Bronze	ARMY- Republic of Vietnam Gallantry Cross Unit Citation	Level of award ("cited before the Army") and additional awards
32		Palm Tree with Swords, Gold	ALL SERVICES- Kuwait Liberation Medal (Saudi Arabia)	No significance- worn upon initial issue
33		Pistol, M1911A1, Bronze	COAST GUARD- Pistol Marksmanship Ribbon	Recipient of Pistol Shot Excellence in Competition Badge (Bronze)
34		Pistol, M1911A1, Silver	COAST GUARD- Pistol Marksmanship Ribbon	Recipient of Pistol Shot Excellence in Competition Badge (Silver)
35		Rifle, M14, Bronze	COAST GUARD- Rifle Marksmanship Ribbon	Recipient of Rifleman Excellence in Competition Badge (Bronze)
36		Rifle, M14, Silver	COAST GUARD- Rifle Marksmanship Ribbon	Recipient of Rifleman Excellence in Competition Badge (Silver)
37		Seahorse, Silver	MERCHANT MARINE- Gallant Ship Citation Bar	No significance- worn upon initial issue

Attachments/Devices Used On American Ribbons

NO	DEVICE	RIBBON USE	DENOTES
38 ★	Star, 3/16", Blue	NAVY- Presidential Unit Citation	Additional awards (obsolete)
39 ★	Star, 3/16", Bronze	ALL SERVICES- National Defense Service Medal, ALL SERVICES (except ARMY) - Philippine Republic Presidential Unit Citation, NAVY, MARINE CORPS and COAST GUARD- China Service Medal	Additional award
40 ★	" " "	ALL SERVICES- Campaign awards since World War II, ALL SERVICES- Philippine Defense and Liberation Ribbons	Major battle participation (one star per major engagement)
41 ★	" " "	ALL SERVICES- American Defense Service Medal	Overseas service prior to World War II
42 ★	" " "	ALL SERVICES- Service awards, NAVY and MARINE CORPS- Unit awards, COAST GUARD- Joint Meritorious Unit Award, MERCHANT MARINE- Expeditionary Medal	Additional awards
43 ★	" " "	AIR FORCE- Outstanding Airman of the Year Ribbon	"One of 12" competition finalist
44 ★	" " "	AIR FORCE- Small Arms Expert Marksmanship Ribbon	Additional weapon qualification
45 ★	" " "	NAVY and MARINE CORPS- Air Medal	First individual award
46 ☆	Star, 3/16", Silver	ALL SERVICES- Campaign awards since World War II	Participation in five (5) major battles/campaigns
47 ☆	" " "	ALL SERVICES- Service awards, NAVY and MARINE CORPS- Unit awards, COAST GUARD- Joint Meritorious Unit Award	Five (5) additional awards
48 ☆	" " "	MERCHANT MARINE- Combat Bar	Crew member forced to abandon ship (1 star per sinking)
49 ★	Star, 5/16", Gold	COAST GUARD- Unit awards, NAVY, MARINE CORPS and COAST GUARD- Decorations, ALL SERVICES- Inter-American Defense Board Medal	Additional awards
50 ☆	Star, 5/16", Silver	COAST GUARD- Unit awards, NAVY, MARINE CORPS and COAST GUARD- Decorations	Five (5) additional awards
51 ★	Star, 3/8" Bronze .... Silver .... Gold	ARMY- Republic of Vietnam Gallantry Cross Unit Citation	Level of award and additional awards: Cited before the Regiment Cited before the Division Cited before the Corps
52 ◎	Target, Pistol, Gold	COAST GUARD- Pistol Marksmanship Ribbon	Recipient of Distinguished Pistol Shot Badge
53 ◉	Target, Rifle, Gold	COAST GUARD- Rifle Marksmanship Ribbon	Recipient of Distinguished Marksman Badge

Medal Clasps and Bars

The appearance of medal bars and clasps to reward subsequent acts of heroism/meritorious service or to commemorate participation in specific battles/campaigns seems to have coincided, once again, with the ascendence of the British Empire in the early 19th century.

As previously described, the "additional award" bar was instituted in 1856 along with the creation of the Victoria Cross. However the battle clasp, which rewards participation in single military campaigns, had its beginnings much earlier when the Army Gold Cross was instituted in 1810. The Royal Warrant of the time established a series of ornate gold clasps, containing the name of the specific engagement, which were attached to the suspension ribbon.

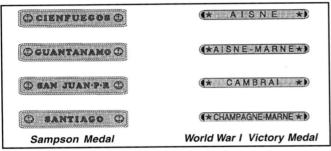

Sampson Medal   **World War I Victory Medal**

The practice made its U.S. debut in 1898 with the appearance of engagement bars to the Sampson Medal and was followed shortly thereafter by the extensive series of battle and service clasps issued with the World War I Victory Medal (see inset for typical examples). No device was authorized for wear on the ribbon bar of the Sampson Medal to denote receipt of these clasps but "battle stars" were extensively used on the ribbon bar of the Victory Medal, one for each battle clasp received.

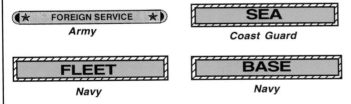

Army   **Coast Guard**

Navy   **Navy**

(1) The individual Services issued a series of clasps to the American Defense Service Medal which indicated that the wearer was serving outside the Continental U.S. prior to America's entry into World War II. A 3/16" diameter bronze star was worn on the ribbon bar to indicate the receipt of any of these clasps (see also the reference to the bronze letter "A" under the "Attachments and Devices" section of this book).

JAPAN   **GERMANY**

(2) The Army of Occupation Medal, issued at the end of World War II, is always worn with one or both of the depicted bars to indicate the area in which the recipient served. It is to be noted that no ribbon device was issued to denote the receipt of either or both clasps.

EUROPE   **ASIA**

(3) As can be seen, The Navy Occupation Service Medal was issued with two differently-named clasps but all of the above comments on the Army medal apply equally to the Navy version.

WAKE ISLAND

(4) In the only case of a battle clasp being named for a specific World War II engagement, the Navy and Marine Corps issued a bar to those military personnel who participated in the heroic defense of Wake Island from 7th to 22nd December, 1941. The clasp is worn on the suspension ribbon of the appropriate Expeditionary Medal and is represented by a silver letter "W" on the ribbon bar.

WINTERED OVER

(5) Military personnel who volunteer to spend a winter on the Antarctic continent may wear a bronze clasp entitled: "Wintered Over" on the suspension ribbon of the Antarctica Service Medal. For a second such period of service, a gold bar containing the same inscription is awarded and for any hearty soul willing to endure a third winter, a similar clasp in silver is bestowed. Only the most senior bar is worn on the suspension ribbon. The bars are represented on the ribbon bar by a disk depicting the Antarctic continent in the same finish as the clasp.

(6) Although not strictly of a military nature, the most ornate clasp in the U.S. repertoire is the second award bar to the Department of Transportation's Life Saving Medals. As before, the finish of the bar corresponds to the actual medal which was awarded, gold or silver. When the width of all U.S. ribbons was standardized in the 1950's, both Life Saving Medals were redesigned. At the same time, the clasp was scaled down to conform with the new 1 3/8" ribbon width and also underwent a minor date change.

(7) The Army Good Conduct Medal uses a unique series of bars in three finishes (bronze, silver and gold) to denote additional awards. Borrowing from the slang expression for a reenlistment ("signing on for another hitch") the clasp, worn on both the suspension ribbon and the ribbon bar, features rope knots (half-hitch knot) to indicate the number of times the recipient has reenlisted.

FLEET MARINE

(8) And finally, there is the "Little Bar That Never Was", a classic case of an overeager bureaucrat jumping the proverbial gun. This bar, inscribed "Fleet Marine", was discovered on an official U.S. Government wall chart of awards and decorations dated 1967 and was intended for wear by Naval personnel who served with Marine Corps units in combat. It was evidently superseded by the present miniature Marine Corps emblem without fanfare.

The evolution of the awards system of the United States may be best characterized as paralleling the American passion for individual freedom. To the casual observer, it might resemble an endless series of unrelated regulations designed to confuse rather than to inform. However upon closer examination, one finds a highly-organized, well-documented system that has been overcomplicated by historical inertia.

When this country won its independence from Great Britain, most British traditions were retained but all trappings of the old regal system were repudiated. As a result, almost 75 years elapsed between the adoption of the U.S. Constitution and the authorization of our first military award, the Medal of Honor. At that time, however, Congress made no provision for a centralized authority to govern awards that may be established in the future. Whether this was due to persistent fears of an "Imperial Presidency" or purely through oversight is still unclear, but once the War and Navy Departments initiated their own systems of decorations and campaign/service medals, it was evident that our Head of State was not even nominally responsible for the execution of the U.S. awards policy (The President traditionally presents the Medal of Honor but does so in the name of the Congress).

As the number of awards grew, responsibility for the approval and presentation of an award to a recipient became (and remains today) a function of the importance of the proposed award. As in most Armed Services around the world, the immediate field commander is empowered to nominate deserving candidates for an appropriate medal but here the resemblance ends. In the U.S. Army, for example, final award authority can be a Company, Regimental, Brigade or Division Commander providing the award is for a campaign, good conduct, achievement, commendation or meritorious service. Only when the upper strata of the "Pyramid of Honor" are attained (i.e., Bronze Star Medal and above) is the senior level of command (The Chief of Staff, Secretary of the Army or Secretary of Defense) required to act upon such recommendations. The other Services follow this pattern closely, some going even further by delegating the authority to issue a few of the more senior awards to lower echelon commanders during wartime situations.

Having thus created their own historical precedent, the individual Services went on to establish distinct and unique regulations for the display of decorations, medals and service ribbons, a policy that lasted from its Civil War beginnings through the World War II era.

In 1947, when the U.S. Armed Forces were unified into the present Department of Defense, one might have expected a series of orderly and clear-cut directives that would totally reorganize all such awards policies. However, with only a few notable exceptions, (e.g., standardization of the height and width of ribbons plus some award criteria) this has not been the case.

Although Joint Service awards committees do exist, they can only recommend general policies for those items shared by all the Armed Forces, but do NOT have the authority to set standards within the individual Services. As a result, some 84 new awards have been authorized since unification, only 20 of which are common to all the Services and the rules governing the display of ribbons and devices now vary so widely as to require a road map.

1. Order of Precedence

The first area of potential confusion is the order of ribbon wear on the U.S. military uniform. A careful examination of the various awards manuals and uniform regulations shows that three distinct arrangements exist among the five Services (the Navy, Marine Corps and Coast Guard share a common scheme).

Arbitrarily taking the Navy method as a baseline, the various award precedence schemes break down into general categories as follows:

A. U.S. Military Decorations
B. U.S. Unit Awards
C. U.S. Non-Military Decorations
D. U.S. Merchant Marine Decorations
E. Prisoner of War and Good Conduct Medals
F. Campaign, Service and Training Awards
G. U.S. Merchant Marine Service Awards
H. Foreign Military Decorations
I. Foreign Unit Awards
J. Non-U.S. Service Awards
K. Marksmanship Awards

The precedence established by the Army is as follows:

A. U.S. Military Decorations
E. Prisoner of War Medal
C. U.S. Non-Military Decorations
E. Good Conduct Medal
F. Campaign, Service and Training Awards
D. U.S. Merchant Marine Decorations
G. U.S. Merchant Marine Service Awards
H. Foreign Military Decorations
J. Non-U.S. Service Awards

<u>NOTE</u>: All U.S. and foreign unit awards (categories B and I above) are worn on the right breast of the Army uniform.

The Air Force has been left for last owing to its unique set of ribbon rules. Not only is the Air Force arrangement different from those discussed earlier but some of their medals and ribbons, designated as "Achievement Awards", do not fit neatly into the previously-defined categories. The Air Force precedence list is as follows:

A. U.S. Military Decorations
B. U.S. Unit Awards
C. U.S. Non-Military Decorations
D. U.S. Merchant Marine Decorations
E. Prisoner of War Medal
—Combat Readiness Medal
E. Good Conduct Medal
F. Campaign, Service and Training Awards
K. Marksmanship Awards
—Air Force Training Ribbon
J. Philippine Service Awards
G. U.S. Merchant Marine Service Awards
H. Foreign Military Decorations
I. Foreign Unit Awards
J. Non-U.S. Service Awards

2. Campaign, Service & Training Awards

In the area of campaign, service and training awards, the Services have again developed different rules and regulations. Air Force award regulations, for example, are roughly chronological, progressing to the present time as follows:

1. Air Reserve Forces Meritorious Service Medal
2. Outstanding Airman of the Year Ribbon
3. Air Force Recognition Ribbon
4. China Service Medal
5. American Defense Service Medal
6. Women's Army Corps Service Medal
7. World War II Campaign Medals (worn in order earned)
8. World War II Victory Medal
9. World War II Occupation Medal
10. Medal for Humane Action
11. National Defense Service Medal
12. Korean Service Medal
13. Antarctica Service Medal
14. Armed Forces Expeditionary Medal
15. Vietnam Service Medal
16. Southwest Asia Service Medal
17. Kosovo Campaign Medal
18. Armed Forces Service Medal
19. Humanitarian Service Medal
20. Outstanding Volunteer Service Medal
21. Overseas Ribbon (Short Tour)
22. Overseas Ribbon (Long Tour)
23. Longevity Service Award Ribbon
24. Military Training Instructor Ribbon
25. Armed Forces Reserve Medal
26. NCO Professional Military Education Graduate Ribbon
27. Basic Military Training Honor Graduate Ribbon

According to applicable Army directives, campaign, service and training awards are worn as follows:

1. Reserve Components Achievement Medal
2. American Defense Service Medal
3. Women's Army Corps Service Medal
4. American Campaign Medal
5. Asiatic-Pacific Campaign Medal
6. European-African-Middle Eastern Campaign Medal
7. World War II Victory Medal
8. Army of Occupation Medal (World War II)
9. Medal for Humane Action
10. National Defense Service Medal
11. Korean Service Medal
12. Antarctica Service Medal
13. Armed Forces Expeditionary Medal
14. Vietnam Service Medal
15. Southwest Asia Service Medal
16. Kosovo Campaign Medal
17. Armed Forces Service Medal
18. Humanitarian Service Medal
19. Outstanding Volunteer Service Medal
20. Armed Forces Reserve Medal
21. NCO Professional Development Ribbon
22. Army Service Ribbon
23. Overseas Service Ribbon
24. Reserve Components Overseas Training Ribbon

Similarly, the Navy, Marine Corps and Coast Guard have assigned each ribbon a specific slot regardless of the dates of service as follows:

1. Naval Reserve Meritorious Service Medal
2. Selected Marine Corps Reserve Medal
3. Coast Guard Reserve Good Conduct Medal
4. Fleet Marine Force Ribbon (Navy only)
5. Navy/Marine Corps Expeditionary Medals
6. China Service Medal
7. American Defense Service Medal
8. American Campaign Medal
9. European-African-Middle Eastern Campaign Medal
10. Asiatic-Pacific Campaign Medal
11. World War II Victory Medal
12. U.S. Antarctic Expedition Medal
13. Navy Occupation Service Medal (World War II)
14. Medal for Humane Action
15. National Defense Service Medal
16. Korean Service Medal
17. Antarctica Service Medal
18. Arctic Service Medal (Coast Guard only)
19. Armed Forces Expeditionary Medal
20. Vietnam Service Medal
21. Southwest Asia Service Medal
22. Kosovo Campaign Medal
23. Armed Forces Service Medal
24. Humanitarian Service Medal
25. Outstanding Volunteer Service Medal
26. Sea Service Deployment Ribbon (Navy, Marine Corps)
27. Arctic Service Ribbon (Navy, Marine Corps)
28. Naval Reserve Sea Service Ribbon
29. Navy & Marine Corps Overseas Service Ribbon
30. Navy Recruiting Service Ribbon
31. Navy Recruit Training Service Ribbon
32. Marine Corps Recruiting Ribbon
33. Marine Corps Drill Instructor Ribbon
34. Marine Security Guard Ribbon
35. Coast Guard Special Operations Service Ribbon
36. Coast Guard Sea Service Ribbon
37. Coast Guard Restricted Duty Ribbon
38. Coast Guard Basic Training Honor Graduate Ribbon
39. Coast Guard Recruiting Service Ribbon
40. Armed Forces Reserve Medal
41. Naval Reserve Medal
42. Marine Corps Reserve Ribbon

Although this makes a foolproof method for checking a ribbon display during a full-dress inspection, it has also created the following anomalies:

A. The China Service Medal (Extended) is worn before all World War II service awards in spite of the prescribed dates of service (1945-57).

B. The U.S. Antarctic Expedition Medal is worn after all World War II ribbons although the qualifying dates lie between 1939 and 1941.

C. World War II Area/Campaign Medals are worn in the specific order shown regardless of when earned. This is also true for the Army which seems to favor alphabetical order for the three awards.

D. The Antarctica Service Medal and Coast Guard Arctic Service Medal are worn after the Korean Service Medal although the service may have been performed as early as 1946.

E. The Navy and Marine Corps Expeditionary Medals take precedence over all except the oldest campaign awards with no regard for dates of service, the most recent being rescue/evacuation efforts in Liberia and Rwanda.

3. Display of Appurtenances

The next area in which the Services have gone their separate ways is in the prescribed arrangement of the various devices used on the ribbons of decorations and service awards.

Pages 125-127 contains a listing of the devices used on U.S. ribbons, but of particular interest are the following:

A. Additional award and campaign devices

B. Bronze Letter "V"

C. Differences in device usage

D. Multiplicity of device types (ribbon clutter)

<u>A. Additional Award and Campaign Devices</u>

In case A, the regulations have created a disparity in the use of the silver device worn in lieu of five bronze devices. For example, The Army and Air Force direct that a silver oak leaf cluster be worn to the right (i.e., the wearer's right) of all bronze clusters on the same ribbon.

The Navy and Coast Guard, on the other hand, have dictated that "a silver star shall be located as near the center of the ribbon as a symmetrical arrangement will permit". They also specify that any bronze or gold star on the same ribbon be "placed to the wearer's right" of the silver star. The Marine Corps has chosen to reverse this procedure and requires the bronze or gold star to be placed on the wearer's LEFT of any silver star.

Because of these conflicting directives, the ribbon configurations depicted on page 132 are required. As can be seen, Navy and Marine Corps devices group around the silver star, while the Army and Air Force move the silver oak leaf cluster to the wearer's right as each new bronze cluster is added.

In almost identical fashion, the grouping of devices ("battle stars") on campaign awards is governed by the various regulations to produce the configurations shown in page 132.

<u>B. Bronze Letter "V"</u>

With reference to case B, the bronze letter "V" (Combat Distinguishing Device) not only has various methods of wear, but the Services vary widely on the ribbons to which it may be attached. It is prescribed in common for use on the Bronze Star and Joint Service Commendation Medals but beyond that point, the usage variations in Table I are seen.

Page 133 shows how the device is worn on the ribbon according to the applicable regulations. At first glance, the schemes might appear identical to that used for decorations (page 132). However, there is now a subtle difference since the Navy, Marine Corps and Coast Guard require that a letter device be absolutely centered on the ribbon bar. The Army and Air Force, as before, move the letter further to the wearer's right as each new oak leaf cluster is added. In the case of the Air Medal, as awarded by the Army, the letter and the prescribed numerals are arranged symmetrically on the ribbon bar.

However, even the "absolutely centered" rule has a variation. If either the Coast Guard Commendation Medal or Achievement Medal is authorized with BOTH the letters "V" and "O" (Operational Distinguishing Device), the two devices are worn on either side of the central white stripe.

Finally, there is the case where all the previously-discussed conditions come together and the letter "V" is displayed with the silver and gold or bronze additional award devices (see page 133). As before, the letter is the senior device in the Army and Air Force displays but, in another quick turnabout, all the Naval-related Services are now in total agreement.

<u>C. Differences in Device Usage</u>

As for case C, the following are examples of conflicting directives in the use of devices:

1. For a good number of years, an additional award of the National Defense Service Medal was denoted by an oak leaf cluster on the Army version and a small (3/16") bronze star by all the other Services. The small bronze star is now used universally.

2. The Army and Air Force use the bronze arrowhead device on the ribbons of the World War II and Korean campaigns and, in the case of the Army, the Vietnam War and Armed Forces Expeditionary Medal (for the Grenada and Panama Operations). Although active participation in assault landings is part of the Navy's mission, they have never authorized the wear of this device.

3. The Navy and Marine Corps use the small (3/16") bronze star on their unit awards (i.e., Unit Commendation, Meritorious Unit Commendation and "E" Ribbon) as an additional award device. The Coast Guard, however, uses the <u>large</u> (5/16") gold star on its equivalent unit awards.

continued on page 134

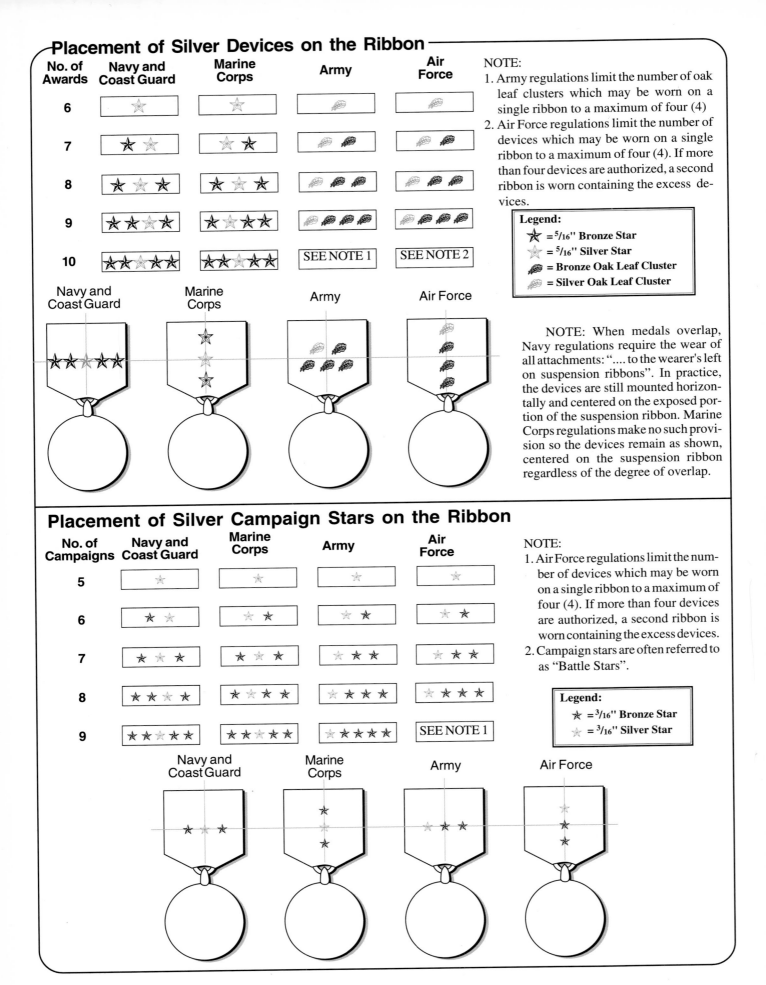

Placement of Silver Devices on the Ribbon

No. of Awards	Navy and Coast Guard	Marine Corps	Army	Air Force
6	☆	☆	🍃	🍃
7	★ ☆	☆ ★	🍃🍃	🍃🍃
8	★ ☆ ★	★ ☆ ★	🍃🍃🍃	🍃🍃🍃
9	★ ☆ ★ ★	★ ☆ ★ ★	🍃🍃🍃🍃	🍃🍃🍃🍃
10	★ ★ ☆ ★ ★	★ ★ ☆ ★ ★	SEE NOTE 1	SEE NOTE 2

NOTE:
1. Army regulations limit the number of oak leaf clusters which may be worn on a single ribbon to a maximum of four (4)
2. Air Force regulations limit the number of devices which may be worn on a single ribbon to a maximum of four (4). If more than four devices are authorized, a second ribbon is worn containing the excess devices.

Legend:
★ = 5/16" Bronze Star
☆ = 5/16" Silver Star
🍃 = Bronze Oak Leaf Cluster
🍃 = Silver Oak Leaf Cluster

NOTE: When medals overlap, Navy regulations require the wear of all attachments: ".... to the wearer's left on suspension ribbons". In practice, the devices are still mounted horizontally and centered on the exposed portion of the suspension ribbon. Marine Corps regulations make no such provision so the devices remain as shown, centered on the suspension ribbon regardless of the degree of overlap.

Navy and Coast Guard — Marine Corps — Army — Air Force

Placement of Silver Campaign Stars on the Ribbon

No. of Campaigns	Navy and Coast Guard	Marine Corps	Army	Air Force
5	☆	☆	☆	☆
6	★ ☆	☆ ★	☆ ★	☆ ★
7	★ ☆ ★	★ ☆ ★	☆ ★ ★	☆ ★ ★
8	★ ☆ ★ ★	★ ☆ ★ ★	☆ ★ ★ ★	☆ ★ ★ ★
9	★ ☆ ★ ★ ★	★ ☆ ★ ★ ★	☆ ★ ★ ★ ★	SEE NOTE 1

NOTE:
1. Air Force regulations limit the number of devices which may be worn on a single ribbon to a maximum of four (4). If more than four devices are authorized, a second ribbon is worn containing the excess devices.
2. Campaign stars are often referred to as "Battle Stars".

Legend:
★ = 3/16" Bronze Star
☆ = 3/16" Silver Star

Navy and Coast Guard — Marine Corps — Army — Air Force

Placement of the Bronze Letter "V" on the Ribbon

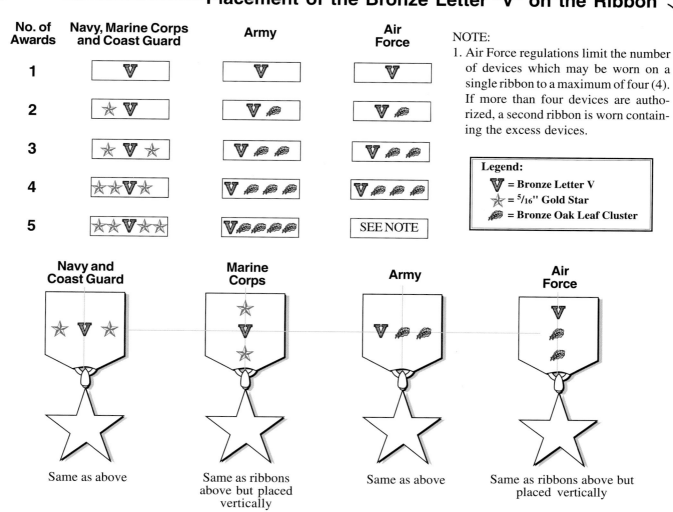

No. of Awards	Navy, Marine Corps and Coast Guard	Army	Air Force
1	V	V	V
2	★ V	V 🍃	V 🍃
3	★ V ★	V 🍃🍃	V 🍃🍃
4	★★V★	V 🍃🍃🍃	V 🍃🍃🍃
5	★★V★★	V 🍃🍃🍃🍃	SEE NOTE

NOTE:

1. Air Force regulations limit the number of devices which may be worn on a single ribbon to a maximum of four (4). If more than four devices are authorized, a second ribbon is worn containing the excess devices.

> **Legend:**
> V = Bronze Letter V
> ★ = ⁵⁄₁₆" Gold Star
> 🍃 = Bronze Oak Leaf Cluster

Navy and Coast Guard — Same as above

Marine Corps — Same as ribbons above but placed vertically

Army — Same as above

Air Force — Same as ribbons above but placed vertically

Placement of the Letter "V" With Other Ribbon Devices

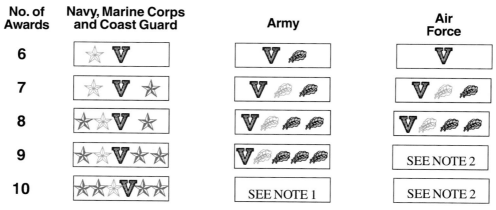

No. of Awards	Navy, Marine Corps and Coast Guard	Army	Air Force
6	☆ V	V 🍃	V
7	☆ V ☆	V 🍃🍃	V 🍃🍃
8	★☆V☆	V 🍃🍃🍃	V 🍃🍃🍃
9	★☆V☆☆	V 🍃🍃🍃🍃	SEE NOTE 2
10	★★☆V★★	SEE NOTE 1	SEE NOTE 2

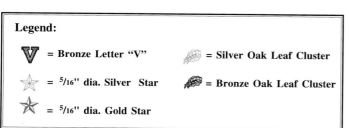

> **Legend:**
> V = Bronze Letter "V"
> ☆ = ⁵⁄₁₆" dia. Silver Star
> ★ = ⁵⁄₁₆" dia. Gold Star
> 🍃 = Silver Oak Leaf Cluster
> 🍃 = Bronze Oak Leaf Cluster

NOTE:

1. Army regulations limit the number of oak leaf clusters which may be worn on a single ribbon to a maximum of four (4).

2. Air Force regulations limit the number of devices which may be worn on a single ribbon to a maximum of four (4). If more than four devices are authorized, a second ribbon is worn containing the excess devices.

Table I - Usage Variations of the Bronze Letter "V"

SERVICE(S)	APPLICABLE MEDALS
Army	• Air Medal, Commendation Medal
Navy, Marine Corps	• Legion of Merit, Distinguished Flying Cross, Air Medal, Commendation Medal, Achievement • Medal (Note: The "V" was no longer awarded with the Legion of Merit and Achievement Medal after the Vietnam War but was reinstituted for awards of the two medals during Operation Desert Storm and thereafter)
Coast Guard	• Legion of Merit, Commendation Medal, Achievement Medal
Air Force	• Commendation Medal, Achievement Medal, Outstanding Unit Award, Organizational Excellence Award

Table II - Regulations for Ribbon Wear

SERVICE (S)	REGULATIONS FOR RIBBON WEAR
Army	• No line will contain more than four service ribbons • Unit awards will be worn with not more than three per row
Navy	• Worn in horizontal rows of three each
Marine Corps	• Normally worn in rows of three, but rows of four may be worn when displaying a large number of awards
Coast Guard	• One, two or three ribbons are worn in a single row
Air Force	• Wear ribbons in multiples of three or four

Continued from page 131

4. Until the Department of Defense standardized the practice, most of the Services used a system of bronze numerals to indicate additional awards of the Humanitarian Service Medal. From the outset, however, the Coast Guard used small (3/16") bronze and silver stars to denote one and five additional awards of the medal respectively. It is the Coast Guard system that is now in effect for all Branches of the Service (page 95).

5. Contrary to other policies covering personal and unit awards, no provisions are made to denote the fifth and subsequent awards of the Navy "E" Ribbon. Upon receipt of the fourth award, the wreathed, silver "E" is worn and no further devices may be affixed to the ribbon thereafter.

6. The Coast Guard has only recently permitted the wear of the oak leaf cluster on its uniform. Anyone earning an additional award of a Joint Service decoration (e.g., DDSM, DSSM, DMSM, etc.) or any award(s) earned while part of the Army or Air Force is no longer required to substitute the large (5/16") gold star for the now universal oak leaf cluster

7. The Army permits the wear of devices on the Republic of Vietnam Gallantry Cross Unit Citation (bronze palms plus gold, silver and/or bronze stars) to denote the level of the award as well as subsequent awards. The other Services only allow the display of a single bronze palm.

D. Multiplicity of Device Types

Case D arises from the fact that many different devices can be worn on the same ribbon. Although two might be acceptable, (e.g., letter "V" with gold star, arrowhead with battle star, etc.), things are definitely out of hand when as many as THREE distinct device types can be affixed to the same ribbon. The most extreme examples in the ribbon clutter category are the following:

1. The Navy, which permits the wear of the Presidential Unit Citation with a gold letter "N", a gold globe and a bronze star at the same time.

2. The Coast Guard, which authorizes the simultaneous display of a bronze letter "V", 5/16" gold/silver stars and a silver letter "O" on the ribbons of its Commendation and Achievement Medals.

3. The Navy and Marine Corps, which use a 3/16" bronze star or 5/16" gold and silver stars plus bronze numerals and the bronze letter "V" simultaneously on the Air

Medal (see below for a more complete discussion of Air Medal device utilization).

4. The Department of Defense, which now prescribes the hourglass (gold, silver & bronze) as well as a bronze letter "M" and bronze numeral on the Armed Forces Reserve Medal (see page 137).

4. Air Medal Devices

Still on the general subject of ribbon appurtenances, we shall now turn our attention to the case of the Air Medal, the classic example of how many different ways the Services can specify the wearing of devices, both now and in the past. As mentioned in the previous section, both the Army and the Navy use the bronze letter "V" on the Air Medal but it is in denoting additional awards that the Services have demonstrated some real Yankee individuality.

Although the Army and Air Force systems (i.e., numerals and oak leaf clusters, respectively) are totally different, they are, at the very least, straightforward and easily understood. It is the Navy, then, that has entered a new dimension by establishing two very distinct categories, strike/ flight and individual award, for all awards of the Air Medal, both initial and subsequent.

Strike/flight awards of the Navy Air Medal are indicated by bronze block numerals worn on the right-hand orange stripe (as seen by the viewer). For individual awards, a small (3/16" dia.) bronze star is used to indicate the first award while the traditional 5/16" gold stars are used to denote additional individual awards (see page 68).

The two different categories have created a situation in which a device is used on a ribbon to denote the INITIAL award of a personal decoration, the first in American medallic history (for purists, it will be noted that the Merchant Marine Gallant Ship Citation Bar is issued with a silver seahorse device and the Navy "E" Ribbon carries a silver letter "E" upon initial issue. Both of these, however, are unit awards rather than decorations).

Just for the record, the Navy had used the above method for many years but discarded it in favor of a system that utilized gold block numerals, placed on the left-hand orange stripe (as seen by the viewer) to denote the total number of individual awards of the Air Medal (see page 137).

Both of the above cases were combined with the bronze strike/flight numerals as described above. Use of the gold numerals was not universal, however, and was resisted vigorously by those senior officers who clung tenaciously to their gold stars. So, with the demise of the gold numeral, there is now another body of dissatisfied Navy men. These were the Vietnam-era pilots who earned the medal in great profusion, but now had great difficulty in displaying their true number of awards using 5/16" gold and silver stars.

The Coast Guard uses ONLY the 5/16" gold and silver stars to denote additional awards of the Air Medal for all

categories of heroic and meritorious achievement in flight. However, strike/flight awards received while serving with Navy units may be worn on the ribbon as prescribed above.

And to close the subject on a final note of confusion, the Marine Corps follows the Navy's lead in using numerals and bronze, gold and silver stars but also allows any gold numerals earned prior to 1989 to be worn on the ribbon.

5. Disparate Regulations

As the next chapter in this "Dissertation on Diversity", the following differences in ribbon wear between the various Armed Services are submitted without further comment:

A. The Air Force is the only Branch of the Service to authorize the wear of miniature ribbon bars on the uniform.

B. The Air Force permits a second ribbon to be worn if more than four (4) devices are authorized for wear on a single ribbon bar. The Army also specifies a limit of four (4) oak leaf clusters on the ribbon bar but makes no provision for excess devices. This leaves the question of a 10th, 14th, 15th, 18th, etc. awards up in the air since the hypothetical recipient has no way to display the requisite number of silver and bronze clusters.

C. Unit awards worn by Army personnel are unique in that the gold frames are physically larger (1/2" vs. 3/8" high) and are worn on the right breast of the Army uniform. This regulation is also applicable to unit awards received from other Services or from foreign governments. If this seems unusual, consider the original Army scheme (circa 1960) that placed the Presidential Unit Citation on the right breast, other U.S. unit awards on the left breast amongst the other ribbons, foreign unit citations below all other ribbons on the left breast pocket flap and the Meritorious Unit Commendation in the form of a sew-on patch on the lower right-hand sleeve.

D. The Navy, Marine Corps and Coast Guard follow the "right-side" precedent to a limited extent, requiring ribbons that have no associated medals (e.g., Combat Action, Unit, Marksmanship, etc.) to be worn on the right breast on those occasions when full-sized medals are authorized. But, as before, there is disagreement on the order of wear. The Marine Corps requires a "top to bottom, wearer's right to wearer's left" arrangement while the Navy and Coast Guard specify an "inboard to outboard" display (see page 50). By contrast, neither the Army nor the Air Force permits these "ribbon-only" awards to be worn on the uniform when full-size or miniature medals are specified.

E. The Army and the Coast Guard Uniform Regulations stipulate that unit awards with gold frames be worn with the laurel leaves on the frame pointing up. The Marine Corps accomplishes the same goal by requiring the laurel leaves to form a "V" (point down). On the other hand, no other awards or uniform regulations mention the subject.

F. The Army is the only Service to permit the wear of unit awards by personnel who did not participate in the action for which it was cited. Any individual joining at a later date may wear the unit award while permanently attached, but must relinquish it upon subsequent reassignment.

G. Army and Marine Corps ribbons may, at the wearer's option, be worn with a 1/8" separation between adjacent rows. The other Services do not permit any such separation.

H. Similarly, the maximum number of ribbons that may be displayed in each row depends on which Service is being discussed. The applicable quotes from the various uniform regulations are offered in Table II (page 134) without comment:

I. The Marine Corps, in an unfortunate reference to the senior status of the color blue in heraldry, specifies the wear of the ribbon for the Merchant Marine Mariner's Medal in the order of blue, white, red (as seen by an observer) thus putting themselves out of step with all of the other Services as well as the dictates of the awarding agency itself.

J. On a number of occasions, the Services have awarded more than one medal for the same combat action as per Table III.

K. Then consider the refusal of some Services to permit the wear of certain awards of the other Branches. As of this writing, the restrictions existing are shown in Table IV.

L. The Coast Guard treats the Department of Transportation (originally the Treasury Department) Gold and Silver Lifesaving Medals, as military decorations. As can be seen in the Coast Guard ribbon chest (page 48) they are afforded a specific position in the Coast Guard order of precedence. All other Services, however, consider them to be nonmilitary decorations with no absolute precedence within the group.

M. As another sidelight to this discussion, the Coast Guard is alone in specifying an additional award device (the large 5/16" gold star) for the Lifesaving Medals.

N. Coast Guard is also the only Service to include awards to civilians in its list of military decorations. The cases in point are the three Department of Transportation awards shown on page 48 which may be worn as shown on the Coast Guard uniform.

O. Another amusing point to ponder is concealed in the Marine Corps Uniform Regulations in the paragraph under Bronze letter "V" (Combat Distinguishing Device). In describing this device, the regulation states that the "...approved bronze letter "V" is gold in color."

P. Finally, the ultimate in awards with little significance is the Army Service Ribbon. Since this ribbon is awarded to all officers or enlisted men who have successfully completed any entry-level training course, EVERY PERSON in the U.S. Army is entitled to wear it. Unlike a true general service award (e.g., National Defense Service Medal), the Army Service Ribbon has no termination date and requires no "service" of any kind.

6. Strange Common Regulations

Thus far, this article has dealt only with the differences between the various U.S. awards regulations. It would have been refreshing to report that the remaining areas, in which the Services all agree amongst themselves, made absolute sense from the standpoints of logic and tradition. Unfortunately, this is not the case as can be seen in the following examples:

A. The medals associated with the Philippine Defense, Liberation and Independence Ribbons, although issued and sanctioned for wear by a friendly foreign government, may not be worn on the U.S. military uniform. All of the applicable Uniform Regulations refer to these awards as "Ribbons" rather than "Medals" and permit only the ribbon to be worn.

B. Ribbon devices, in most cases, are worn to denote the award of clasps to certain service medals (e.g., World War I Victory Medal, American Defense Service Medal, Navy Expeditionary Medal, etc.). The sole exception to the rule is the World War II Occupation Medal, which makes no provisions for a device in cases where both clasps have been awarded.

C. During the United Nations' first 50 years of existence, the U.S. permitted only two medals associated with UN missions to be worn on the military uniform. These were the UN Korean Medal and the United Nations Medal for participation in all other United Nations operations. In a recent policy change, a total of 9 additional ribbons were authorized. However, there is still a peculiar twist as only the first ribbon earned may be worn, with all subsequent UN service denoted by bronze stars. U.S. soldiers have participated in seven additional UN missions but wear of those ribbons is still pending. For further information, see *United Nations Medals and Missions* referenced in the bibliography (page 139).

D. A second award of the Philippine Presidential Unit Citation (for service during disaster relief operations in 1972) is denoted by a small bronze star on the ribbon. However, a similar second award of the Republic of Korea Presidential Unit Citation for the same operation goes unrecognized.

E. Finally, consider the case of the "Wintered Over" clasps and disks used on the Antarctica Service Medal. In a classic example of reverse logic, the time-honored sequence of bronze, silver and gold was altered to bronze-gold-silver to denote 1, 2 and 3 winters respectively.

Former Device Usage on the Navy Air Medal

Navy and Marine Corps (Individual Awards)

No. of Awards	(Circa 1966-1978)	(Circa 1978-1991)
1		
2		
3		
4		
5		

Legend:

★ = 5/16" dia. Gold Star

★ = 3/16" dia. Bronze Star

1, 2 etc. = Gold Block Numerals

Placement of Devices on the Armed Forces Reserve Medal

WITH NO CALL UP TO ACTIVE SERVICE	WITH CALL-UP TO ACTIVE SERVICE PRIOR TO 10 YEAR PERIOD	WITH CALL-UP TO ACTIVE SERVICE AFTER INITIAL 10 YEAR PERIOD
 After 10 years of reserve service	 With 1 mobilization	 After 10 years of reserve service and 1 mobilization
 After 20 years of reserve service	 With 2 mobilizations	 After 10 years of reserve service and 2 mobilizations
 After 30 years of reserve service	 With 3 mobilizations	 After 10 years of reserve service and 3 mobilizations
 After 40 years of reserve service	 With 4 mobilizations	 After 10 years of reserve service and 4 mobilizations

Legend:

 = Bronze Hourglass

 = Silver Hourglass

 = Gold Hourglass

M = Bronze Letter "M"

3 = Bronze Block Numeral

Table III - Occasions On Which Multiple Awards Were Authorized

DATE	EVENT/ACTION	AWARDS PRESENTED
1937	Attack on gunboat "Panay" (China)	1. Navy Expeditionary Medal 2. China Service Medal
1941	Defense of Wake Island	1. Asiatic-Pacific Campaign Medal 2. Navy (or Marine Corps) Expeditionary Medal with "Wake Island" clasp 3. Navy Presidential Unit Citation
1941	Defense of the Philippine Islands (U.S. Army personnel)	1. Bronze Star Medal 2. Asiatic-Pacific Campaign Medal 3. Army Presidential Unit Citation 4. Philippine Defense Ribbon (Philippine Government)
1975	Evacuation of Saigon, Republic of Vietnam	1. Armed Forces Expeditionary Medal 2. Humanitarian Service Medal 3. (Some personnel): Combat Action Ribbon plus Navy Unit Commendation or Navy Meritorious Unit Commendation
1991	Operation "Desert Shield" & "Desert Storm"	1. National Defense Service Medal 2. Southwest Asia Service Medal 3. Medal for the Liberation of Kuwait (Saudi Arabia) 4. Medal for the Liberation of Kuwait (Kuwait)

Table IV - Inter-Service Restrictions on Ribbon Wear

SERVICE	REGULATIONS
ARMY	(a) Air Force Longevity Service Award Ribbon (b) Air Force and Navy Marksmanship ribbons (c) Marksmanship Badges awarded by other U.S. Services
MARINE CORPS	(a) Army Combat Medical or Combat Infantryman's Badge must be "traded in" for the Combat Action Ribbon (b) Any award that has no direct Marine Corps equivalent (e.g., Navy Marksmanship Ribbons, Air Force Training and Recognition Ribbons, Army Service Ribbon, etc.)
NAVY	(a) Army badges per the Marine Corps (above) (b) Coast Guard Commandant's Letter of Commendation Ribbon (c) All other awards having no direct Navy equivalent
COAST GUARD	(a) All training and marksmanship medals/badges/ribbons earned in another branch of the Service (b) Any award that has no direct Coast Guard equivalent (e.g., Air Force Longevity Service Ribbon, Combat Readiness Medal, etc.)
AIR FORCE	(a) No comparable restrictions instituted

As indicated in the Introduction to this book, certain errors/omissions have been noted by the authors subsequent to the preparation of the color plates. In addition, there are certain areas of text which require further clarification where space was at a premium. These will be referenced to the applicable page(s).

Page 20, 21: Lifesaving medals are awarded to military personnel only if the individual is on a leave or liberty status. Otherwise, a military decoration is more appropriate.

Page 21: The Bronze Star Medal for meritorious service was authorized for those awarded either the Combat Infantryman Badge or Combat Medical Badge between 7 December 1941 and 2 September 1945. Since the two badges were not awarded until July, 1943, those Army infantrymen and medics whose meritorious achievements in combat prior to July, 1943 are confirmable in writing may still be eligible for the Bronze Star.

Page 22: The Army Commendation Medal, originally a ribbon only, is authorized for award to any Army member who received a letter or certificate of commendation signed by a Major General or higher for meritorious achievement between 7 December 1941 and 1 January 1946.

Page 22: The Navy Commendation Medal is authorized for award to any member of the U.S. Navy, Marine Corps or Coast Guard who has received a letter of commendation from the Secretary of the Navy, the Commander in Chief of the Pacific or Atlantic Fleet or Commander of the Fleet Marine Force, Pacific for an act of heroism or meritorious service performed between 6 December 1941 and 11 January 1944. Subsequent to the above period, personnel may apply for the medal if they possess a letter of commendation from the same higher authority providing the award is specifically mentioned.

Page 28: The award criteria for the two Occupation Medals are worth repeating since they rank highest on the list of items which many veterans forget to claim. The guidelines are the same for both, requiring a member of the Army, Navy, Marine Corps or Coast Guard to have served 30 consecutive days in any of the occupied territories after VE-Day and/or VJ-Day.

Page 28: The Navy Occupation Service Medal was issued with two distinct reverse designs, one for Navy and Coast Guard recipients and one for the Marine Corps.

Page 30: The Armed Forces Reserve Medal is issued with six reverse patterns; one each for the Army, Navy, Marine Corps, Air Force, Coast Guard and National Guard.

Page 32: Some confusion seems to exist on the criteria for the Philippine Independence Ribbon/ Medal. The original standard ("...present for duty in the Philippines on 4 July 1946...") was modified in 1953 and, since that time, sentiment (and some very competent authorities) seem to favor the award to U.S. personnel who won either the Philippine Defense or Philippine Liberation Ribbons. However, U.S. military regulations require the receipt of **both** the Defense and Liberation Ribbons.

Page 139: The Army has recently followed the Air Force's practice and now allows a second ribbon to be worn if all authorized additional award devices cannot be accommodated on a single ribbon.

Bibliography

Abbott, P.E. and Tamplin, J.M.A.- *British Gallantry Awards*, 1971

Adjutant General of the Army- *American Decorations 1862-1926*, 1927

Belden, B.L.- *United States War Medals*, 1916

Borts, L.H.- *United Nations Medals and Missions*, 1997

Committee on Veterans' Affairs, U.S. Senate- *Medal of Honor Recipients 1863-1978*, 1979

Dept. of Defense Manual DOD 1348.33M- *Manual of Military Decorations & Awards*, 1996

Dorling, H.T.- *Ribbons and Medals*, 1983

Gleim, A.F.- *United States Medals of Honor 1862-1989*, 1989

Gleim, A.F.- *War Department Gallantry Citations for Pre WWI Service*, 1986

Inter-American Defense Board- *Norms for Protocol, Symbols, Insignia and Gifts*, 1984

Kerrigan, E.- *American Badges and Insignia*, 1967

Kerrigan, E.- *American Medals and Decorations*, 1990

Kerrigan, E.- *American War Medals and Decorations*, 1971

Mayo, J.H.- *Medals and Decorations of the British Army & Navy*, 1897

McDowell, C.P.- *Military and Naval Decorations of the United States*, 1984

National Geographic Magazine, December, 1919

National Geographic Society- *Insignia and Decorations of the U.S. Armed Forces*, 1944

Strandberg, J.E. and Bender, R.J.- *The Call to Duty*, 1994

U.S. Air Force Instruction 36-2903- *Dress and Personal Appearance of U.S.A.F. Personnel*, 1994

U.S. Air Force Instruction 36-2803- *The Air Force Awards and Decorations Program*, 1994

U.S. Army Regulation 670-1- *Wear and Appearance of Army Uniforms and Insignia*, May, 2000

U.S. Army Regulation 600-8-22- *Military Awards*, 1995

U.S. Coast Guard Instruction M1020.6A- *U.S. Coast Guard Uniform Regulations*, 1985

U.S. Coast Guard Instruction M1650.25B- *Medals and Awards Manual*, 1995

U.S. Marine Corps Order P1020.34F- *U.S. Marine Corps Uniform Regulations*, 1995

U.S. Navy Instruction SECNAVINST 1650.1F- *Navy and Marine Corps Awards Manual*, 1991

U.S. Navy Instruction SECNAVINST 15665H- *United States Navy Uniform Regulations*, 1991

U.S. Navy Manual NAVPERS 15,790- *Decorations, Medals, Ribbons and Badges of the United States Navy, Marine Corps and Coast Guard, 1861-1948*, 1 July 1950

Vietnam Council on Foreign Relations- *Awards & Decorations of Vietnam*, 1972

Wilkins, P.A.- *The History of the Victoria Cross*, 1904

Wyllie, Col. R.E.- *Orders, Decorations and Insignia*, 1921

Index   *NOTE: Numbers in Bold Italics Denote Illustrations*

Achievement Medal, Aerial *22, 69*
Achievement Medal, Air Force *23, 74*, 134
Achievement Medal, Army *23, 73*
Achievement Medal, Army Reserve Components *25, 79*
Achievement Medal, Coast Guard *23, 74*, 131, 134
Achievement Medal, Joint Service *23, 72*
Achievement Medal, Navy and Marine Corps *23, 73*, 134
Additional Award and Campaign Devices 131
Aerial Achievement Medal *22, 69*
Air Force Achievement Medal *23, 74*, 134
Air Force Basic Military Training Honor
   Graduate Ribbon *36, 114*
Air Force Combat Readiness Medal *24, 75*, 138
Air Force Commendation Medal *22, 71*, 134
Air Force Cross *18, 57*
Air Force Distinguished Service Medal *19, 59*
Air Force Good Conduct Medal *25, 78*
Air Force Longevity Service Award Ribbon *36, 113*, 138
Air Force Medal of Honor 16, *17, 55*
Air Force Military Training Instructor Ribbon *36, 113*
Air Force N.C.O. Professional Military
   Education Graduate Ribbon *36, 114*
Air Force Organizational Excellence Award *36, 118*, 134
Air Force Outstanding Airman of the Year Ribbon *26, 81*
Air Force Outstanding Unit Award *36, 117*, 134
Air Force Overseas Ribbon (Long Tour) *36, 113*
Air Force Overseas Ribbon (Short Tour) *36, 113*
Air Force Presidential Unit Citation *35, 116*
Air Force Recognition Ribbon *26, 81*, 138
Air Force Small Arms Expert Marksmanship Ribbon *31, 98*
Air Force Training Ribbon *36, 114*, 138
Air Medal *21, 68*, 134
Air Medal Devices *68*, 124, 135, *137*
Air Reserve Forces Meritorious Service Medal *25, 80*
Airman's Medal *20, 63*
American Campaign Medal *27, 84*
American Defense Service Medal *26, 83*, 136
American Defense Service Medal (clasps/devices) *128*
Andre Medal 5
Antarctic Expedition Medal, U.S., (1939-41) *27, 87*, 131
Antarctica Service Medal *28, 91*, 131
Antarctica Service Medal (devices) *128*, 136
Arctic Service Medal (Coast Guard) *29, 91*, 131
Arctic Service Ribbon (Navy, Marine Corps) *35, 110*
Area/Campaign Medals, World War II 131
Armed Forces Expeditionary Medal *29, 92*, 131, 138
Armed Forces Honor Medal, Republic of Vietnam *33, 101*
Armed Forces Reserve Medal *30, 96, 137*, 139
Armed Forces Service Medal *29, 95*
Army Achievement Medal *23, 73*
Army Commendation Medal *22, 70*, 134, 139
Army Distinguished Service Cross *18, 56*, 124
Army Distinguished Service Medal *18, 58*, 124
Army Gold Cross (Great Britain) 128
Army Good Conduct Medal *24, 76*
Army Good Conduct Medal (devices) *128*
Army Medal of Honor 16, *17, 53*
Army Meritorious Unit Commendation *34, 118*
Army N.C.O. Professional Development Ribbon *34, 109*
Army of Occupation Medal (World War II) *28, 88*, 136
Army of Occupation Medal (clasps) *128*
Army Overseas Service Ribbon *34, 110*
Army Presidential Unit Citation *34, 116*, 138
Army Reserve Components Achievement Medal *25, 79*

Army Reserve Components Overseas
   Training Ribbon *34, 110*
Army Service Ribbon *34, 109*, 136, 138
Army Superior Unit Award *34, 119*
Army Valorous Unit Award *34, 117*
"Asia" Clasp (Navy) *128*
Asiatic-Pacific Campaign Medal *27, 85*, 138
Atlantic War Zone Medal, Merchant Marine *38, 51*
Attachments/Devices Used on American Ribbons (table) 125
Attachments and Devices 124
Award Certificate Samples *123*
Award for Superior Achievement, D.O.T.
   (Coast Guard) *48*, 49
Background of United States Awards 5
Badge of Military Merit (Purple Heart) *5, 66*
"Base" Clasp (Navy) *128*
Basic Military Training Honor Graduate
   Ribbon, Air Force *36, 114*
Basic Training Honor Graduate Ribbon,
   Coast Guard *37, 115*
Bicentennial Unit Commendation, Coast Guard *37, 120*
Bosnia Medal (NATO) *33, 104*
Bronze Star Medal *21, 65*, 129, 131, 138, 139
Bronze Letter "V" 131
Bronze Letter "V", Usage Variations (table) 134
Claiming or Replacing Medals 52
Clasps and Bars, Medal *128*
China Service Medal *26, 83*, 131, 138
Civil Actions Medal, Republic of Vietnam *33, 101*
Civil Actions Unit Citation, Republic of Vietnam *37, 121*
Civil War Awards 6
Coast Guard Achievement Medal *23, 74*, 131, 134
Coast Guard Arctic Service Medal *29, 91*, 131
Coast Guard Basic Training Honor Graduate Ribbon *37, 115*
Coast Guard Bicentennial Unit Commendation *37, 120*
Coast Guard Commandant's Letter of
   Commendation Ribbon *23, 74*, 138
Coast Guard Commendation Medal *22, 72*, 131, 134
Coast Guard Distinguished Service Medal *19, 60*
Coast Guard "E" Ribbon *36, 120*
Coast Guard Expert Pistol Shot Medal *31, 99*
Coast Guard Expert Rifleman Medal *31, 98*
Coast Guard Good Conduct Medal *25, 79*
Coast Guard Medal *20, 64*
Coast Guard Meritorious Team Commendation *36, 119*
Coast Guard Meritorious Unit Commendation *36, 119*
Coast Guard Pistol Marksmanship Ribbon *31, 99*
Coast Guard Reserve Good Conduct Medal *26, 81*
Coast Guard Recruiting Service Ribbon *37, 115*
Coast Guard Restricted Duty Ribbon *37, 115*
Coast Guard Rifle Marksmanship Ribbon *31, 99*
Coast Guard Sea Service Ribbon *37, 115*
Coast Guard Special Operations Service Ribbon *37, 114*
Coast Guard Unit Commendation *36, 118*
Combat Action Ribbon *23, 75*, 138
Combat Bar, Merchant Marine *38, 51*
Combat Readiness Medal (Air Force) *24, 75*, 138
Commandant's Letter of Commendation
   Ribbon, Coast Guard *23, 74*, 138
Commemorative Medals (Unofficial) *121*
Commendation Medal, Air Force *22, 71*, 134
Commendation Medal, Army *22, 70*, 134, 139
Commendation Medal, Coast Guard *22, 72*, 131, 134
Commendation Medal, Joint Service *22, 70*, 131